Law Stories

Law, Meaning, and Violence

The scope of Law, Meaning, and Violence is defined by the wide-ranging scholarly debates signaled by each of the words in the title. Those debates have taken place among and between lawyers, anthropologists, political theorists, sociologists, and historians, as well as literary and cultural critics. This series is intended to recognize the importance of such ongoing conversations about law, meaning, and violence as well as to encourage and further them.

Series Editors:

Martha Minow, Harvard Law School
Michael Ryan, Northeastern University
Austin Sarat, Amherst College

Narrative, Violence, and the Law: The Essays of Robert Cover, edited by Martha Minow, Michael Ryan, and Austin Sarat

Narrative, Authority, and Law, by Robin West

The Possibility of Popular Justice: A Case Study of Community Mediation in the United States, edited by Sally Engle Merry and Neal Milner

Legal Modernism, by David Luban

Surveillance, Privacy, and the Law: Employee Drug Testing and the Politics of Social Control, by John Gilliom

Lives of Lawyers: Journeys in the Organizations of Practice, by Michael J. Kelly

Unleashing Rights: Law, Meaning, and the Animal Rights Movement, by Helena Silverstein

Law Stories, edited by Gary Bellow and Martha Minow

Law Stories

Edited by Gary Bellow and Martha Minow

Ann Arbor
THE UNIVERSITY OF MICHIGAN PRESS

Copyright © by the University of Michigan 1996
All rights reserved
Published in the United States of America by
The University of Michigan Press
Manufactured in the United States of America
⊗ Printed on acid-free paper

1999   1998   1997   1996   4   3   2   1

A CIP catalog record for this book is available from the British Library.

Library of Congress Cataloging-in-Publication Data

Law stories / edited by Gary Bellow and Martha Minow.
    p.   cm. — (Law, meaning, and violence)
   ISBN 0-472-10718-6 (hardcover : alk. paper)
    1. Practice of law—United States—Anecdotes.   2. Lawyers—United
States—Anecdotes.   3. Law—United States—Anecdotes.   I. Bellow,
Gary.   II. Minow, Martha, 1954–   .   III. Series.
   K184.L377   1996
   340–dc20   96-16551
                                                           CIP

To Jeanne
  Douglas
  Courtenay and
  David

  Joe and
  Mira

story tellers and story listeners all

Contents

Introduction: Rita's Case and Other Law Stories   1
    Gary Bellow and Martha Minow

Welfare Stories   31
    Anthony V. Alfieri

Maintaining the Status Quo: Institutional Obstacles in a
    Child Custody Dispute   51
    Lenora M. Lapidus

"We Are All We've Got": Building a Retiree Movement in
    Youngstown, Ohio   77
    Alice and Staughton Lynd

What's Wrong with These Pictures? The Story of the
    Hammer Museum Litigation   101
    Nell Minow

Public Defender, Public Friend: Searching for the "Best
    Interests" of Juvenile Offenders   131
    Charles Ogletree

On Representing a Victim of Crime   149
    Abbe Smith

Daily Log of Independent Fieldwork   169
    Lynne Weaver

On the Vision and Practice of Participation in Project
    Head Start   197
    Lucie E. White

Afterword: Constancies and Commonalities in This
Volume's Law Stories 219
Gary Bellow and Martha Minow

Contributors 231

Introduction: Rita's Case
and Other Law Stories

Gary Bellow and Martha Minow

War stories is the phrase used by academic lawyers to disparage the ways practicing lawyers talk about their experiences. Still much of what matters about law eludes most academic writings. Perhaps, as a consequence, legal scholarship is awash in new methodologies designed to illuminate how law shapes and is shaped by its enforcers, interpreters, and those it regulates.

The approach that particularly interests us in these new inquiries is best described as participant-narrative. Celebrating storytelling, books by lawyers and law review articles for more than a decade have featured autobiographical accounts by lawyers, law professors, and law students; tales of fiction, fantasy, or allegory; retellings of strategies and tactics in famous cases; and reflections on the role of storytelling in conventional law practice. But despite this flowering of such narratives, stories of the actual experiences of clients and lawyers in concrete legal contexts remain few and far between. Because we believe that only such stories can convey how law is used and experienced by people enmeshed in its workings, we solicited the stories collected in this volume.

Our goal, begun here, is to develop a body of narrative work that reflects (*a*) multiple points of view; (*b*) textured depictions of conventional practices and institutional cultures; and (*c*) insights into how the legal workers and those affected by law make their choices, understand their actions, and experience the frustrations and satisfactions they entail. Scholars and interested observers of law need more of this kind of writing by practitioners to ground generalizations or critique about the

Thanks to Laurie Corzett for help with preparing the entire book.

functions law plays in social ordering. Power, language, institutions, customs, and relationships shape the meanings and constraints of law as both a regulative activity and a social institution; stories by participants uniquely expose these dynamics to view.

Business schools and public policy schools have, for many years, produced case studies for this purpose: a case writer, with no prior involvement in the situation, interviews key players and writes up a description of a setting and a problem to be used in a classroom for a variety of pedagogical purposes. In the process students are asked to assume the role of one or more of the protagonists and engage the dilemmas that the study highlights.

Some law schools have similarly experimented with this pedagogical approach. The resulting case studies are, indeed, more nuanced and far richer in detail than what is typically found in an appellate opinion. But the pedagogical purpose—and the usual authorship by someone with no involvement in the experience—tend to tilt the narratives away from the layers of emotion and perspective that legal institutions create for people caught or working within them. Moreover, case studies usually fail to offer the voice of the self-reflective practitioner and the insights of self-conscious practice. Our interest in this volume is to add to the stories being told about law more first-person accounts that address some of these experiential dimensions.

Unsurprisingly, our interest in the possibilities and limitations of the case study approach itself grows out of a case—originally handled by Gary Bellow as counsel for one of its participants and turned into a case study by Leila Kern, a student working under Martha Minow's supervision. The experience of writing, telling, and discussing this case not only made us more aware of its methodological limitations, but gave us some glimpse of what there was to be learned from practitioners describing the dilemmas they face and the institutional settings they navigate. What follows here is that study, as produced for our students,[1] and a discussion by Gary and Martha of what it left out or failed to convey.[2] We then turn to three general themes, and the ques-

---

1. The case is reprinted with permission from Lance Liebman and Philip Heymann, *The Social Responsibilities of Lawyers: Case Studies* (Foundation Press: Mineola, N.Y. 1988).

2. Before writing this chapter, we talked together many times about its themes and about Rita's case. We also recorded a conversation on tape on January 12, 1995, in which Martha interviewed Gary about Rita's case. We drew on that interview for this chapter.

tions they generated, that emerge from reflections on the story and animate all of the essays in this book.

The first of these themes concerns the significance of context: particular legal institutions and bodies of law produce particular patterns of activity familiar to those who participate in them but baffling to others. Each particular context—framed by law but influenced as well by social, economic, bureaucratic, political, and cultural factors— creates constraints for the legal worker and the client. How does this process work? On what sanctions, communications, and social processes does it rely? To what extent is familiarity the key to its ability to control behavior? The second theme addresses the incompleteness and indeterminacy of most constraints, the opportunities that exist in each situation for individuals to pursue their own purposes, to win their desired ends, or to invent their ends. How do such opportunities arise? How are they recognized? What conditions, psychological as well as social, are required for them to be realized? Finally, there are questions concerning the construction and alteration of identities in the process of accommodating and challenging limits in law practice. As they engage a legal problem, clients and legal workers experience shifts in the ways they see themselves and often change the way they relate to and are seen by others. How common, permanent, and typical are these occurrences? What is their significance in the roles law plays in social conflict?

Of course, none of these themes can be used as a template for understanding all the stories included in this volume. Nor is any specific reading of any story the only or best one that can be offered. In this sense, this collection cannot satisfy the criteria of truth, typicality, or theoretic significance that has been, at times, offered for evaluating story-writing in law.

Rather, as we found in our ruminations on Rita's case, each chapter offers partial descriptions, unsatisfying explanations, and ambiguous characterizations. But they also invite challenge to assumptions too readily held and understandings too shallowly conceived. And they encourage an imaginative consideration of alternative tellings and

---

The quotations from "Maynard" and "Kiladis" come from the "Rita's Case" chapter in *The Social Responsibilities of Lawyers*.

more subtle conclusions concerning the messages they convey. Or, at least, so we hope. We leave that judgment to you.

Rita's Case

Introduction

In April 1982, Keith Maynard, director of Philadelphia Legal Aid (PLA), sat down to consider whether he would encourage one of his young attorneys, Joan Kiladis, to pursue a child custody case for which she had done an intake the previous day. There would be no problem with PLA handling such a suit—the client appeared to meet the income requirements of the organization and the lawyers at PLA routinely handled child custody cases.

But the issue for Maynard was whether he wanted Kiladis, a young lawyer in her third year out of law school, on this suit. She had devoted most of her time for the past year to a child custody case and although that legal battle had ended—Kiladis's client having gained custody of her eleven-year-old grandchild—Kiladis's involvement with the client, Gladys, and her granddaughter, Rita, had really just started. Kiladis still saw the family regularly: she took Rita to the zoo or to the museum or on other day trips, she often helped Gladys by driving her to and from her therapy appointments or to the grocery store or to Rita's school, and from time to time she dropped by their apartment with food for the family or gifts for Rita.

Maynard, although proud of Kiladis's work on Rita's case, had two concerns: first, he was worried that another custody case would again occupy Kiladis's time with extralegal affairs. He could not afford to have one of his lawyers spend as much effort on such a routine manner; nor, Maynard thought, could Kiladis afford to spend so much emotional energy on her lawsuits. Second, he was concerned that Kiladis's intense involvement in Rita's case was not proper for a lawyer. Maynard had been taught that a lawyer must be a detached advocate for—not intimately involved with—her clients' interests. He was worried that Kiladis might be departing from limitations on the lawyer's proper role with her participation in her clients' lives.

For her part, Kiladis wanted nothing more than the opportunity to handle another custody case. Rita's case was the highlight of her time at PLA; rather than shuffling forms and preparing memos, she had had an opportunity to get involved with a family and had had what she had considered a positive impact on their lives. She relished the personal dimension of the case. But she also knew that Maynard would be reluctant to let her delve immediately into a new custody suit; so she wrote him a note asking him to consider the work she had done on Rita's case and asking for an opportunity to discuss this new case with him.

Before he called Kiladis in to discuss the new case with her, Maynard did as Kiladis asked—he pulled out the file to reconsider Rita's case and to think again about Kiladis's involvement in that case.

Rita's Background

Rita was born in Bellevue Hospital in New York City in December 1971. Her mother, Carllota, had entered the hospital in labor, just four hours after taking a shot of heroin. Rita's father, who had been living with Carllota for a number of years and who had fathered her two other children, was not present, nor was his name entered on Rita's birth certificate. Carllota abandoned Rita in the hospital, where the infant remained for three months, being treated for both heroin addiction and syphilis. Rita's maternal grandmother, Gladys, obtained legal guardianship and took Rita home in March 1972.

When Maynard later discussed Rita's case, he could not recall how Gladys had been named guardian; grandparents had no special status in guardianship cases and certain factors in Gladys's home life argued against her being named guardian. Maynard guessed that some social worker had filed the necessary papers and pushed the guardianship through.

Rita lived with her grandmother for the next two and one-half years. First they resided in New York City; then, with the New York court's approval, they moved to West Philadelphia where they lived in a house next door to a low-income public housing project. Although many members of the family—aunts, uncles, cousins—also lived with Gladys at various times during this period, two others were relatively permanent members of the household, both in New York and in Philadelphia. One was Manuel, Rita's first cousin. Three years older than Rita, Manuel had also been born out of wedlock, to Rita's aunt, Maria, and had been raised by Gladys from birth. Maria, like her sister Carllota, was addicted to heroin. The second semipermanent member of the household was Juan. Born in 1950, Juan had been brought up by Gladys since he was 15. In 1977, when he was 27 and Gladys was about 51, Juan became Gladys's third husband, thus becoming Rita's stepgrandfather.

In August 1974, Gladys turned to the Department of Public Welfare in Philadelphia (DPW) for help with Rita. The child, although only two and one-half years old, was very difficult to handle; according to Gladys, she had become manipulative, aggressive, and unmanageable. Gladys was scheduled for gallbladder surgery and needed help caring for Rita. The department suggested that Gladys place Rita in the Catholic Home for Children where the child could be evaluated and receive appropriate therapy, if needed. The home requested that St. Christopher's Hospital evaluate and provide therapy for Rita while she resided at the home.

Maynard later remembered that Gladys's feelings toward Rita seemed to indicate ambivalence: "Gladys loved Rita, but also couldn't control her, was somewhat older and not feeling well. There was this, 'I want her away, I want her back.'" Perhaps this ambivalence explains why, when she had recuperated from her gallbladder operation, Gladys did not bring Rita back from the Catholic Home for Children. Maynard remembered, "Once Gladys got home, and a period of time passed as she recovered from major surgery, she found she had a situation that was not so bad. So Gladys left things alone. It is similar, I think, to what some parents in other class settings who are ambivalent about their children do; they put their children in boarding school."

From August 1974 until June 1976 Rita seemed to thrive at the Catholic Home. She visited her family frequently on weekends, and her grandmother was often at the home during the week as well. But Gladys could not adapt to the boarding school regime; she was not comfortable with the rules. "I think the home found Gladys to be a pain in the ass," added Maynard. She could not do anything on time. She came to visit Rita during the week; she baked birthday cakes for other children's birthdays. She often brought Rita back late after a weekend home visit. Sometimes after such visits Rita's face and clothes were dirty and her hair uncombed, which shocked home personnel.

Although Gladys viewed the Catholic Home as a temporary residential facility where children could receive help and then return to their families, the DPW often used the home as a clearinghouse for children needing foster care. Because of Gladys's erratic behavior, the home decided that Rita would be better off in foster care. This decision was reinforced by Gladys's failure to state clearly that she wanted Rita back. Accordingly, in June 1976, the home decided to place Rita with a foster family in a lower-middle-class Philadelphia suburb. Gladys continued to visit Rita and take her home on weekends during the seven months Rita lived there.

Relations between Gladys and Rita's foster family quickly became strained. The foster parents complained to the home that Gladys was not sticking to the visitation schedule, and Gladys complained to DPW that Rita's foster parents were abusing Rita. Maynard commented:

> I believe that Gladys intentionally undermined this placement. She was extremely threatened that she had failed as a mother again and that she

was going to lose Rita permanently. Gladys did not have the ability to say directly to the home, "I want my child back." So, I think she made it very difficult for the foster family. When she talked to Rita about it, Rita picked up signals about what Gladys wanted to hear. So Rita started saying things about what was being done to her. There's no way of knowing whether they were true or not.

Nonetheless, Gladys complained to the DPW social worker about the alleged abuse and corroborated her tale with a description of bruises on Rita's buttocks, back, and sides; the social worker had Rita returned to Gladys within three days. By this time, February 1977, Juan and Gladys had married.

At first, everything seemed fine when Rita returned to Gladys. But soon Gladys became depressed. She could not handle Rita at all, and something seemed to be wrong with the child—she was aggressive and difficult, biting other children and throwing temper tantrums. Gladys turned to her social worker therapist, Elizabeth Reilly, who had Rita evaluated at the Learning Disabilities Center where Reilly worked. Reilly doubted Gladys's ability to care for Rita given her own physical problems and Rita's antics. Reilly was finally able to convince Gladys to place Rita back at the Catholic Home for Children. She also began a process of convincing Gladys to put Rita up for adoption.

During the following 18 months, Rita again settled into the routine at the home. Although there were still many home visits, Gladys was again having difficulty maintaining the visiting schedule. She often did not arrive when she had promised to, and she frequently left early. Occasionally, Rita's mother, who had herself moved to Philadelphia, visited Rita at the home. Home personnel noted that Rita often returned from visits to Gladys appearing distressed.

Within a year of Rita's return to the home, when Rita was six years old, plans were again made to move her to a foster family. Maynard remarked:

> The planning came from the judgment of the people at the home that Rita really ought to be permanently placed somewhere, and that grandma should remain grandma. There should be visits, but Rita should slowly be weaned away from her grandmother. This was a judgment that was concurred in by Elizabeth Reilly, Gladys's therapist. And there was something in writing—some document from the home that indicated consent by Gladys to an adoption. Interestingly enough, when we got discovery, that document was missing; but I had seen it.

The plans to move Rita into a foster placement were greatly accelerated when a young, inexperienced psychology student, after six play-therapy sessions with

Rita, concluded that Rita had been sexually abused. Looking back on Rita's case, Kiladis commented:

> The student was being supervised by someone whose "thing" was sexual abuse. What wasn't so clear to us and took us a while to find out was that half the children in the home had been placed there as a result of being sexually abused. This student felt that Rita was acting out various sexual behaviors. What was somewhat unfair about it was that apparently this went on all the time. Kids often playacted, partly as a way of working through some of what they've been through, and obviously it rubbed off on some of the other kids. But this student really freaked out about what was going on.

Although it was possible that Rita had been exposed to some sexual behavior, it was not clear exactly what had occurred or where. The home suspected Juan, Rita's stepgrandfather, and filed with DPW a form CY47 report of possible abuse. The home also decided to place Rita out of Gladys's reach. Although the home stated that it was cutting off visitation because of the sexual abuse issue, Gladys's failure to cooperate with the first foster care placement was also a major concern of the home's. "All of the social workers' notes were loaded with things like that, that Gladys was and had continuously been difficult." Rita was then moved to a foster placement with the Biancos, a middle-class family in Jenkintown, a well-to-do suburb of Philadelphia about 20 miles from Gladys's home in West Philadelphia. Gladys was not given Rita's address or her phone number.

The home promised Rita's new foster parents in Jenkintown that the child was theirs to adopt. Kiladis later reflected that this promise might have been part of "a deliberate cover-up" of Rita's exposure to either sexual abuse or sexual activity at the home itself. At first Gladys reacted passively to Rita's placement in a foster home, as she had when Rita was placed in Germantown the first time. But when the new DPW worker on the case, who had met Gladys only once before, bluntly told her that Rita was being placed a second time—adding, "I'm not going to let you see her"—and furthermore made accusations about sexual abuse of Rita by Juan, Gladys's attitude suddenly altered. Maynard recalled: "Gladys went to her therapist Reilly and Reilly's staff and drove them crazy, screaming at them, 'You've got to help me!' and they in turned called us." Maynard added:

> I got a call from Reilly saying that we had to help this woman. There had been accusations of sexual abuse and her child had been taken away. Reilly

didn't say anything to me about the fact that she had been moving Gladys toward adoption, that she herself felt that that might be both in Gladys's and Rita's best interests. I learned of these things only after the case came to us.

Maynard, after some investigation, took Gladys as a client. In a complicated series of moves he was able to negotiate a visitation schedule for Gladys while Rita was being evaluated by a group of specialists at St. Christopher's who dealt with sexually abused children. After several weeks, however, the "games began again." As Kiladis later put it, Gladys and the Biancos competed for Rita like divorcing parents. Gladys was never on time when she brought Rita back and never returned her to the Biancos in the same clothes in which she had left. The Biancos often dressed Rita inappropriately—for example, dressing her in a party dress when they knew that Gladys was taking Rita on a picnic. The Biancos would then complain when Rita's dress became soiled. Each family criticized the other's way of life. The Biancos were not Hispanic, and Jenkintown had essentially no Hispanic population. Rita, who had been bilingual, could no longer speak much Spanish. In fact the Biancos severely reprimanded her for any tendencies to use Spanish. At school in Jenkintown she was exposed to racial slurs and made to feel inferior for being Spanish. Rita claimed that the Biancos told her that if she returned to West Philadelphia she would become "scum like the rest of them" and that their home offered a fine suburban lifestyle.

Legal Strategy

Taking the Case

Maynard remembered how he analyzed the case after getting the call from Reilly:

> Invariably I begin investigating these sorts of cases as if the facts are there to be assembled for decision at some future date. But in my gut I know that the decision will not be the same once the investigation is completed. Memories, perceptions, and positions will all have been affected—influenced by the investigation itself. What might look very bad for a client before a lawyer gets into a case can look very different after the lawyer's influence is felt. On the other hand, what are the choices? This is not an extreme case where I suspected that the child was being abused by my client. Rita had Carllota's phone number and often spoke to her, and

Carllota was often at Gladys's house. In addition, Rita went over to her mother's house more often than any of us realized, and the exposures over there that would be bad for a child were enormous. But this wasn't enough to alter what I did in the case. I simply chose the right of Gladys to make the decision about her grandchild over the right of other people to make it. I did not decide that I was the lawyer to decide what was best for Rita. Within certain limits, I really did and do allow my role as an advocate in the situation to take its course.

By the time Kiladis entered the case, then, Maynard had gotten to know Gladys well: he did not believe that there was sexual abuse in Gladys's home, and he believed that losing Rita permanently would be a terrible blow for Gladys. If, during the course of the prolonged legal maneuverings, Gladys's anger and anxiety would dissipate and she committed herself to adopting Rita, Maynard would be amenable.

Kiladis's approach to representing Gladys was somewhat different. Kiladis had let Maynard know, when she first became involved with the case, that she had to speak with Rita before she could make a commitment to represent Gladys. If DPW was correct in its evaluation of the situation and if Rita had developed a strong positive bond with the Biancos, then Kiladis felt she would not have "the emotional energy for the case." But if Rita reported that life with the Biancos was very different from the way both the home and the DPW described it, then "it would be very important to help her." Kiladis recalled:

> Ultimately it put me in a bit of a bind. It wasn't clear whose attorney I was, what I was advocating for, and so on. Knowing Rita's needs as well as Gladys's and eventually even Carllota's created a lot of tension for me. Their needs were different, and it was not clear how to bargain them out; whether to try to get the maximum good for everyone or just for our client, Gladys.

Aside from the question of what might or might not be in Rita's best interests, Maynard had first been confronted with the problem of Gladys's best interests. Gladys wanted Maynard to move immediately to get Rita back for her. Here Maynard had two concerns: first, that he might lose if he went to court at a time when suspicions of sexual abuse were being raised; and second, that a court battle would take its toll on Gladys herself. Gladys was not emotionally able to withstand the upheaval of a prolonged court procedure.

Early in the case Maynard had come to realize that it would be extremely painful for her to be evaluated as a parent by an outsider.

Although he intended to be Gladys's advocate and to try to intervene with DPW, Maynard's legal instincts told him he could best manage the case by drawing things out for a while, despite Gladys's desire that he act immediately. Maynard therefore decided that it did not make sense to force the issue to a hearing right away:

> One, I couldn't win. Two, I thought this would be bad for Gladys. And three, the expert who had been doing therapy all of this time could not make a good witness for Gladys. So I went back to Gladys and I said: "I don't think that I can win it now. I don't think I can even get you visitation now, although if you tell me that I have to, I will try. I also don't think that Elizabeth Reilly will be as good a witness for you as she needs to be. I have got to do a lot of work with her, and you should start talking to her as well."

Initial Legal Maneuvers

From March through May, Maynard asked for visits at critical times: a confirmation ceremony in the family, illness of a close relative, a whole range of similar events. Each time, the visits were refused, yet there was constant negotiation with DPW about visits.

On May 10, 1979, more than two months after Gladys had come to him, Maynard drafted a letter for her. Essentially the letter was a statement by Gladys that she wished to terminate DPW's custody of Rita and demand that Rita be returned to her. Maynard knew that this would precipitate action on the part of the department, and it did. Since the time Gladys had voluntarily placed Rita with DPW, the department had had custody of the child. Now, on May 25, 1979, the department moved to formalize its custody by filing a motion in the appropriate Philadelphia court. Judge Warren granted temporary custody to the DPW, pending further proceedings.

But by then Maynard had begun the process he described as "obtaining information from, and trying to neutralize" the professionals involved in the case, and he was ready to proceed in court. On June 8, 1979, Maynard filed two motions: one for visitation and one for the payment of expert assistance for a psychological evaluation of Rita concerning the alleged sexual abuse. When he went into court on June 11, Maynard did not press the first motion:

What I said to them was that Gladys should be allowed to visit. I asked them why they felt that she shouldn't. They told me that it was too dangerous, that Gladys, or someone in her household, was going to sexually abuse the child. Then I brought up the notion of having an independent expert decide that issue. I used the two motions to get them to concede to the motion for expert assistance.

In fact, the court never acted on the visitation motion. Maynard continued to pursue that goal through negotiation. On the other hand, Judge Warren allowed the motion for payment of expert assistance because DPW did not oppose it. All parties agreed that expert assistance was a good idea; that Gladys really could not afford it; and, moreover, that it should be provided by the team of specialists at St. Christopher's. Maynard's choice of that team was a deliberate one:

> Before I went on the motion, I went to St. Christopher's. I had two meetings with the people there. They had never seen Gladys, but I had two meetings with them. I had a long talk with them about what I saw was going on and about how important it was that they look into it. I also went to see the fellow who runs the clinic, knowing that at that time St. Christopher's was involved in an internal struggle over whether to support DPW's approach to child custody issues, an approach which many saw as extreme intervention.

Maynard felt that many of the specialists on the team at St. Christopher's had attitudes that were ideal for his client. They were internally involved in a fight about whether they should be supportive of DPW's approach to removing children from their homes; they were sympathetic to poor people; they did not respect social workers (who generally stood at the bottom of the hierarchy of mental health professionals); and they believed that the social workers' decisions were often ill-advised and unsympathetic to poor people. Maynard recalled, "I knew they would bend over backwards to be noninterventionist in a case with PLA; I knew they would take the general position that these kids belong at home." In this particular case, where a child was being taken from an Hispanic environment and being removed to a distant suburb where she was not being allowed to see her relatives, Maynard thought the team would surely begin with an attitude sympathetic to Gladys. By the time Maynard had met with them twice, he knew that he had a "fairly receptive audience."

Maynard told Judge Warren that he had been to see the people at St. Christopher's. He indicated that they would be willing to accept the appointment from the court. Maynard was relieved that neither David Slade—a lawyer the court had appointed to represent Rita—nor the DPW counsel objected to the choice of St. Christopher's as evaluator. Had he been on the other side, Maynard noted, he would have demanded a different appointment, recognizing that the attorney who got to the expert first established a relationship that was likely to set up the case to some extent in his favor. But, in Maynard's words, "they were so relieved to give up this fight on visitation for a period of time that they went along with the appointment of St. Christopher's as an evaluator."

It was not until August 1980 that Rita's court-appointed lawyer, Slade, voiced concern about the evaluation being done by St. Christopher's. At that time he moved for an additional psychological evaluation and payment of costs. Although this evaluation was also to be conducted by St. Christopher's, Slade specified that the report evaluate Gladys's household as a potential home for Rita rather than limiting itself to the question of whether or not abuse had occurred there. Although Maynard knew that Slade might have realized that the St. Christopher's team was going over to Gladys's side, Maynard went along with the motion for a new evaluation because "I knew we had St. Christopher's; once you've got them that far, you've got them."

Lull

The evaluation process was very drawn out. But that also, Maynard thought, worked in Gladys's favor in the long run. In the interim, the Philadelphia Legal Aid attorneys had succeeded in building up Gladys's visitation with Rita, bit by bit. They also were able to speak with all of the actors in the case—a therapist in Jenkintown to whom the Biancos had taken Rita, a nun at the home, the DPW social workers, and Gladys's therapist, Reilly. Every interview had a dual purpose: it was an opportunity to get information and an opportunity to "neutralize" the speaker to ensure passive acquiescence in (if not active support for) a result favoring Gladys. Maynard commented that "all of those contacts were negotiations as well as interviews. The whole strategy was to bring the professionals around so that they saw Rita's placement as something that ought to change."

A great deal had changed under the influence of PLA. A schedule of day visits had been established. The St. Christopher's team was evaluating the situation, and though Gladys was cooperating fully with them, Betty Bianco was not. Because Betty refused to bring Rita to Philadelphia to go to St. Christopher's, Joan Kiladis was driving out to Jenkintown to pick up Rita and bring her downtown. Gladys was still in therapy with Elizabeth Reilly, whom Maynard felt was now moving toward siding with Gladys.

The team at St. Christopher's was aware that Rita was feeling tension because of the racism in the Jenkintown school she was attending. By March 1980, a talk between Gladys's attorneys and the staff at St. Christopher's indicated that the St. Christopher's evaluators were coming to three conclusions, summarized in a memo in the PLA file:

(1) While the St. Christopher's team cannot state categorically that there has been no sexual abuse, nothing in Rita's language or behavior indicates any basis for the CY47. If she was abused, she is no longer cognizant of the fact. The team believes that the filing of the CY47 was ill-advised; that a lot of the behavior cited is characteristic of institutional living.

(2) Rita wants to go home to her grandmother, cannot understand why she is moved from place to place, and is apprehensive that her therapists will be taken away from her.

(3) Because of the above, the team would recommend that Rita be returned to Gladys's home and continue in therapy at St. Christopher's.

Yet St. Christopher's was unwilling officially to exonerate Juan of sexual abuse, nor would the evaluators address the possibility that Rita was being beaten at the Biancos. Rita had written a letter to her therapist at St. Christopher's, saying that she was being beaten and generally mistreated by the Biancos and that she wanted to go home to her grandmother and "pappy," her name for Juan. Although Kiladis had not actually handed Rita the pencil and paper to write it, she felt somewhat implicated in the letter-writing process because she frequently urged Rita to be frank with the people she saw at St. Christopher's, reassuring her that what she told her therapist there would not get back to the Biancos.

Kiladis had also told Rita to be frank with David Slade, but as it had turned out, Rita never got to talk with Slade. Although he was the child's attorney and, according to Maynard, had left "no legal stone unturned," Slade never went out to see the child or asked to have her brought to his office. Maynard recalled, "We did not sit down with Slade and say, 'you should see the kid.' If we had, I think that he would have gone. But we didn't do that." Kiladis said that both Rita and Gladys had called Slade's office on numerous occasions and left messages on his answering machine, but their calls were never returned. Maynard added:

> Slade lived in another world. He lived in the downtown world of big firms. Those attorneys don't go to Jenkintown, and they don't go out to people's houses. The last thing he was going to do was to go to Gladys's house in West Philadelphia. I think that that is part of the class structure of the bar, and I think it's a shame. Those attorneys miss the chance for the type of practice that a doctor who is a general practitioner has. I have a life as full of people as of law, law as a human service. It's not for everybody, but it's for more people than you'd think if they'd give it a chance.

It was also clear to Maynard what Slade was advocating. At first, Maynard said, Slade had gone along with DPW, but later he opposed them as well and asked for continuances. He seemed to feel that Rita had already lost her identification as a Hispanic, and that therefore ethnicity was no longer at issue. "Slade was not even present at the final two hearings in the case," Maynard noted.

The PLA attorneys were able to turn to Rita's advantage Kiladis's friendship with two of the women at DPW who were involved with the case. Memos in the PLA file indicate that Kiladis had long telephone conversations with Susan Goldman, the supervisory social worker. Goldman had often called Kiladis at her home to discuss Rita's case. They also discussed the form CY47 report of possible abuse that the home had filed with DPW more than two years earlier but that had never been substantiated or officially pursued. Goldman felt that the psychology student who had made the first report of sexual abuse had been under considerable pressure—pressure to find instances of such abuse for her supervisor's book. Goldman and Kiladis discussed the question of why the home had chosen to move Rita into foster placement at a time when many of the professionals involved were warning against any change. Kiladis told Goldman of her own belief that Juan was a stabilizing influence on the family and that his youth counted in the family's favor if any concerns about Gladys's failing health might arise. Kiladis reassured Goldman that DPW need not rely upon its own judgment that Gladys and Juan were "okay as parents," since St. Christopher's was certainly very competent and would be making a favorable report.

Similarly, Kiladis was continually in contact with Grace Myers, the counsel for DPW. Before Myers became the attorney of record on the case, Kiladis had met her at the Philadelphia courthouse. Kiladis explained:

I had several long conversations with Grace. I knew her from law school. When I talked with her at the courthouse, I knew that some of what I was saying would get back to the department. I told her that we had a lot of cases with the department in which we concurred with the moves that the department was making, but that we had a few where we felt that the department's behavior was off the wall. The department occasionally overreacted, and Rita's case was an example of that; they were much more upset than was warranted.

Kiladis knew that her relationship with Myers "cut a lot of red tape." Kiladis did not tell Myers that she thought Gladys would fall apart if she had to take care of Rita without the necessary support services from DPW. Instead she told her that there were support mechanisms in place, that Gladys was doing well with them, that Gladys was being very cooperative, and that when the department told Gladys to do something differently with Rita she did so. Myers, according to Kiladis, "knew that I believed in what I was saying, that Rita wanted to go to Gladys, that Gladys wanted her, and that there were support mechanisms at work that I had no objection to."

Final Legal Matters

On January 29, 1981, Kiladis filed a petition for Gladys and Juan to adopt Rita. By then Kiladis herself had been with the case for six months and knew all of the professionals involved, as well as the principals—Rita, Gladys, Betty Bianco, Carllota, and Juan. Since Juan spoke very little English, Kiladis's acquaintance with him was limited. She had participated in a conference at St. Christopher's and knew that the hospital team's second report, which would come out on February 1, 1981, would contain a recommendation that Rita be returned to Gladys after a period of gradually increased visitation. The adoption petition, although filed, was not immediately acted upon.

DPW agreed to St. Christopher's recommendations, and Rita returned to live with Gladys, Juan, and Manuel in March 1981. She was, however, still under the legal custody of DPW. Rita and Gladys attended therapy sessions each week at St. Christopher's. Juan refused to go from the beginning. Kiladis believed that his resistance arose from a combination of his residual distress about having been accused of sexually abusing Rita and the traditional macho notion that men do not talk about their feelings. For whatever reasons, Juan said that if he had to attend therapy sessions he would move out. And shortly thereafter he did so, moving in with a woman his own age.

Gladys, Rita, and Manuel—Rita's cousin—were now living together at Gladys's home in West Philadelphia. Gladys was in therapy with Elizabeth Reilly, and Rita and Gladys continued to go to therapists at St. Christopher's. DPW remained involved. Finally, in January 1982, Kiladis convinced Susan Goldman that it was time for DPW to release Rita from its custody by moving to dismiss the original DPW motions for custody and to dispense with Carllota's consent to Rita's adoption. A hearing was set for February 2. Because Rita was ill that day, she and Gladys did not attend. Kiladis was there, along with Grace Myers for DPW; David Slade was not present. Since there was no opposition to the dismissal of the two motions filed by DPW, the judge was willing to dismiss them. But, he asked, who would then be Rita's guardian? Myers mentioned that Gladys was legally Rita's guardian because of the New York court order. Kiladis, not convinced of the validity of that order in Pennsylvania, told the judge that she had filed an adoption petition for Gladys and Juan. Myers voiced some concern about allowing Rita to be adopted by Gladys and Juan. Both women were concerned about the possibility that if adopted, Rita might become the object of a custody dispute between Gladys and Juan in the event that their separation ended in divorce. Judge Warren ordered a continuance.

In April Rita's case appeared before Judge Warren again. Rita and Gladys were present with Kiladis, and DPW was represented by Grace Myers and Susan Goldman. David Slade again did not appear. The judge allowed DPW to dismiss its two motions, entered into the record an agreement between Gladys and DPW for aftercare services, and allowed the petition for Gladys and Juan to adopt Rita, even though Juan was not present and the judge knew that Juan and Gladys were living separately. Rita ran up to the bench and hugged the judge.

Conclusion

After he finished reviewing Rita's case, Maynard concluded that it was Kiladis's involvement that had won the case for Gladys. Kiladis not only spent many hours talking with Susan Goldman and Grace Myers, she also spend a great deal of time with Gladys and Rita. While Rita lived in Jenkintown, Kiladis drove her to and from St. Christopher's and to and from Gladys's for visits. She met Carllota and recognized the extensive contact that Rita still had with her mother. Kiladis in many ways became an advisor and counselor to Gladys, talking with her about the best school placement for Manuel and, eventually, Rita, as well as answering Gladys's questions about various presents for Rita while the child was still living with the Biancos. Maynard recalled Kiladis had told him, "I had to set limits or I would have been making up grocery lists for her."

But Maynard was still not convinced Kiladis had successfully set those limits:

> She came as a new lawyer and gradually became more experienced. As she began to grow and I had more confidence in her, I gave her more and more of the case. She developed an excellent relationship with Gladys. I was anxious for that to happen because I needed to separate myself from it psychologically. But what I also saw develop was the classic problem of overcommitment. It seemed to me that Joan took every little piece of anything that was there and blew it up. At the same time she was driving Rita around town and making Gladys's domestic arrangements. She made the case because of the amount of energy and effort that she put into it.

Before Kiladis went in to speak with Maynard, she thought about the many things she knew about Rita's case that Maynard did not know. She thought of Carllota's continuing involvement with Gladys and Rita and the potential dangers in Rita's exposure to a drug-dominated environment. Moreover, there was the fact that Gladys received a full monthly allowance from the federal AFDC (Aid to Families with Dependent Children) program, even though (unbeknownst to the welfare department) Gladys and Juan owned the building that Gladys and the children were living in and had not reported the rent they were receiving from the two apartments in the building; and the couple also had previously owned a building in Puerto Rico that, since it was not occupied by either of them, would have disqualified Gladys for welfare as well. Additionally, Kiladis knew that Gladys was working one job under a false Social Security number. Where did Kiladis's duty to her client begin and end?

Contingency and Change: A Commentary on Rita's Case

All tellings are unique, incomplete, and inaccurate. This can be said of each of the stories that follow; it turned out to be true of Rita's case as well.

"Rita's Case" is based on a problem brought by Rita's grandmother to Harvard's Legal Services Center in Jamaica Plain, Massachusetts.

The context is the linked institutions of foster care, state social services, local courts addressing family law matters, and legal services for poor people. The dominant institutional mode in this context is delay and the preservation of the status quo, whatever it currently is. The prevailing norm, regularized into a pattern of practice followed by judges and practitioners alike, is consensual agreement. Against this background, the case study presents lawyers who pursue active, strategically oriented courses of action, trigger or channel conflicts, and adopt partisanship as their norm and ethic. Working with and against relatively passive lawyers for the state and the child, these lawyers win the return of a grandchild to her grandmother from state custody and foster care placement.

The study disguises crucial facts: the location was moved from Boston to Philadelphia; the names of all involved and some of the peripheral facts were changed. Gary Bellow—renamed Keith Maynard—served as the actual senior attorney; Joan Zorza, renamed Joan Kiladis, was the younger attorney. Leila Kern, at the time a law student, wrote the case under the supervision of Martha Minow. "Rita's Case" became part of a case-writing project directed by two other Harvard Law professors, Lance Liebman and Philip Heymann, who developed teaching materials aimed at professional ethics issues. Liebman and Heymann published "Rita's Case" along with other case studies in *The Social Responsibilities of Lawyers: Case Studies* (Foundation Press, 1988).

The final form of the study was constructed from several sources. Working like an investigative reporter, Leila Kern gathered the facts several years after the events it recounts had occurred in the early 1980s. She initially received the lawyers' files of the case and then interviewed the major actors involved with it; she interviewed Gary as one of the actors, but without reference to his being a colleague of the involved faculty. He deliberately refrained from any role as author or editor so, as he put it, "my voice would not get blurred with my role as a teacher." She also interviewed Joan Zorza and staff members from the State Welfare Department and the Department of Social Services.

Martha reviewed the issues with Leila, commented on drafts, and helped develop questions for teachers and students on the issues the case presented. The study has now been read and discussed in many law school classes, in seminars in continuing legal education, and in judicial training programs. It has been the subject of a videotape production by the Georgia Chief Justice's State Commission on Professionalism and has found its way into several texts on professional responsibility. In this process it has been interpreted and reinterpreted in ways not foreseen by either its participants or its chroniclers. As the essays in this book began to be gathered, our experience with "Rita's Case" prompted both of us to ask ourselves what we had learned and are learning from such efforts at storytelling in law. What is the relationship between the study and what actually happened—or perhaps, better put, what other stories might be fairly told about what happened?

The study, as written, conveys two implicit narratives. The first is the dramatic and heroic rescue of Rita, a Hispanic child, from the clutches of an overbearing, white middle-class child protective system. The Legal Services attorneys come in on the side of Gladys, the beleaguered and wronged grandmother; the child is rescued from the state and the alien foster family; the sexual abuse that Rita experienced is presented as a terrible, but past event and characterized as more likely to have happened while in state custody than anywhere else. Her return to the home of her grandmother is sealed with the kiss of adoption so the state cannot easily reenter Gladys's life and take her grandchild again.

This version poses questions about tactics but not ends because its background assumption views the state as bad and the client as deserving. It questions not the outcome of the case, but whether the attorneys acted properly in purposely orchestrating the result: to what extent can a lawyer take advantage of a bureaucracy that appears less biased than lethargic in exercising its independent authority to protect the child? Are there limits to such conduct in the profession's regulative norms?

The second narrative questions the client's ends and the problematic consequences of the lawyers' conduct. This version stresses the continuing presence in Rita's life of her mother, Carllota, who remains drug-involved and a danger to her; the grandmother's ambivalence and inconsistency as a parent figure, her own questionable marriage to Juan, a man many generations her junior; and Rita's opportunities for a safe and secure life in the suburbs with a foster family interested in providing her a permanent home. The lawyers secure the return of Rita to Gladys, and an adoption by her and her husband Juan, despite his virtual abandonment of the home for another woman. Rita grows up to adulthood in her grandmother's home. In this version the reader is left with troubling questions about the hubris of the lawyers and their choice to pursue the grandmother's expressed desires in a situation in which her granddaughter's best interests might dictate a different course. What is the lawyer's responsibility for the consequences of his or her actions? By what criteria should a judgment about consequences—immediate or long-term—be made?

How a reader resolves the questions posed by either version depends, of course, not only on the reader's values and attitudes, but on his or her evaluation of the child protective system and the perceived risks to this child both in and out of it. If the reader thinks the system works well for children, this child's future might properly be guided by it and the lawyers should fail in their efforts to bring her back to her grandmother's home. If the reader thinks the system is not helping this child, but instead is exposing her to abuse and yanking her from her family with little regard for her cultural identity, then the lawyers are heroes reuniting the child with her family and her world.

Such judgments are further influenced by the way the writer presents the narrative. In "Rita's Case," the outcome is presented as a function of the competing choices made by the lawyers about the roles they should play and the normative commitments that should guide their conduct. Perhaps because of the desire to use the case in teaching professional responsibility, particular emphasis is placed in the study on one such set of decisions: the choices concerning how much involvement or distance from the client and her goals the lawyers should permit or encourage at various stages of the representation. The younger, inexperienced lawyer is pictured as deeply involved in her client's life, concerned and committed to both grandmother and grandchild, and willing to take on responsibilities (grocery shopping, transportation) well beyond other professional obligations. The older, experienced lawyer maintains sharper boundaries, maintaining a distance between himself and the client that permits him to stay focused on his partisan role in making judgments on options and strategies as they are presented to him. The suggestion is that this clarity of posture and purpose overrides the younger lawyer's doubts about the relative claims of grandmother and granddaughter and largely accounts for the trajectory the case followed. The title of the case study, which references the grandchild rather than the grandmother—the client whom the lawyers represent—underscores the writer's doubts about the outcome.

As we reread the case, both of us were struck by how many alternative versions of these events this interpretation left out. It treats the actions and motives of the participants as too unidimensional and static, paying too little attention to the ambiguities they reflect and the ways they changed over time. In one such possible scenario, closer to Gary's own memory, the two lawyers did, indeed, start with differing conceptions of their roles. Gary (Maynard), who focused primarily on the client's stated preference, was prone to carry the case forward, down entitlement-oriented lines, with an eye to what he could get for the client, regardless of the consequences. Joan (Kiladis), who believed that her own views of a just result should finally guide her conduct, was more prone to exercise independent judgment about what an appropriate outcome would be in this kind of case. She tended to look to the potential consequences of her advocacy to evaluate whether a case should be taken at all or how it should be handled. But neither lawyer's views are readily captured by the reduction of these orientations to singular choices, or by contrasting each of their views concerning detachment and involvement in legal work.

As Gary recalls, both believed, and discussed with each other, that they both needed to be distant enough to make the kind of prudential judgments that are called for in giving advice in uncertain and emotional circumstances, and yet committed enough to gain the client's trust and the psychological energy to press the client's cause. The study conflates the tensions in the lawyer-client relationship relating to involvement and detachment with a secondary set of tensions flowing from the problem of reconciling devotion to client preferences with concern for consequences. In so doing, the complexities of each, and the difficulty of integrating them with each other, are blurred or lost.

Nor do attitudes and approaches necessarily remain constant over time. Rather, each changes as the case, and the choices and actions that influence it, change. Seen from this vantage point, the story's attempt to make the protagonists representative of a particular ethical position takes an unexpected turn: the lawyers shift places on the primary ethical issue the study poses. Gary offers the following retrospective on what occurred:

> Over time I began to be more concerned about the results we were going to produce, ironically because the advocacy strategies we were pursuing were working so well. . . . Suddenly Joan and I had become so effective that we were taking advantage of the inability of the system to actually give voice to and protect all the parties,

including Rita. I began to become somewhat uneasy about that. . . . Joan, on the other hand, perhaps because of her involvement with grandmother and granddaughter, had stopped speaking of what was desired by, or best for, each of them individually. Her concern more and more focused on preserving the connections that their living together fostered. As the case progressed, we essentially reversed roles.[3]

Pursuing every possible legal avenue to protect the relationship between grandmother and granddaughter meant even pursuing a questionable adoption—so the Department of Social Services would be out of Rita's and Gladys's lives permanently. The facts that Gladys's marriage was falling apart and that Carllota, Rita's mother, remained addicted to drugs and very much in Rita's and Gladys's lives became much less significant than the possibility that, at some later date, the department might reintervene in the family. Although it could still do so if Rita were adopted, the department then would be required to prove Gladys's unfitness in order to remove Rita from her home. Without pursuing an adoption, Gladys's guardianship could be set aside on a showing relating solely to Rita's best interests.

Certainly some, if not all, of this was known to the attorneys as they prepared for the adoption hearing, but neither the department nor the court knew these facts or, if they "knew" them, neither was focusing adequately on their long-term significance. Gary recalls becoming more and more concerned that, without even discussing the factual and legal circumstances of the case with the court, the client might well win what her lawyers sought on her behalf: adoption of her granddaughter and complete insulation from continuing involvement by any outside agency. In fact, this occurred.

Ironically, this dilemma, and its emergence in a particular proceeding, is downplayed in the case study narrative, despite its powerful ethical implications. The central ethical issue in the case for Gary was not the question of the terms on which the case was taken, or the abstract choice of detachment or involvement with the client, or even the general issue of the obligation owed the client, Gladys, as opposed to Rita. Central instead was the particular decision, at a given point in

---

3. We have no doubt that Joan would have still another version of these events, the case study, and this new retelling of its narrative.

the relationships that the lawyers had structured and influenced, to seek adoption, with its long-term consequences for all involved. A discussion of overinvolvement and detachment in the lawyer-client relationship does not begin to come to grips with the complexities of this choice—for both of the lawyers involved.

A similar difference between the study and alternative tellings arises from the way the study deals with the senior lawyer's relationship with Gladys. The study presents Gladys, at least after the Department of Social Services excluded her from Rita's life, as unequivocally committed to Rita's return to her home. It also treats these feelings as constant over the course of the case. Gary's recollections offer a more complex picture. A counselor—named Elizabeth Reilly in the case study—asked Gary to take the case. She emphasized the client had felt victimized by the state's removal of her granddaughter from her home; that act by the state was an assault on Gladys's dignity. Yet Elizabeth Reilly's own goal as a counselor was to help Gladys agree to release Rita for adoption. From her perspective, Gladys's sense of personal insult stood in the way of a result that Gladys "really" wanted and that was both in Gladys's and Rita's interests. The referral to a lawyer was intended to remove the barriers to this process, not to generate strategies for Rita's return.

Gary also noted that his office had an independent interest in having a good working relationship with Reilly, who saw many of the office's clients and was an important resource for the work Gary's own office was doing in this area. It was not clear (it never is) what role this agenda would play, or the initial expectations surrounding the referral, in the events that followed.

Gary recalls liking Gladys immediately; although distracted by many personal issues, she was strong, capable, and intelligent. She also obviously felt better having a lawyer. Gary learned from her immediately that, as Reilly had suggested, Gladys felt insulted by the state's removal of Rita from her home, but also she was well along in accepting Reilly's plan to release Rita for adoption—without really facing up to what this would mean in her own life. Gladys seemed to want the option to have Rita returned to her, an option that she was then willing to relinquish. This goal was further complicated by the fact that no effort to regain custody of Rita would be likely to succeed without expert testimony on Gladys's behalf. Elizabeth Reilly, as the counselor and expert who knew the case best, would most likely report that neither Rita nor Gladys would benefit from efforts to reunite them. Moreover, Reilly, unknown to Gladys, felt that Gladys had been pushing Rita away, seemed too tired to care properly for Rita, and seemed unable to shield Rita from the drug world of her mother, Carllota. Acknowledging that she "needed" Reilly, Gladys told Gary that Elizabeth Reilly "would certainly tell the judge that Rita should come home to her." She had no idea that Reilly could well be a witness against her.

A client, thus, arrives at a legal services office seeking help in achieving ends about which she is deeply ambivalent. She holds a variety of misunderstandings about what could be accomplished, who would help her, and what would lie ahead. She readily acknowledges that what she wants is not what she might want later. She is sufficiently hurt by the events that preceded her coming to the lawyer that she is willing to disrupt her granddaughter's life in ways that she also acknowledges might not be in her granddaughter's interest, or even in her own. In such circumstances, what directions or interests of the client should be followed?

As Gary recalls, he tried his best to talk these issues through with Gladys as forthrightly as he could, and then recommended to Gladys a lengthy process of "positioning" the department. The delay could permit them to build a case that had some chance of success and would allow Gladys to figure out what she really wanted and how she felt about the risks both of seeking custody and losing—and of seeking custody and winning—the case. It would also give Gladys and Gary an opportunity to work out their own relationship. The case study truncates into a single paragraph several months of discussion, thinking, and strategic action, as Gary sought and strengthened the client's trust in him.

Gary believes that he initially won Gladys's support by suggesting a strategy to use the welfare department's antagonism against her to her own advantage, inviting denials by the department of requests for visits by Rita on holidays and to family events. The idea was to create a credible story, which could be documented and presented to a court, that the department was acting punitively toward Gladys rather than out of concern for her grandchild. By offering to work on issues that Gladys cared strongly about—confirming the negative treatment by the state that so offended her—Gary sought to establish a relationship with her that, over time, would more truly facilitate her making decisions about how she wanted the dispute with the department to be resolved. Nothing in the study quite captures this constructed quality of a client's wants, interests, and preferences, and the role a lawyer plays in their evolution.

The countless interactions that compose a case's history have this quality. Gradually, through multiple interactions within ongoing relationships, a client's perceptions and expressed interests change—or achieve clarity—and the lawyer may or may not fully appreciate which is the better characterization.

Gary arranged for Children's Hospital to become involved and to evaluate Gladys and Rita; that is, to provide the professional support crucial to tipping the case in Gladys's favor. The case study documents the way the involvement of the hospital was obtained, but it does not address what the resulting contact with experts meant for Gladys. About three weeks after the court's order, Gary drove Gladys to the hospital for her first visit with the Children's Hospital professionals. He remembers how nervous Gladys was—how much she wanted to convey to the experts at the hospital that she loved Rita. The anger had dissipated; she now felt loss and grief; this was her grandchild; she would raise her; she would raise her as she saw fit; and she would raise her in her own culture.

Were these new feelings for Gladys, or had time permitted her to express a view previously dominated by anger and humiliation? What became of her plan to guide Rita toward adoption? At any given moment, a client may have many different feelings and ways of organizing responses to the world; the client may present one view as the dominant one, or the lawyer may pick one up because it is most suited to the legal options or most congenial to the lawyer's own values. Moreover, what the client presents to the lawyer may bear only a peripheral relationship to the way the client crafts her own self-presentation to others. Gary remembers that, on the trip to Children's Hospital, Gladys did not so much express her desire to regain custody of Rita as her acceptance of her identity as the person in Rita's life who knew what illnesses her child had, what she eats, how she sleeps. In anticipating questions on these issues, Gladys experienced and embraced her feelings as Rita's parent. As she talked with the hospital experts who recognized her as the central figure in Rita's life and who credited her with the hard work she had done, Gary recalls watching Gladys undergo a transformation, recognizing her need for support and her desire to be that parent. It was this transformation, and its attendant self-understandings, that sustained her in the many, many months that the case required. This moment is as much a part of this law story as the maneuverings of the lawyers in the courtroom or across the bargaining table.

The case study quotes Gary (Maynard) as saying

> Invariably I begin investigating these sorts of cases as if the facts are there to be assembled for decision at some future date. But in my gut I know the decision will not be the same once the investigation is completed. Memories, perceptions, and positions will all have been affected, influenced, by the investigation itself. What might look very bad for a client before a lawyer gets into a case can look very different after the lawyer's influence is felt.

This insight should be taken not as a cynical statement concerning the legal manipulation of reality but, instead, as a glimpse into the significance that each relationship, each conversation, may have for those engaged in a particular case. Investigation, counseling, and bargaining are not just instrumental opportunities to achieve clients' already known and expressed desires, but experiences, often arranged and structured by the lawyers themselves, that permit clients to learn what they actually or come to want, and to define and understand themselves.

The same dynamics affect not only clients—the most common focus of these and other law stories—but the many others to whom the stories refer. Consider, for example, the treatment in Rita's case of Slade, the appointed counsel; Grace Myers, counsel for the department; Susan Goldman, the social work supervisor assigned to the case; and the Biancos, the unheard-from foster parents in the drama. Only Joan's and Gary's characterizations of their motives, roles, and actions in the case are included. Place yourself, for a moment, in the shoes of these other participants, and view the events from their perspectives. What other tellings of Rita and Gladys's story might they offer?

The story is presented by the study as a very difficult one to win. Even if Rita had been Gladys's child, and her unfitness to care for Rita the standard to be applied, agreements of the court and the state workers would typically have to be obtained before Rita was returned to her home. Experts would testify on both sides; hearings would be held and delayed. Visitation—supervised and eventually unsupervised—would have to occur. Cooperation of all concerned at each stage of the process would have to be secured, whether given helpfully, grudgingly, or obstructively with an eye to eventual removal of the child from the home. This is, at best, an arduous, difficult process.

In Rita's case, moreover, the applicable standard to be applied was whether returning Rita to Gladys was in Rita's best interest. The Massachusetts requirement that the unfitness of the parent must be established to remove a child from a parental home does not apply when the parenting figure is not the child's mother or father. Given Rita's history in institutional placements, her grandmother's inconsistent behavior, and the availability of an alternative placement that promised long-term stability and continuity, it is hard to imagine how the state actors would have been willing to support the return of Rita to Gladys, or to acquiesce in any of the steps set out in the study that moved toward that end. Indeed, it is likely that, if presented to the court at virtually any of the early stages in the case, the court would have supported Rita's removal.

Nevertheless, Rita, by agreement of both court and agency, is finally placed with and adopted by her grandmother. How was this agreement obtained? The case study suggests that the dominant factor was the advocacy efforts of the lawyers. The lawyer appointed to represent Rita was inactive. None of the lawyers who ultimately agreed to the resolution of the case had any stake in the original decision. Overworked and underappreciated, they were easy marks for an advocacy strategy that gained control of most of the primary sources of information about risks to Rita and about how and whether she had been abused. The foster family's voice, unrepresented and unrecognized, is never even heard.

In contrast, the grandmother's lawyer obtained high-profile outside experts. The lawyers put in unusual time and attention. The junior lawyer had a prior relationship with the lawyer for the Department of Social Services; this cut through the red tape. The evidence of abuse was indeterminate. All of these elements are worked into the narrative to explain the outcome. But both of us—participant and chronicler—are left unsure. None of the people working for the state (by appointment or otherwise) were quite the dupes the story suggests. All were mature, experienced players in this system. They surely could see (and, on several occasions said they could see) what Joan and Gary were trying to do. They had been too often supported by an accommodative court to believe that they could not have forced a different result. They worked too hard and knew too much about the cases they handled to so easily be labeled indifferent.

What we think occurred, at least in the case of the department's lawyers and employees, is that they wanted their instinct—that Rita would be better off with the foster family—to be wrong. It had been right too often. Generalized, it meant that large numbers of kids in low-income areas should just be removed wholesale to other environments. For people who chose to do the work they did, and who often wished that what they saw was not as true as it seemed, this conclusion was intolerable. Maybe what they saw in Joan and Gary's efforts was not just advocacy. Maybe they saw in those efforts a well-founded belief in Gladys that, given confidential access to "secrets" and information about the family, only her lawyers could have fairly held. Surely, Gladys loved her granddaughter. That they could see without persuasion. Why not, this once, let love and connection take its course? This is what we both now think occurred, although this was only implied to Gary by the department's workers. Seen in this light, their concurrence in the process, including the adoption, takes on a very different cast. They may have been far less objects of persuasive advocacy than willing participants in the story's conclusion. A focused study often attributes more influence to the subjects of the study than is warranted.

This leads us finally to a word about endings. A case study needs an end, if only as a point of decision to prompt discussion. But actually, there is no end, only breaking points and partial resolutions. A million things could happen. The household could fall apart. The welfare department could accuse Gladys of fraud; Gladys could win the lottery. Gary could adopt a Hispanic child (he did).

The case study does offer a useful clue to the artifice of endings; it leaves the reader with many questions about what the attorneys for Gladys said and did not say to each other. Like the quotation about the way an investigation creates facts, the case also suggests much about the artifice of presentation. The reporter who wrote the case study shaped the facts the same way a lawyer does; the reporter selects what to tell and what to keep secret, just as a lawyer does. So the reader is alerted to the ways that the story is invented, crafted, and partial.

The lawyers at some point withdraw, because, after all, it is the client's life. If their lens is wide, they leave this and every case with secrets, ironies, and, perhaps, a story to tell.

Welfare Stories

Anthony V. Alfieri

I met Mrs. Celeste[1] one morning during my first weeks of practice as a welfare lawyer in a neighborhood legal aid office. She told me that her electricity had been shut off and that her food stamps had been stopped. Of the many stories I heard in those first weeks, I found Mrs. Celeste's story especially compelling. At my urging, the legal aid office accepted Mrs. Celeste's case for investigation. Assigned to conduct the investigation, I interviewed witnesses, inspected documents, and searched statutory and doctrinal materials. After reviewing the results of the investigation with senior colleagues, I was appointed to represent Mrs. Celeste at a food stamp hearing and, subsequently, to join a litiga-

---

1. At my client's request, I refer to her in this essay as Mrs. Celeste. For five years, I served as cocounsel on a litigation team that brought a class action lawsuit on behalf of Mrs. Celeste and other food stamp recipients. During much of this period, I was responsible for virtually all lawyer-client communications.

With Mrs. Celeste's permission, the narratives recollected in this essay are drawn directly from the administrative hearing transcript and pretrial deposition compiled in the above-mentioned lawsuit. In scrutinizing these materials, I discovered a bundle of narratives that together compose Mrs. Celeste's story. At first glance, the narratives appeared disjointed both spatially and substantively, due in part to the haphazard interrogatory style used by questioners at the hearing and deposition. However, after close and repeated readings supplemented by case notes, I was able to discern recurring patterns and a logical order. Adopting this order, I assembled four different interlocking narrative strands, gathering pieces from both the hearing and the deposition.

Reconstructing the narratives required judgments of both form and substance. As to form, I sought to preserve the original text, except where redundant or ungrammatical due to its original oral expression. For reasons of privacy, names have been changed and specific institutional references have been omitted. As to substance, I erred toward textual inclusion. My method of reconstructing Mrs. Celeste's narratives from the hearing transcript and the deposition demonstrates both the availability and suppression of client narratives in daily advocacy.

tion team challenging the outcome of that hearing in a federal class action lawsuit. The litigation ended five years later in a consent decree.[2]

In the years since, I often have revisited Mrs. Celeste's case to gather lessons of lawyering for my teaching and to settle doubts that have arisen when these lessons were tested by clients, colleagues, students, and my own research. What I have discovered is that the story Mrs. Celeste told me at the outset of the case is neither the story I originally heard nor the one I retold in state hearing offices and federal courtrooms.

The story Mrs. Celeste told me is the story of an impoverished welfare recipient struggling against bewildering bureaucratic institutions to pay rent, retain gas and electricity, feed her children, and preserve her family's dignity. The story I heard and retold in the context of advocacy is different. It is a story about statutory eligibility and the state-sanctioned victimization of economically dependent women and children. In that story, Mrs. Celeste appears as a divorced Hispanic foster parent and a longtime food stamp recipient dependent on public assistance for survival. Because of a state food stamp reduction and economic need, she reallocates her public assistance income to pay rent and to purchase food and clothing. The reallocation causes her twice to forego payment of gas and electricity until the local utility company acts to discontinue her service, at which time she seeks out emergency assistance.

The state reduction of a client's welfare benefits and the resulting shortage or loss of basic necessities is a common story in impoverished communities. For poverty lawyers devoted to serving those com-

---

2. The setting of Mrs. Celeste's story is a mixed food stamp/foster care household composed of a three-generation natural family and foster children from three unrelated families. The regulatory conduct at issue is the legality of counting foster children as members of their foster care households, and the counting of foster care payments as household income for food stamp purposes. The issue raised novel substantive questions under the Food Stamp Act and conflicting federal regulations. See 7 U.S.C. §§ 2011-2030 (West 1988 & Supp. 1990); 7 C.F.R. §§ 273.3(ii), 273.9(b)(2)(ii) (1986).

At Mrs. Celeste's administrative hearing, the New York State Department of Social Services upheld the New York City Human Resources Administration's decision to reduce her monthly food stamp allotment, citing federal regulatory requirements. After legal aid lawyers filed federal class action lawsuits challenging the regulations on behalf of Mrs. Celeste and others in New York, Vermont, and Minnesota, the United States Courts of Appeals for the Second and Eighth Circuits invalidated the regulations. See Foster v. Celani, 849 F.2d 91 (2d Cir. 1988), aff'g per curiam, 683 F. Supp. 84 (D. Vt. 1987); Murray v. Lyng, 854 F.2d 303 (8th Cir. 1988), aff'g, 667 F. Supp. 668 (D. Minn. 1987).

munities in situations of crisis, the conventions of legal discourse, the constraints of institutional practice, and the inequalities of social relations dictate an instrumental method of storytelling. Stories must be quickly heard and retold to fit the settled traditions of law. The task is to deploy the tactics and strategies of lawyering to obtain the right fit; that is, to tell the right story.

This essay will not review the wisdom of poverty lawyer tactics and strategies in Mrs. Celeste's case. For my purpose, it is sufficient to observe that the tactics and strategies applied satisfied the twin objectives of safeguarding Mrs. Celeste's entitlement to food stamps and invalidating federal regulations abrogating that entitlement. The essay turns instead to poverty law advocacy as a medium of storytelling.

My thesis is that the poverty lawyer's telling of his[3] client's story in advocacy silences powerful client narratives. Stories contain multiple narratives, some heard, others unheard. Embedded in each narrative is a normative vision of the self and the world. The story Mrs. Celeste first told me contains powerful narratives of dignity and caretaking. Yet, these and other narratives are absent from lawyer storytelling in Mrs. Celeste's case. That absence provides the focal point of this essay. The essay is divided into three parts. Part 1 recollects Mrs. Celeste's narratives. Part 2 examines the traditional method of lawyer storytelling in poverty law practice. Part 3 explores reconstructive methods of lawyer storytelling.

Client Storytelling

Rereading Mrs. Celeste's original story and the story I retold in advocacy from case notes, state hearing records, and federal litigation documents[4] reveals four narratives silenced by lawyer storytelling. Due to their limited accessibility and shifting content, my understanding of Mrs. Celeste's narratives is partial. Even a partial understanding, however, grasps their normative power. That power is expressed in the norms of dignity, caretaking, community, and rights. Drawing upon Mrs. Celeste's state hearing transcript and federal court deposition,

---

3. To underscore the interconnection between gender and the traditions of poverty law advocacy, I use the male pronoun when referring to the lawyer and the female pronoun when referring to the client.

4. I employed these materials in an earlier version of this essay. See Anthony V. Alfieri, "Reconstructive Poverty Law Practice: Learning Lessons of Client Narrative," *Yale Law Journal* 100 (1991): 2107.

below I stitch these norms into a narrative framework. It is important to note that these narratives are singular to Mrs. Celeste and should not be extrapolated to construct an essentialist vision of impoverished clients.

Dignity

My food stamps were decreased from November to approximately February. Four months. Of course it caused me hardship. First of all, there were a lot of things that my kids, I couldn't afford to buy them. I couldn't buy them fresh vegetables, fresh fruits. Everything had to come from cans. Sometimes I run out of rice for my kids and they don't eat no rice. They eat anything; maybe they eat Cheerios or something like that. No-frills food, you know, things that had no frills. I paid less money for them.

But not all the time I have the money. When I don't have the money they have to go without it. There were a lot of things that I had to make cut-downs. I remember what they were. The foods was there, and both my boys always go into the baseball league. They couldn't go because I couldn't afford it. Christmas, they didn't have nothing. You know, there are a lot of things that they didn't do. They couldn't go to the movies, they couldn't go to the Skate Key, where they skate. Sometimes I had to buy in the thrift shop, you know, Salvation Army to buy some things that wasn't even fit to use, so I could use the money for food.

Caretaking

I first became a foster parent way back about 1983 some time, March 25, 1983. In that same day I got four kids, that night. When the lady came to my house, she put me down for two; I got four. Right now I have six foster children. You can never say. It could change tomorrow. I received the prior four. All of a sudden I had five, then six. That's the way it goes.

The kids age from eleven years to seven months. Starting with the oldest one, Nilsa, she is eleven years old; she's been with me since June of 1986. Salas is eight, Vilma is six, and Sarmiento is five; they have been with me three and a half years. Pablo is two, he has been with me since he was fifteen days old. Tyrice is seven months; she has been with me on and off, six months.

I didn't know about the foster care money. I found out when I went to the interview. It wasn't much, but you'd get something to provide for the kids. I take them in because I love kids. I always loved kids. And to have six kids in your house you have to love kids, because money is not everything, you know. The money they give you is not even enough to go around. If you think you are going to get rich on that money, forget it. Don't take care of no kids, then, because it's not going to work out. You really have to have some love, consideration, and know what these kids need.

I don't mix their money, the foster payment of the kids, with my money. I keep it in a separate place in the top drawer in an envelope. When the check comes, I just go and cash it. Then I go out and buy all their food. And, whatever is left, then you're going to have to go out and buy clothes and Pampers. Maybe at the end of the month I will have like, twenty or thirty dollars left, and still that's, you know, that's their money. You have to have that money with you at all times to keep the kids. I mean, I want to keep them.

The girls have gone back to their home and they have come back even worse than when I first had them. From their mother's house. They came back dirty and everything. I even had to buy special shampoo for lice because these children, when they came back to me, they came back with lice, bugs. I had to buy special shampoo and I had to buy Tylenol. They were sick with a cold. They come out worse, they got bad habits, swearing and everything. They come to my house and they stop all this. The judge orders the child to go back to the mother and nine months later the child has to be ordered to my house again.

Community

You have to go once a month for a meeting and they tell you the rule what you can do and what you cannot do with a child. How to discipline the children. What you could do with them, what you can't do with them. When the child is taken out of your house, how to prepare you to be disattached from that child. And when a child comes into the house, how you should behave with them, what to expect. If you get a child that is in need, like a special-need child, maybe he has muscular dystrophy, how to deal with him. If he has a mental or physical problem, how to deal with that. And we have to go to these meetings every month.

There is a psychologist in the agency. And there are other people that come from the outside, talk to you about it. People that go there, you know, the experts, whatever they call them. It's a lot of people that go there. The psychologist talks to us about how to behave with the kids, how to discipline the kids. This meeting has been going on for three and a half years that you have every month, starting in October and ending in June.

Rights

In order for me to become a foster mother, I have to have earned income for me and my kids. And, the welfare and the food stamps and the Medicaid, that's my only income. And, that's what makes me, you know, a foster mother. If I had no kind of income, I couldn't be a foster mother. They will take them out of the home, you know, they would figure that I wouldn't have enough income to really take care of them.

I don't care if they don't pay me. I consider Sarmiento and Pablo my kids even though I have no authority over them. I consider them my kids, and unless the judge orders them to go back to the mother, it is going to be hard on me, but I want to adopt. If they take Pablo and Sarmiento out of my house, I lose the priority of adopting them, and that is my main concern.

I don't want to lose Pablo because supposing you are a mother, how would you feel if they take a child away from you two and a half years old when he comes to you fifteen days old? What trauma is that baby going to feel? It is like putting a child through so many things. The child needs a head start and Pablo has it. He has a head start with me, and if they put him out, I lose the priority of adopting the child. That is the one I want.

I have a baby in the hospital, Tyrice. I don't care if you pay me the money, I want Tyrice. I went to the hospital every day and I don't get paid for that, but I am there every day, not the mother. Tyrice, she will be put in the hospital, and nobody is going to adopt a child who has problems, problems with her nerves, muscular problems. I look at Tyrice and how sick she is. I say she is a baby and she needs love, and that is what I am here for, to give her love. A lot of people don't want this work because it is too much trouble, but if you love kids like I do, it is not too much trouble.

Traditional Lawyer Storytelling

Poverty law advocacy is a field of storytelling where client narratives like Mrs. Celeste's are silent. Narrative silence is not a natural order; it is a constructed order imposed through acts of legal violence. Law's discursive conventions, institutional practices, and social relations render storytelling violent. The violence is interpretive. Indeed, silencing is a form of interpretive violence. Mrs. Celeste's case illustrates the contextual, normative, and hierarchical dimensions of silencing.

Contextual Silencing

Acts of silencing occur within contextual layers of legal discourse, institutional procedure, and social relations. Because these layers merge in advocacy, it is difficult to locate a single contextual act of silencing. Often the sites shift and the acts multiply. What may appear to be a discursive act of silencing may in fact prove to be procedural or relational.

Legal Discourse

Legal doctrine, statutes, and regulations all give rise to discursive acts of client silencing. Here, for example, federal regulations deemed Mrs. Celeste's foster children members of her natural family's food stamp household. Moreover, the regulations deemed foster care payments household income for purposes of computing her family's monthly food stamp allotment. Because these deeming rules constituted conclusive inferences, the scope of Mrs. Celeste's story was narrowed to matters of statutory construction. Hence, in state hearing offices and in federal courtrooms, legal aid lawyers told a story of legislative history, nutrition policy, and statutory income classification. Matters outside this statutory ambit were omitted.

Institutional Procedures

Institutional procedures also generate acts of client silencing. The procedures may be formal and rule-based or informal and conduct-related. At Mrs. Celeste's state hearings, the informal conduct of administrative law judges affected her *ability* to tell her story. On repeated occasions, judges sought to engage me and agency officials in a colloquy to adduce evidence and to assemble legal argument rather than directly elicit Mrs. Celeste's testimony. Although this informal method of gathering facts and parsing arguments may promote administrative efficiency, it limited Mrs. Celeste's opportunity to speak.

By comparison, in federal district court, formal rules of procedure influenced Mrs. Celeste's *willingness* to tell her story. Fearing an adverse decision, legal aid lawyers not only declined to bring controversial issues before the court but also elected to draft pleadings conventionally. Controversy erupted when legal aid disputed the federal defendant's (i.e., the Secretary of the U.S. Department of Agriculture's) prerogative to take Mrs. Celeste's deposition in the office of his counsel, the U.S. Attorney for the Southern District of New York. Citing Mrs. Celeste's family caretaking responsibilities and the costs of alternate child care, I argued that the deposition should take place in the legal aid office near Mrs. Celeste's home. When party negotiations failed to resolve the dispute, procedural rules governing discovery convinced me to abandon the argument for fear of pressing an issue the court might regard as frivolous. The lack of a safe place to tell her story is likely to have inhibited Mrs. Celeste's willingness to speak during discovery.

In the same way, procedural rules governing pleading persuaded legal aid lawyers to set forth a conventional—short and plain—statement of Mrs. Celeste's story in her complaint instead of a more lengthy, narrative version. Putting forward such an alternative statement risked inviting additional discovery requests and pretrial motions. Discovery requests threatened to slow our litigation strategy, burden Mrs. Celeste, and tax the scarce staff resources of legal aid. Pretrial motions subjected Mrs. Celeste to the danger of court dismissal and delay. The vexations of discovery, pleading, and motion practice restrained us and Mrs. Celeste from speaking out in advocacy.

Social Relations

Social relations as well engender acts of client silencing. Fundamentally, a poverty lawyer may believe his client to be dependent and inferior. Alternatively, he may view client dependency as a strategically necessary construction required to gain sympathy from adjudicators and to minimize client participation in case management, thus speeding the favorable disposition of a mass caseload. Whether his motivation flows from formal belief or instrumental knowledge, a poverty lawyer plans and manages the advocacy process—interviewing, counseling, negotiation, discovery, trial, and motion practice—in a manner that restricts his client's opportunity to speak.

To be sure, some clients prefer silence to speech. Theories of identity and role construction suggest that this preference is mutable. Identity theory implies that a client constructs a vision of the *self* out of competing norms: dependence and independence, competence and incompetence, power and powerlessness. Role theory indicates that a client constructs a sociolegal *role* embodying the social practices of lawyers, bureaucratic agents, and adjudicators.

The conjunction of contradictory private norms and acquired public roles in lawyer-client social relations provokes tension. Privately, a client appears both dependent and independent, competent and incompetent, powerful and powerless. Publicly, in her sociolegal role, a client looks only dependent, incompetent, and powerless. The contextual constraints of legal discourse and institutional procedure fail to account for this public-private dichotomy. A fuller explanation calls for the study of normative and hierarchical forms of silencing.

Normative Silencing

Acts of silencing are predicated on a normative *preunderstanding* of a client's world. Preunderstanding is a method of social construction that operates by applying a standard, normative reading to a client's story. In the context of welfare law, that reading implies dependence. Welfare readings of dependence, however, displace the meaning of client norms.

A poverty lawyer lacks the critical distance from preunderstanding to grasp the machinations of client-accommodated dependence. Situated in a position of power and interpretive privilege, he cannot see the illusion of dependence projected by his own preunderstanding and reflected back by a client. Indeed, my own reading of Mrs. Celeste's story rested on a preunderstanding of client dependence and inferiority. This generalized reading portrayed Mrs. Celeste as an *object*—foster parent, food stamp recipient, client—acted upon but incapable of acting. The image appeared in litigation team planning conferences, negotiations with cocounsel and opposing counsel, state hearing arguments and lines of questioning, and federal court arguments, pleadings, and memoranda of law. This objectified image excluded Mrs. Celeste from participation in telling the story of her struggle to preserve her family's food stamp entitlement and to maintain her foster care parent eligibility. Client exclusion from storytelling is a consequence of accommodation, distrust, and translation.

Accommodation

The lawyer's dependent characterization of client story is reinforced by a client's withholding of her narratives from storytelling. Withholding is induced by the lawyer but executed by the client in a strategic accommodation to the normative world projected by the lawyer's preunderstanding. Accommodation does not confirm the lawyer's narrative reading of the client's story, but it does create the illusion of the rightness of his interpretation.

Mrs. Celeste accommodated the violence of normative silencing by withdrawing to the private domains of her family and foster parent community. There she continued her struggle to procure emergency assistance grants, feed, clothe, and house her natural children, care for her foster children, assist other foster parents threatened by food stamp reductions, and obtain adequate child support payments for her granddaughter. Legal aid lawyer narratives failed to assign normative meaning to Mrs. Celeste's talk of emergency assistance applications and delays, food stamp budgets and reductions, and child support payments. Likewise, the narratives failed to grant normative significance to Mrs. Celeste's talk of troubled foster children, uncertain agency placements, unpredictable family court decisions, and monthly foster parent meetings. The absence of this kind of talk from advocacy is indicative of client accommodation to lawyer silencing.

Distrust

Client accommodation to lawyer silencing is rooted in distrust. The impoverished client distrusts her poverty lawyer's interpretive practice of storytelling. Interpretive distrust thwarts lawyer-client participatory forms of advocacy. The inclusion of client narrative in storytelling will not cure client distrust. Nor will it restore a previous condition of lawyer-client trust. Talk of healing and restoration is misplaced. There is no remedy to enjoin distrust. Further, there is no a priori state of trust to revisit.

Difference militates against interpretive trust. Diverse categories of difference—class, ethnicity, gender, race—intensify the experience of client distrust. For each category, the lawyer conflates difference and dependency. On this logic, if all impoverished Hispanic women are dependent, then Mrs. Celeste is dependent. The accumulation of difference—age, disability, sexual orientation—expands the degree of dependency inferred.

Translation

Even if difference carried no inference of dependency, a poverty lawyer could not accurately translate client narratives into advocacy stories. He is constrained by the imperfection of translation. Discursive imperfection cannot be rectified through simple narrative revision. No advocacy story can embody the fullness of a client's narratives. Furthermore, no lawyer-told story can guarantee that client narratives are entirely reliable or reconcilable.

Holding a client to a standard of wholly consistent narratives defies the public/private ambiguity of client identity and the conflicts of client role. Mrs. Celeste's narratives establish neither perfect coherence nor total stability. What overcomes this ambiguity is her normative vision of dignity, caretaking, community, and rights. That vision is subverted by hierarchy.

Hierarchical Silencing

Acts of silencing are hierarchical insofar as they favor and disfavor specific client narratives. Favored narratives attain a privileged position in story. Disfavored narratives slip to a marginal position. These positions are not fixed. Dominant and subordinate narratives fluctuate, moving up and down, switching from top to bottom. This unsteady movement characterizes lawyer storytelling in Mrs. Celeste's case at discursive, institutional, and relational levels.

Legal Discourse

At a discursive level, the statutory language of the Food Stamp Act privileged the narrative of client eligibility. Employing the statutory categories of eligibility (i.e., household size, income, and resources), legal aid lawyers established the basis of Mrs. Celeste's claim of food stamp entitlement. This showing was crucial. Nonetheless, it marginalized Mrs. Celeste's alternative, rights-based narratives of caretaking and community.

Mrs. Celeste's narrative of caretaking did not explicitly speak of rights and entitlements. She put no great store in the abstract talk of rights. But, in the concreteness of her daily life, she aggressively asserted rights on behalf of her family, including child support, emergency assistance, and food stamps. Each assertion implied an instrumental usage: child support and food stamps to feed her natural family, emergency assistance to resupply gas and electricity.

Mrs. Celeste's commitment to rights survived the capriciousness of both bureaucratic and judicial enforcement. With respect to emergency assistance, she points out, "To my knowledge, if I don't sign [recoupment papers] I don't get the money for the gas and electricity." With regard to food stamps, she complains, "I don't know why the food stamps go down. I don't know why they go up either." Even when court enforcement of her granddaughter's child support right proves meager, Mrs. Celeste never abandons rights. She explains, "He [the father] wanted to give Azalia only ten dollars. I said, 'No, that is not going to be the way. You have to go by the court.' The court made it thirty-five dollars."

Equally significant is Mrs. Celeste's commitment to the interpersonal connections unsanctioned by rights. Mrs. Celeste's narratives confirm an extant connectedness beyond conventional rights discourse. She notes, "I consider Sarmiento and Pablo my kids even though I have no authority over them." At the same time, her narrative asserts the need for the minimal protection of rights, the rights of bare subsistence.

An adjoining narrative also relates to Mrs. Celeste's role as a foster parent. This narrative carries the distinctive voice of community, a voice heard when she spoke of other foster parents. I am unsure whether Mrs. Celeste looked upon these parents as distant colleagues or friends. But it is clear that she considered herself one among these parents and deemed them members of an extended community. At times, she would speak about this community, mentioning "good" and "bad" parents and calling my attention to parents suffering under the same threat of food stamp reduction. On such occasions, she would stop and describe the parent, tell where and how they met, what they talked about, and whether the parent would call me for help.

From these talks, I learned that Mrs. Celeste participated in a regular meeting of foster parents sponsored by her private foster care agency. Organized ostensibly for the purpose of training, in time the meetings acquired the more profound purpose of providing foster parents a safe forum for the sharing of experiences and the telling of stories. It was here, I discovered, that Mrs. Celeste shared a fuller story of her struggle to protect her natural family's food stamp entitlement. As the story evolved into a litigated defense of that entitlement, Mrs. Celeste's narrative gained power. Emboldened, several foster parents joined the lawsuit. Several more made inquiries to their private agencies or to legal aid.

Yet, when discussion turned to Mrs. Celeste's awareness of other similarly aggrieved foster parents, I limited her participation to the identification and referral of prospective plaintiffs-intervenors. Once prospective clients had been contacted and evaluated, I ended Mrs. Celeste's participation. I did not offer her an opportunity to meet and talk to the various plaintiffs-intervenors, nor did I make arrangements to allow her to visit additional foster care agencies in order to address groups of affected foster parents. Moreover, I did not invite Mrs. Celeste and the other plaintiffs collectively to attend litigation sessions, negotiation conferences, or federal court arguments.

Institutional Procedures

At an institutional level, bureaucratic procedures privileged the narrative of client victimization. Those procedures—legal aid case intake policies, state hearing regulations, and federal rules of jurisdiction—required evidence of compensable injury to trigger remedial action. The narrative of the injured victim shaped the construction of Mrs. Celeste's case not only at legal aid, but also at the state hearing office and the federal courthouse. To retain counsel, to obtain a hearing, and to acquire standing to sue, Mrs. Celeste accommodated the narrative of victimization. Although this narrative established the predicate of harm necessary to award Mrs. Celeste compensatory relief, it belied alternative narratives of dignity.

Mrs. Celeste's narrative of dignity chronicles her struggle to maintain her individual dignity and the dignity of her natural and foster families in the context of poverty. She tells of this struggle when she describes her two utility "shut offs," explaining the exigent logic of balancing food, rent, and clothing against gas and electricity. She also talks of the "hardship" caused by her food stamp reduction, mentioning the "no frills" canned food, "cut downs," and Salvation Army clothing "that wasn't even fit to use."

Mrs. Celeste's narrative of dignity is not restricted to her struggle for subsistence living. Her concept of dignity also encompasses independence and self-sufficiency. When economic circumstances and the inadequacy of state welfare benefits overwhelm her ability to sustain her natural family, she confronts the state public welfare bureaucracy. She remarks: "I went right up to the Department of Social Services and I told them. I had to pay the rent and to buy food." Mrs. Celeste's narrative speaks forcefully of her struggle to endure impoverishing conditions consistent with the norms of dignity, independence, and self-reliance.

Social Relations

At a relational level, social practices privileged the narratives of client dependency and inferiority. These narratives of inequality and difference permeated Mrs. Celeste's lawyer-client and client-state relations. The structure of the legal aid case intake interview, for instance, presumed Mrs. Celeste's helplessness. I controlled the interview, posing questions and demarcating answers. Additionally, in planning her administrative hearing, I presumed Mrs. Celeste incompetent to understand the legal theory and strategy of the regulatory challenge under preparation. Thus, I did not fully include her in discussions regarding the constitutional and statutory bases of her case or the strategy of litigation designed to attack the food stamp regulations. Nor did I provide her with legal materials (e.g., statutes, regulations, legislative history, case law) to explicate the theory of the case. When planning escalated to pretrial strategy, once again I declined to invite Mrs. Celeste to participate in meaningful discussion, limiting communications with her to discovery preparations and brief apprisals of litigation progress.

Similarly, the framework of the state hearing presumed Mrs. Celeste incompetent. The administrative law judges conducting the hearings tended to direct questions to me and to agency officials. In doing so, they addressed us by name. Only after I pressed further inquiries on cross and redirect examination did the judges question Mrs. Celeste more thoroughly. Even so, they tended to interrupt her answers and refer to her as "the claimant."

Each of these lawyer and state-derived social practices overlooked Mrs. Celeste's narrative of caretaking competence. The narrative of caretaking pertains to Mrs. Celeste's role as a foster parent, describing a world both random and rule bound. Certified for the household care of two foster children, Mrs. Celeste immediately received four and subsequently six. She observes: "You can never say. It could change tomorrow." Supervision of the children is regulated: "They come to find out how much food, the clothing, the sleeping area, how I keep the kids, you know, what are the privacy, what are the things they do." Reimbursement is minimal: "The money they give you is not even enough to go around."

The prominence of Mrs. Celeste's narrative of caretaking is shown by her dedication to an unwieldy group of foster children during the five-year period I represented her. That dedication tolerates the unpredictability of foster care placement: "The judge orders the child to go back to the mother and nine months later the child has to be ordered to my house again." That same dedication withstands the likelihood of disruptive placement: "The girls have gone back to their home and they have come back even worse than when I first had them."

Instrumental Defenses of Silencing

Contextual, normative, and hierarchical acts of lawyer silencing ally with narratives of client eligibility, victimization, and dependency to fashion the traditional method of lawyer storytelling in the field of public welfare. At bottom, this method is instrumental: the goal is to win the case. In Mrs. Celeste's case, the relevance of eligibility and victimization is evident. Eligibility is the source of her statutory right. Victimization is the source of her remedy. Yet, neither exhausts the meaning of Mrs. Celeste's experience as a food stamp recipient or a foster parent, nor does dependency adequately capture that meaning.

Ignoring this untapped meaning, a poverty lawyer justifies his traditional method of storytelling on necessitarian and positivist bases. On necessitarian grounds, he argues that the absence of alternative client narratives is demanded by legal discourse and institutional practice. Legal discourse, he maintains, imposes rhetorical constraints. Institutional practice, he insists, adds procedural barriers.

On positivist grounds, a poverty lawyer contends that alternative client narratives are unknowable. He points to the boundaries of class, gender, and race spawned by social inequality and difference. These boundaries, he complains, obstruct human understanding. Even if client narratives are in fact knowable, he claims that the contradictions of client identity—dependence and independence, competence and incompetence—diminish their utility in advocacy. To be useful, he declares, client narratives must be stable. They must tell coherent and consistent stories. For the trier of fact—a judge or a jury—unstable narratives imply a lack of credibility and therefore imperil a client's chances of winning.

Reconstructive Lawyer Storytelling

Poverty lawyers cannot wholly eradicate the interpretive silencing of traditional storytelling, but they can seek to decipher the powerful normative meaning of client narratives and to integrate that meaning into the contexts of advocacy. Normative integration affirms a client's ability to assert power both in the lawyer-client relation and in the associated legal settings of welfare centers, state hearing offices, and federal courtrooms. For Mrs. Celeste, the demand for an emergency assistance grant constitutes an assertion of power. Her insistence on the court-ordered increase of her granddaughter's child support payments is a second assertion. Her request for an administrative hearing to halt the reduction of her family's food stamps is a third, and her sharing of information with other foster parents about her effort to challenge the reduction in a lawsuit is a fourth.

Every one of these assertions of power is tailored expressly to the context in which Mrs. Celeste found herself. When the context switched, in this case, from welfare office to foster parent meeting, the substance of her assertion changed. Mrs. Celeste's ability to adjust her assertion to the fluctuating contexts of impoverishment shows her power as an autonomous subject. But, as Mrs. Celeste's demands for emergency assistance grants demonstrate, the moments of power recounted by a client may seem mundane and even redundant to the lawyer.

At the investigative stage of Mrs. Celeste's case, for example, I attended several foster parent group meetings to gather information about the foster care system, explain the developing litigation, and search for additional plaintiffs. To my surprise, during the meetings I became aware of the gradual subversion of my storytelling power and the shifting of that power to the foster parents. This shift flowed out of the foster parents' control over the context of story, a power that made my own narratives tentative and uncertain, and hence more reliant on the foster parents for normative affirmation. Mrs. Celeste's foster parent community meetings, though ordinary, give evidence of client narrative power and normative authority. To reconstruct traditional storytelling, poverty lawyers must reinscribe, redescribe, and recontextualize that power and authority in advocacy.

Reinscription

Reinscription is a method of reinstalling client narrative into the text of legal story. The aim is to enable a client to narrate her own story in advocacy. By writing down her story, alone or with the aid of family and friends, a client may be better able to inscribe the story with her own images and meanings. In this way, a client's transcribed images and meanings may become a source of normative reference for her lawyer.

In the instant case, Mrs. Celeste's spoken and transcribed narratives supply a fertile source of normative reference. The norm of dignity, for example, represents a narrative of family struggle to survive a state levied food stamp reduction. The norm of caretaking signifies a narrative of foster parenting, particularly the desire to adopt Pablo and Tyrice. The norm of community symbolizes a narrative of foster parent association. And the norm of rights signals a narrative of food stamp entitlement and parent-child connection.

The possibility of multiple, internally inconsistent client narratives secluded outside of a lawyer's view may shake the confidence of pre-understanding, but that possibility does not preclude the reconstruction of client story. Reconstruction may go forward with the understanding that the fullness of story is contingent on the ongoing articulation of client narratives. The point is to strive to tell client story consonant with the norms of client narratives heard in daily struggle. Sifting out the normative meaning of client narrative omitted by traditional practices of lawyer interpretation and announcing that meaning in advocacy entails the redescription of story.

Redescription

Redescription seeks to discern and invert the client-based normative hierarchies—dependence/independence, competence/incompetence, power/powerlessness—of lawyer storytelling. The redrawing of advocacy images should not be discounted. Poverty lawyers have altered images, albeit modestly, by encouraging clients to take notes at administrative hearings, attend judicial arguments, and conduct trial examinations. Reconfiguration has been limited to modest gains because the images of dependency saturate legal discourse, institutional procedure, and social relations. Insulated by tradition, a lawyer is incapable of single-handed narrative redescription. For this reason, lawyer-driven narrative redescription is an errant and futile labor. Certain peripheral images and narratives may be redrawn and rewritten, but the central image of a client as a dependent and an inferior object will be reproduced substantially intact. To decenter this image, lawyers must recontextualize poverty law advocacy.

Recontextualization

Recontextualization demands both the shifting of advocacy to client community settings and the emplacement of client community networks in traditional lawyer settings. Emplacement is a tactic focusing on client community integration in traditionally lawyer-dominated contexts. The contexts include poverty law offices, welfare bureaucracies, administrative and legislative hearings, and courts. Emplacement redescribes these contexts by physically introducing the powerful images and narratives of individual clients and client community groups.

In poverty law offices, emplacement of client community support groups facilitates lawyer-client collaboration in interviewing, investigation, counseling, negotiation, and litigation strategy. To be effective, emplacement must be implemented by institutional procedures that ensure lawyer-client collaborative practices. Consistent with their purpose, the procedures should be collaboratively formulated, not lawyer enacted. To form client community support groups, a lawyer must look to his client base and search out those willing to participate in the education and organization of potential group members. Client support groups may be organized around activities (e.g., negotiation or counseling), member status (e.g., foster parent or food stamp recipient), or subject matter (e.g., food stamp reductions).

In welfare bureaucracies, emplacement may involve direct client–case worker negotiation, instead of lawyer intervention. At administrative hearings, emplacement may entail client-led legal argument and witness examination. In courts, emplacement may require client argument, testimony, and note taking. At legislative hearings, emplacement may call for client testimony. Whatever the setting, emplacement recontextualizes the storytelling of poverty law advocacy, redescribing story in a way inclusive of client narratives.

Conclusion

The reconstructive methods of reinscription, redescription, and recontextualization in no sense constitute a renunciation of the instrumental tradition of lawyer storytelling reproduced in poverty law. To renounce this long-accepted tradition without a well-formulated and historically tested alternative is heedless of the professional responsibilities of poverty law advocacy. Yet, these same responsibilities urge reconstruction if only to mitigate the violence of lawyer silencing and thereby make room for a client to speak her narratives as an autonomous subject. Notwithstanding the claims of traditional advocates, narrative room is available in legal discourse, institutional procedure, and social practice. Locating that room requires faith in the possibility of human understanding and in the power of human agency. Deprived of that faith, poverty lawyers tell impoverished stories.

Maintaining the Status Quo: Institutional Obstacles in a Child Custody Dispute

Lenora M. Lapidus

Introduction

Mary Biaggi[1] came to the Harvard Legal Aid Bureau seeking a divorce and custody of her ten-year-old daughter, Gina. Without Ms. Biaggi's knowledge, her husband, Tony Biaggi, from whom Ms. Biaggi was separated, had already filed for divorce and obtained an order for temporary custody of Gina. The story of Ms. Biaggi's struggle to regain custody of Gina is a story of institutional stagnation, inertia, and delay. Although in the end Ms. Biaggi was granted sole custody, it took her more than three years of fighting in the Probate and Family Court (Family Court) and the Department of Social Services (DSS) to accomplish her goal.

This case study makes apparent the ways in which these two state institutions—the Family Court and the Department of Social Services— fail to serve the needs of those for whom the institutions were created. In the area of child custody, neither institution issues determinations based on in-depth investigation and assessment of the circumstances of the parties and neither abides by legal standards set forth in state statutes and regulations. Because they lack an understanding of the parties' actual needs and abilities and simultaneously are unwilling to rule based on legal principles, judges and administrators who serve in these state institutions operate based on a status quo: they refuse to order any

---

1. This essay is based on a true case study. However, all names have been changed to protect the confidentiality of the persons involved.

change, even when such change would be "in the best interests of the child." The arbiters delay and prolong a determination by waiting for evaluations, reports, and expert opinions. They delay even when the result is that a child remains in an unsafe environment or in foster care.

This essay presents a case study of a custody battle waged, simultaneously, in the Family Court and the Department of Social Services. The first section presents the chronology of the case and the parties involved. The second section analyzes the ways in which the institutions that were created to meet the needs of families in crisis fail to meet these needs because the roles assigned to players within the systems— including guardians *ad litem,* Family Services officers, and DSS caseworkers—prevent the parties' voices from being heard. The third section discusses ways in which the multiple professional players obstruct rather than expedite the process. The final section presents concluding thoughts.

The Biaggi Family

Mary Biaggi, a poor African American woman, and Tony Biaggi, a white man from a lower-middle-class Italian American family, had an unstable fourteen-year marriage. Mr. Biaggi frequently lived away from the family home, during which time he maintained little contact with the Biaggis' child, Gina, and paid no child support. Ms. Biaggi had been the primary caretaker for Gina throughout the child's early years. In April 1988, Ms. Biaggi became pregnant. The father was not Mr. Biaggi, but a man with whom Ms. Biaggi had a short relationship. After discovering she was pregnant, Ms. Biaggi decided to enter a short-term residential drug and alcohol treatment program to help her overcome her substance abuse problems. Unaware of support services, and believing that the best place to send Gina while she was in treatment would be to the child's father, Ms. Biaggi asked Mr. Biaggi if he would take Gina to live with him temporarily. Mr. Biaggi agreed.

At the time Ms. Biaggi sought the assistance of the Harvard Legal Aid Bureau, in October 1988, she had successfully completed the treatment program and was living in a drug-free and alcohol-free halfway house. From the very first meeting, Ms. Biaggi presented herself as a deeply concerned and loving mother who was responsibly trying to put her life in order. She had not seen Mr. Biaggi or Gina for four months, since the previous June when Mr. Biaggi cut off contact with her. Ms.

Biaggi did not know the address or phone number of her husband or child because Mr. Biaggi had moved from his former residence and disconnected the telephone. Ms. Biaggi suspected that while she had been in the treatment program her husband might have initiated divorce or custody proceedings against her, but she had not received notice of any action. Ms. Biaggi wanted desperately to reestablish contact with her daughter.

As a law student member of the Harvard Legal Aid Bureau, I began preparing divorce papers on Ms. Biaggi's behalf and attempted to locate Mr. Biaggi and Gina.[2] I discovered that, as suspected, Mr. Biaggi had already filed for divorce and temporary custody of Gina. Although Mr. Biaggi knew where Ms. Biaggi was living, he listed her address as "parts unknown" and sent a copy of the notice to what he claimed was her "last known address," a residence that he knew she had vacated several years earlier. As a result, Ms. Biaggi never received notice of the custody action and did not appear in court to contest it. The Family Court granted Mr. Biaggi's ex parte petition and awarded him custody of Gina. Because Mr. Biaggi had gotten to the courthouse door first, the order granting him custody, although always open to modification, would establish a significant obstacle in the future custody dispute.[3]

Initially, Ms. Biaggi attempted to rebuild her relationship with Gina through visitation. Because she was living in a halfway house, Ms. Biaggi was not yet ready to have Gina return to live with her. After an initial court appearance, at which Mr. Biaggi failed to appear, we tracked down Mr. Biaggi and Gina and worked out a visitation plan. Although Ms. Biaggi would have liked to see Gina more frequently, Mr. Biaggi insisted that visits be limited.

---

2. At the time, I was a law student member of the Harvard Legal Aid Bureau, working under the supervision of a member of the Massachusetts bar, pursuant to Sup. Jud. Ct. R. 301.3.

3. The Supreme Judicial Court's Gender Bias Study of the Court System of Massachusetts, 61 (1989) (hereinafter "Gender Bias Study"), found that fathers frequently seek and obtain custody through ex parte proceedings in which the mother is not present to offer counterarguments or evidence. Temporary loss of custody, even if lost through an ex parte hearing, creates extreme difficulties for mothers who want to regain custody. The study found that a temporary loss of custody causes more severe ramifications for women than it does for men; if a mother has lost custody in a prior court determination, questions frequently arise about her fitness, and these questions may be difficult to refute (id. at 64–65).

In January 1989, Ms. Biaggi began visiting with Gina first every other Saturday, and then every Saturday. For a while, Ms. Biaggi was content with this short-term visitation. As the spring progressed, however, Ms. Biaggi began thinking about her future plans. She intended to graduate from the halfway house in June and hoped to move to an apartment in Boston with her newborn daughter. At this time, she began to express an interest in having Gina return to live with her and in obtaining custody of her daughter.

Meanwhile, the situation at Mr. Biaggi's home was deteriorating. Often, when Ms. Biaggi would call the house in the evenings to speak with Gina, she would find no one home. On several occasions when Ms. Biaggi reached the child at home in the morning, Gina reported that Mr. Biaggi had not been home all night and that she had been left alone. The child began staying out late at night and getting into trouble with the police. She also began performing poorly in school. Gina told her mother that Mr. Biaggi was gambling and using drugs. The child expressed to Ms. Biaggi that she was unhappy living with her father and wished to come back to live with her mother again.

Ms. Biaggi feared that Mr. Biaggi was not providing the care and control that the child needed and decided that she wanted Gina to return to live with her before Gina suffered further or got into serious trouble. However, because Mr. Biaggi would not consent to this arrangement, and he had been awarded custody, Ms. Biaggi needed to strengthen her bond with Gina through increased visitation before the Family Court would grant a change of custody. This was particularly true because custody had been awarded to Mr. Biaggi at a time when Ms. Biaggi was in a drug treatment program. Indeed, because Ms. Biaggi was consistently honest and forthright about her prior drug use and efforts to remain drug-free, while Mr. Biaggi, who continued to use drugs, kept this information secret, Ms. Biaggi was viewed as the less suitable parent.

When Gina's sixth-grade school year ended in June 1989, Ms. Biaggi grew concerned that the child would be restless with nothing to do. Ms. Biaggi therefore suggested that Gina go to summer camp. Ms. Biaggi's sister offered to pay for Gina's camp costs at the camp that Gina's cousin attended. Mr. Biaggi, however, refused to allow Gina to enroll in camp. As Ms. Biaggi had feared, in the first few weeks of summer Gina stayed out late at night, got into trouble with the police, and finally ran away from home.

The first time Gina ran away she was picked up by the police, detained overnight because she refused to give the police her real name, and released to her father the next morning, once her identity was discovered. Approximately a week later, Gina ran away again. When Mr. Biaggi found her, the two got into a fight. Gina hit Mr. Biaggi with a bag containing a bottle and cut his face. Mr. Biaggi went to the hospital. A hospital worker contacted the Department of Social Services to take the child into protective custody. DSS persuaded Mr. Biaggi to sign a voluntary agreement to place Gina in foster care. DSS did not attempt to contact Ms. Biaggi to inform her about what had happened or to discuss options with her before placing Gina in foster care.

The DSS officials relied only on information that Mr. Biaggi provided. The department did not consult with or involve Ms. Biaggi in the development of an appropriate service plan and did not investigate the possibility of placing the child in her mother's home or the home of any other relatives. Gina was placed in foster care in August 1989 and spent the next year in six different foster homes.

In September 1989, DSS placed the child in a psychiatric hospital for a twenty-one-day evaluation. Gina was diagnosed as having a conduct disorder and being undersocialized and aggressive. The report indicated that a primary difficulty evidenced during the child's hospitalization was mistrust of adults. The hospital stated, repeatedly, that the child indicated she was extremely angry toward and disapproved of her father and did not wish to elaborate on her reasons. The report stated that she appeared to have something to hide. Based on Gina's descriptions, the report concluded that the prior year living with her father had been very traumatic for the child. According to the discharge report, Gina specifically many times requested that she not be returned to her father. With regard to her mother, the report indicated that Gina often became silent, nonverbal, and somewhat sad in talking about her mother and repeatedly expressed a specific wish to return to live with her.

Upon Gina's release from the hospital, Ms. Biaggi requested that DSS allow Gina to return to live with her and that DSS provide Ms. Biaggi with support services. Despite this request and Gina's stated wish to return to live with her mother, DSS placed Gina in another foster home. Gina also entered a special school for children with behavioral problems and began psychological counseling.

In December 1989, the parties attended a pretrial conference at the

Middlesex Probate and Family Court. After hearing of the child's current placement in foster care and her refusal to visit or speak with Mr. Biaggi, the judge transferred legal and physical custody from Mr. Biaggi to DSS. The judge concluded that DSS was in a better position than the court to evaluate the child's needs and determine a proper placement. Further, because DSS was already involved in the case, the judge deferred to the department's determination that Gina should remain in foster care.

In January 1990, DSS held a Foster Care Review at which a panel assessed the appropriateness of the child's current foster home placement and the extent to which each member of the family and service team was in compliance with the service plan. The panel found that placement in the foster home was appropriate and that the long-term goal of the department was to return the child "home," with a goal date of January 1991. During the Foster Care Review, DSS officials were unwilling to clarify whether by "home" they meant the mother's or the father's residence. Ms. Biaggi objected to the department's unwillingness to state an intention to return Gina to her home and its adoption of January 1991 as the return home date.

At a subsequent meeting, the DSS area director stated that the department's goal was to return Gina to Ms. Biaggi's home. Mr. Biaggi, who was present at the meeting, said he agreed to this goal. The area director said, however, that Gina could not return to live with her mother immediately because the child had begun showing signs of drug and alcohol use, which had to be treated before the child could return home. The department indicated that, in its view, the child should be placed in a drug and alcohol residential treatment program and should continue psychological counseling before she returned to her mother's home.

In May 1990, Gina entered a teen alcohol and drug abuse treatment program where she spent three months. Through this program, Gina received counseling about her drug use, her behavior, and her relationship with her family. She and Ms. Biaggi participated in family counseling together. After Gina completed the program, the clinical caseworker and the director recommended that the child return to live with Ms. Biaggi. They also recommended that Gina not be forced or coerced into seeing her father.

In July 1990, DSS filed a motion with the Family Court recommending that Gina reside with her mother upon release from the residential treatment program, stating that the department believed that temporary replacement in substitute care would be detrimental to Gina in her efforts to strengthen her relationship with her mother. The Court granted the motion, and Gina returned to live with Ms. Biaggi.

Although physical custody was transferred to Ms. Biaggi, DSS retained legal custody and continued to provide social services to Ms. Biaggi and Gina. In December 1991, DSS filed a motion to remove the department as custodian and return custody to Ms. Biaggi. Finally, in January 1992, after more than three years of battling DSS and the Family Court, the court granted the department's motion and ordered full legal and physical custody to Ms. Biaggi.

The Failure of Institutions: The Operation of the Family Court and the Department of Social Services

Both the Family Court and the Department of Social Services were established to serve the needs of families in crisis. The court's mission, with regard to custody, is to resolve disputes in the "best interests" of the child.[4] The primary mandate of DSS is to strengthen the family unit, reunite children with their parents, and establish permanency.[5] The department is required to keep a child in substitute care only as long as the family is *unable* to provide necessary care and protection.[6] Irrespective of these articulated standards, however, Ms. Biaggi spent more than three years fighting to regain custody of Gina, while Gina lived first in the increasingly unsafe environment of her father's home and then in foster homes approximately 60 miles away from her mother. The child remained apart from her mother despite the mother's and daughter's requests that they be reunited.

These institutional systems—composed of Family Court judges, guardians *ad litem*, Family Services officers, and DSS caseworkers—share certain operational features that led to this predictable delay. Contrary to their avowed purposes, each institution became an obstacle rather than an aid in Ms. Biaggi's attempt to reunite with her daughter.

---

4. Mass. Gen. L. ch. 208, § 28 (supp. 1995).
5. Mass. Gen. L. ch. 119, § 1 (1993); Mass. Gen. L. ch. 18B, § 3(A)(1) (1994); Mass. Regs. Code. tit. 110, §§ 1.01, 1.02, 6.00 (1993).
6. Mass. Regs. Code tit. 110, §§ 1.01, 1.02. (1993).

The Middlesex Family Court

The Middlesex Family Court has established two institutional structures to assist judges in resolving contested custody disputes. The court
frequently appoints a guardian *ad litem* (GAL) to investigate the family
situation and make a recommendation to the court about what
custodial arrangement would be in the best interests of the child. The
GAL is usually not a lawyer, but rather a social worker or other professional. The GAL holds the position of investigator and recommender,
yet she will appear in court on all temporary motions and may file her
own motions as well.

The second institutional structure is Family Services. Parties filing
motions for custody or visitation are sent to Family Services prior to
appearing before a judge. The Family Services officers (FSOs) act as
both investigators and mediators. The goal of the FSO is to meet with
the parties and their counsel to reach an agreement that can then be
presented to the judge for approval and order. If the two parties cannot
agree, the FSO may present her own recommendation to the judge.

Generally, the presiding judge will not permit the parties an opportunity for an evidentiary hearing or allow the parties to testify to additional facts upon which the judge may base her decision. Judges usually
adopt the recommendations of the GALs and FSOs whether or not the
parties agree. When the GAL or FSO has not conducted a complete
investigation or has reached a recommendation based on personal
biases, the true facts are never made known to the judge, and as a result
the rulings do not take account of the full circumstances of the parties.

Guardian Ad Litem

> Gina's birthday here again. I want to give her a party. We have to go
> to court to approve it. GAL was laughing and talking with a man
> before court. Court starts. The man the GAL was talking to was the
> judge. GAL looks to Tony and his lawyer as if to say it's in the bag.
> And it was. (We lost.) No Gina for the weekend or her birthday.
>   —Mary Biaggi

A guardian *ad litem* was appointed to our case in May 1989. Ms.
Biaggi had filed a motion for the court to appoint an attorney to represent Gina. We thought that Gina should have her own attorney because,

on several occasions, I had found myself in the position of presenting to the court the child's stated interests; yet, because my primary role was to represent Ms. Biaggi, my claims on behalf of Gina frequently were disregarded. The court denied our request to appoint a lawyer for the child, but instead appointed a GAL. Although GALs present a judge with their opinions concerning the best interests of a child, GALs do not act as the child's attorney and have no obligation to represent to the court a child's stated preferences.

The GAL appointed to our case met with Gina only two times during the summer of 1989 and did not meet with her at all after Gina entered foster care. Nevertheless, the GAL repeatedly argued to the court her view of what would be in the child's best interests. Gina was never given the opportunity to speak to the judge on her own behalf, even after she reached age twelve, the age at which minors are generally considered mature enough for their views to be taken into account by a judge deciding custody. On several occasions throughout this protracted litigation, Ms. Biaggi asked me, "When will Gina get a chance to come to court and speak for herself? Why can't she say what she wants; why can't the judge see her and determine what would be in her best interests rather than have all these other people speaking for her and saying what is in her best interests?" Judges, however, do not always feel comfortable talking with children. And because the court has created investigative structures, including GALs, judges who do not wish to hear directly from the child can, and do, rely entirely on the "professionals." As a result, judges making custody determinations, in essence, often remain ignorant of the child's desires and needs.

Initially, we attempted to work with the GAL to persuade her that it was in Gina's best interests to return to live with her mother. At first the GAL appeared to agree with Ms. Biaggi. Later, however, when Ms. Biaggi graduated from the halfway house and moved into her own apartment in Roxbury—a predominantly African American community in Boston—a few weeks earlier than the GAL thought she should, the GAL changed her mind. She then shifted her allegiance to Mr. Biaggi and argued that the child should continue to live with her father.

After Gina was removed from Mr. Biaggi's home and placed in foster care, the GAL took the position that the child should not be returned to either parent but should remain in foster care or be placed in institutional residential treatment. The GAL adopted and maintained this position throughout the litigation, notwithstanding the child's own statements to counselors and others that she wanted to return to live with her mother and the view of therapists that reuniting with Ms. Biaggi would be in Gina's best interests. The GAL continued to express the view that the child should not return to live with her mother—the parent with whom she had grown up—although the GAL never visited Ms. Biaggi's home nor discussed the situation with Gina. Neither did the GAL ever present to the court any evidence to support her recommendation. She never identified anything wrong with Ms. Biaggi or her home but merely stated that, in her view, it was not in the child's best interests to return to live with her mother in Roxbury.

Without the GAL's support, Ms. Biaggi's efforts to regain custody became significantly more difficult. The Family Court gives extreme deference to the views of GALs. Moreover, the usual judicial deference was compounded in our case by the fact that the appointed GAL was an active, regular player who appeared in the Family Court on various matters almost daily.

In October 1989, when Gina was about to be released from the hospital where she had been undergoing psychiatric evaluation, we filed a motion for joint legal custody. At that time, Mr. Biaggi still had custody—awarded by the Family Court in an ex parte hearing at which Ms. Biaggi was not present. Mr. Biaggi had signed a voluntary agreement to place Gina in the care of DSS. DSS had developed a service plan that entirely excluded Ms. Biaggi. The department had failed to investigate the mother or any maternal relatives before placing the child in foster care, because Mr. Biaggi had said he did not want Ms. Biaggi involved. The department remained unwilling to inform Ms. Biaggi of Gina's treatment or service plan on the grounds that Mr. Biaggi had custody and he did not want Ms. Biaggi involved. DSS believed that its hands were tied. If Ms. Biaggi were awarded joint legal custody, the department would be free, and indeed obligated, to involve her in the service plan and keep her informed of Gina's situation.

Massachusetts law establishes a presumption of joint legal custody pending final resolution of a divorce and custody action.[7] Shared legal custody is defined as "a continued mutual responsibility and involvement by both parents in decisions regarding the child's welfare in matters of education, medical care, emotional, moral and religious develop-

---

7. Mass. Gen. L. ch. 208, § 31 (supp. 1995).

ment."[8] Joint custody is presumed to be in the child's best interests, unless a court makes findings to the contrary. Until a judgment on the merits is rendered, the statute mandates that legal custody shall be shared absent emergency conditions, abuse, or neglect. If a judge enters an order for temporary legal custody to one parent, written findings must be made that shared custody would not be in the best interests of the child. Despite this law, when the Family Court awarded custody to Mr. Biaggi no written findings were made and no emergency conditions, abuse, or neglect were cited. Accordingly, legal custody should have remained shared by the parents, pending resolution of the divorce and custody action.

The joint custody statute was enacted, in part, to eliminate the race to the courthouse by parents contesting custody—each parent seeking to secure a temporary order of sole custody as leverage to support continued sole custody in the permanent order.[9] Indeed, the statute was enacted to prevent precisely the type of situation that arose in this case: Mr. Biaggi sought a temporary custody order, without Ms. Biaggi's knowledge, without proper service or notice, to gain advantage in the divorce proceeding.

At the hearing on our joint custody motion, I argued that pursuant to the statute, the court should order temporary joint legal custody, so that Ms. Biaggi could participate in Gina's service plan—involvement that was in the child's best interests. I explained how Ms. Biaggi had attempted to work with the Department of Social Services in order to develop a plan to meet the child's needs and how the department had been reluctant to involve Ms. Biaggi because she did not have legal custody of Gina.

The guardian *ad litem* argued simply that the court should make no changes. The GAL asserted that the child was in foster care, she was being released from the hospital, having undergone a psychiatric evaluation, the hospital had not yet issued its report and recommendation, the GAL had not yet prepared her report and recommendation, and therefore, no changes should be made until these reports had issued. The GAL argued that the court should not alter the current custodial arrangement until it received the reports, which were to be issued within a few weeks.

---

8. Id.

9. H. Freeman, ed., *Massachusetts Family Law Manual*, vol. 1 (Boston: Massachusetts Continuing Legal Education [20 West Street], 1989), § 16, 4.

The status quo prevailed. Despite my argument based directly on legal authority in support of joint legal custody, the judge ruled that it was premature to determine legal custody, that we should wait until the reports were issued, and that, following the issuance of the reports, we could return to argue the motion for joint legal custody again. The judge accepted the GAL's status quo argument and left custody with Mr. Biaggi, despite the fact that he had shown his inability to properly care for or control Gina, that the child had been removed from her father's home and placed in foster care, and that she refused to communicate with Mr. Biaggi.

Judicial deference to the GAL was also evident in a hearing on our motion for visitation in November 1989. At the time, Gina was living in a foster home in a suburb of Worcester. She had been out of the hospital for approximately four weeks. She was behaving and doing well in school for the first time in months. As a reward for her progress, Ms. Biaggi and the foster mother thought it would be beneficial to allow the child to spend her birthday with her mother. Ms. Biaggi and I spoke to the social worker. DSS agreed to conduct a home visit of Ms. Biaggi's house and, if the home visit was favorable, to allow overnight weekend visitation. DSS conducted a home visit, and the social worker was satisfied that Ms. Biaggi's home was safe and secure and would be an appropriate environment for the child to stay overnight. Visitation was scheduled to take place the following weekend.

Gina grew excited about the weekend visit. Her hopes were raised that she would have a chance to come to Boston to spend time with her mother, her infant sister, and her brother. I knew the visit meant a lot to both Gina and Ms. Biaggi. I also believed it would be in the best interests of the child and would aid significantly in her continued emotional development.

The GAL learned of the planned visitation and decided it should be stopped. In part, she was bothered by the fact that DSS had made a decision without discussing it with her. The day before the planned visit, the GAL filed an emergency motion to prevent the visit and requested an immediate expedited hearing. DSS did not appear in court because the agency had not been subpoenaed or served with a copy of the GAL's motion. The GAL argued that weekend visitation would be too great a change for the child. Although the GAL agreed that nothing was wrong with the mother or her home, and pointed to no specific risks to the child from overnight visitation, she stated that the status quo should be maintained. She argued that Gina was beginning to adjust, and that the court should not disrupt her progress by ordering weekend visits. The GAL made this argument notwithstanding Gina's eagerness to visit and the determination by DSS that such visitation would foster the child's emotional and behavioral improvement.

Not surprisingly, the judge ruled: no change at this time. Weekend visits were denied. The judge never spoke with Gina, who was almost twelve years old, and never obtained any information about the possible ramifications of weekend visitation. The judge simply adopted the GAL's recommendations and denied the visits.[10] The child's hopes were shattered. Ms. Biaggi was terribly disappointed. And there seemed to be nothing that I could do.

It was clear that the court would continue to follow the recommendations of the court-appointed GAL and maintain the status quo. The judge simply rubber-stamped the recommendations of the GAL, although her opinions were frequently unsupported by the facts and often were made without allowing the parties any opportunity to influence those decisions.

On several other occasions, the court similarly adopted the GAL's recommendations despite clear legal and factual bases for doing otherwise. Indeed, the only time that the court did *not* adopt the GAL's recommendation was during one pretrial conference, in which we appeared before a new judge who had recently transferred to the court and was not closely tied to the court regulars, including our GAL.

During this conference in December 1989, the GAL argued that Gina should be placed in a residential treatment program and that DSS should be ordered to establish visitation between the child and Mr. Biaggi. I argued that Gina was progressing well in the foster home, had made dramatic improvements since her release from the hospital, and should not be taken out of a stable environment and placed in a more restrictive one. I also argued that Mr. Biaggi should not have any visitation because the hospital report clearly stated that Gina did not want to return to live with her father and indicated that Gina was angry at her father but would not say why. Reading between the lines, the report suggested possible sexual abuse. The judge perceived this unstated concern, found it absurd that Mr. Biaggi still had custody, awarded custody to DSS, and suspended any visitation with the father for the

---

10. See additional discussion infra at 66–67, 69.

immediate future. The GAL was manifestly flustered by her inability to persuade the judge to adopt her view. For the first time, it seemed that the Family Court had actually done some justice, and it had taken a judge who was new to the court to do so.

Yet, more typical are the episodes in which the Family Court refuses to act, even if such action is mandated by statute or necessitated by the facts of the case at hand. Instead, judges rely on recommendations of GALs and opt to maintain the status quo, despite legal arguments and strong evidence that the facts require particular changes. Change—any change—appears to be dangerous. Instead, the court adopts a position of inertia, refusing to order any change.[11] As a result, litigation proceeds slowly. Months pass and nothing happens. The court prefers this sluggish pace, even when moving slowly means keeping a child in foster care, separated from her family, longer than necessary. Indeed, the status quo is maintained even when the status quo is damaging and not in the best interests of the child.[12]

Family Services

A second structural and operational problem with the Family Court is the role played by Family Services. In cases involving child custody and visitation, the Family Court refers the parties to Family Services prior to their appearance before a judge. The purpose of a meeting with Family Services is "to dispose of the issues quickly so that a full judicial hearing is not necessary."[13] As arms of the court, the FSOs both investigate

---

11. Maintenance of the status quo may be inherent in the statutory provisions governing child custody. Mass. Gen. L. ch. 208 § 28 establishes that a custody determination, once made, may be modified "provided that the court finds that a material and substantial change in the circumstances of the parties has occurred." Thus, the language of the custody statute itself ensures that, without a showing of changed circumstances, it will be difficult to alter a custodial arrangement, even if the initial order was not made in the best interests of the child.

12. The court's preference for the status quo is particularly harmful to *mothers* who have lost custody and seek to alter the custodial arrangement. It is extremely difficult for a mother to regain custody once a court has awarded custody to a father, even if such award was not supported by the facts and was obtained through an ex parte proceeding. "In most families, mothers have temporary physical custody of children while the divorce is pending. . . . If, however, mothers did not have continuous custody of their children . . . they are likely to be judged much more harshly than fathers whatever the reasons for the temporary separation" (Gender Bias Study at 64). Fathers who actively seek physical custody are successful over 70 percent of the time (Id. at 59).

13. Opinion of attorneys meeting in focus group sessions (Gender Bias Study, supra note 2, at 24).

and mediate child custody matters. Unlike voluntary, independent, community-based mediation, however, parties to a contested custody dispute are *required* to meet with Family Services. Through this meeting, the FSO attempts to facilitate a stipulation agreement between the parties. If this effort is successful, the FSO presents the agreement to the judge for approval. If the parties cannot reach an agreement, the FSO makes her own determination and presents a recommendation to the judge. Family Services officers are enormously influential. Agreements mediated by FSOs are likely to be approved and findings and recommendations, if they are made, are likely to be accepted by judges.

Family Services officers receive some training but are not required to have degrees in social work or law, and their backgrounds vary. FSOs generally handle a case only once, on the day it is scheduled for a hearing. Therefore, although parties may appear in court several times during pretrial motion practice—on motions for temporary visitation or changes in custodial arrangements—each time they appear they meet with a new FSO, who is unfamiliar with the case and the family members involved. The FSOs usually ask to meet with the lawyers alone first. Sometimes the FSOs make their determinations without ever hearing from the parties themselves.

In March 1990, we appeared in court on a motion for visitation. The clerk sent us to Family Services. A Family Services officer met with the DSS lawyer, a DSS caseworker, the GAL, Mr. Biaggi's lawyer, and myself. Mr. Biaggi wanted to participate. He kept approaching the table where we sat to ask if he could join in the discussions. During the three years this case was litigated, Mr. Biaggi fired, or attempted to fire, his three consecutive attorneys, in part so that he could speak for himself. On this particular occasion, Mr. Biaggi again said he wanted to fire his attorney and represent himself so he could join in the discussions. Only *he* knew what was best for his daughter, and only *he* knew all the details of the situation, Mr. Biaggi insisted. But no one wanted to hear from him. No one allowed him to say what it was he actually wanted or thought of the situation. In the end, he was reluctant and almost refused to sign the stipulation agreement his attorney had negotiated on his behalf.

Sometimes the role of the FSO becomes additionally problematic because she and the GAL are both court-appointed professionals. Although custody and visitation matters are generally referred to Family Services prior to appearance before a judge, if a GAL has been appointed, Family Services will sometimes forgo the FSO mediation and defer to the GAL to play the mediating role.

In November 1989, when we were in court seeking weekend visitation for Gina's birthday, which the GAL opposed,[14] the FSO's deference to the GAL posed particular problems. In that instance, we were unwilling to have the GAL take the place of Family Services. The GAL had filed a motion to restrain DSS from allowing weekend visitation. Ms. Biaggi opposed this motion. DSS, however, was not in court to present its position supporting visitation. As a result, I was forced to present the view of DSS in support of visitation; yet, I also represented an interested party and spoke on behalf of both the child and the mother.

To avoid representing these multiple positions, I requested that Family Services meet with us and not abdicate its role simply because a GAL had been appointed. Reluctantly, the FSO agreed. At the meeting, I informed the FSO of the Department of Social Services' position. I explained why DSS thought that weekend visitation would be beneficial to Gina. The GAL argued that visitation should be prohibited. The FSO appeared to accept the GAL's argument; after all, the GAL worked closely with Family Services—indeed the GAL had been in the Family Services office chatting with the FSO when I requested the meeting—and she did not want to go against her buddy. I requested that the FSO call DSS herself to hear the department's view. She agreed.

The FSO returned from her call, persuaded that, contrary to the GAL's view, the department thought visitation was a good idea. The FSO asked if the GAL would withdraw her motion to prevent weekend visitation. The GAL refused. Our case was next on the calendar. I requested that the FSO remain in the courtroom to present DSS's opinion so that I would not have to speak for the department. The FSO responded that she was busy and had to get back to her office; if the judge wanted to hear from her, he could contact her. The FSO's unwillingness to remain and present a view in opposition to the GAL, despite the fact that she believed visitation was in the child's best interest, exemplified the difficulty of breaking through the barriers erected by the repeat players.

The judge called our case. The GAL presented her motion to restrain DSS from allowing weekend visitation. I argued in opposition and presented DSS's view. Mr. Biaggi's attorney said that Mr. Biaggi supported the expert opinion of the GAL. I requested that the judge call

---

14. See discussion *supra* at 62–63.

the FSO—who had spoken with DSS—to hear DSS's view. He refused. The judge granted the GAL's motion and enjoined weekend visitation.

By adding Family Services as a substructure of the Family Court, with the assigned task of gathering evidence and recommending resolutions, the court has delegated much of its judicial function to untrained nonlawyers. If the FSOs actually gathered sufficient information about the interests and strengths of the parties and presented this information, and well-based recommendations, to the judges, such delegation might be appropriate. Perhaps informal mediation could serve the needs of families better than the traditional adversarial litigation process. When the system does not operate as it should, however, and FSOs fail to gather sufficient information or to present fair recommendations to the court, the legal process cannot function justly.

Moreover, the presence of repeat players, such as GALs, who have ongoing relationships with the court, influences the FSOs' actions and these actions, in turn, determine the judges' rulings. As a result, bureaucratic laziness and wheel greasing replace individualized justice.

Department of Social Services

Christmas coming and Gina can't be with her family. We have Christmas at the foster home. Cassandra is a year now. Gina is missing her grow up.

—Mary Biaggi

Within the Department of Social Services, caseworkers are responsible for evaluating families and making recommendations to the administrators. The administrators then make final decisions regarding placement and visitation. "The caseworker plays a key role in locating, linking, and maintaining services and assessing their effectiveness in protecting the child."[15] Frequently the caseworkers fail to establish adequate relationships with the families, however, and are therefore unable to make well-informed recommendations. Like the Family Court rulings based on incomplete investigations by the GALs and FSOs, when DSS caseworkers neglect to gather full information about their clients, the administrators' determinations are not supported by the facts.

---

15. D. Ratterman, D. Dodson, M. Hardin, *Reasonable Effort to Prevent Foster Placement: A Guide to Implementation*, 2d. ed. (Washington, D.C.: ABA National Legal Resource Center for Child Advocacy and Protection, 1987).

My relationship with the Department of Social Services, like that with the GAL, shifted between one of ally and one of adversary. At the outset, the department appeared oppositional. DSS had placed Gina in foster care without involving Ms. Biaggi or investigating the mother as a potential placement. The department was clearly more aligned with Mr. Biaggi than with Ms. Biaggi: Mr. Biaggi had custody, he had signed the voluntary request for services, he lived in the central Massachusetts service area where this DSS office was located, and the department staff considered him the client to whom they were providing services. My initial efforts focused on persuading DSS to involve Ms. Biaggi in the service plan and to keep her informed of the department's goals. The department was reluctant to do so because it did not want to disregard Mr. Biaggi's wishes.

Yet, Mr. Biaggi was not truly a voluntary client. His "voluntary" request for services, typical of many DSS placements,[16] in fact represented a choice on his part only in comparison to the less attractive alternative of involuntary placement. Mr. Biaggi signed a voluntary request only after Gina had run away from his home and hit him with a bottle. While Mr. Biaggi was being treated at the hospital, DSS received the call to take the child. Mr. Biaggi's only choice was to sign the agreement voluntarily or risk having DSS take the child away against his consent. Despite the circumstances of this "voluntary" agreement, and despite the overwhelming evidence that Mr. Biaggi had failed to provide adequate parental care and control for his daughter, the department accepted, without question or investigation, the father's statement that no other family members were available to take the child.

The service plan for placing Gina in foster care indicated that the department did not contact any relatives because "no relatives were available." Ms. Biaggi, however, remained fit, able, and willing to take the child throughout this time. Rather than conduct a complete investigation and assessment of the family, as required by the regulations governing the department,[17] DSS relied solely upon information supplied by Mr. Biaggi and placed Gina in a foster home with strangers, instead of her mother's home.

---

16. Most placements with DSS are through "voluntary" agreements between the parent(s) and the department that arise out of serious difficulties in the parental home. D. Chambers and M. Wald, "Smith v. Offer," in R. Mnookin, ed., *In the Interest of Children: Advocacy, Law Reform, and Public Policy* (New York: W. H. Freeman, 1985), 70.

17. Mass. Regs. Code tit. 110, § 5.00 (1993).

Even after the department was informed of the mother's avail-ability and willingness to take the child, the department kept Gina in a foster home approximately 60 miles away from her mother's residence for a year and a half. In doing so, DSS violated its own regulations.[18] Although Gina refused to see or speak to her father, and despite the fact that the child came into the care of DSS because of problems in the father's home, DSS placed her in a foster home close to Mr. Biaggi's house. Ignoring Gina's repeated requests that she be sent to live with her mother or be allowed to visit her mother more often, the depart-ment did not consider placing the child with her mother or even in a foster home in the Boston area close to Ms. Biaggi. During most of the time Gina was in the care of DSS, the department did nothing to reunite the child with her mother and family in Roxbury.[19]

Initially, the department believed that it could not involve Ms. Biaggi in Gina's service plan because Mr. Biaggi had so requested. When I threatened Mr. Biaggi with a motion for joint custody, on the ground that DSS believed it could not fully involve the mother as long as Mr. Biaggi had sole legal custody, Mr. Biaggi signed an agreement allowing the department to release information to Ms. Biaggi and in-volve her in the service plan.

Following this release of information and inclusion of Ms. Biaggi in the service plan, DSS became more allied with our position. The depart-ment agreed that overnight visitation with the mother would be benefi-cial for Gina. DSS saw that Mr. Biaggi exhibited emotional problems and the department acknowledged that Gina wanted to avoid contact with him. DSS began to take stands in opposition to the GAL, particu-larly when she indicated that she believed the child needed institutional residential treatment.[20] I attempted to strengthen our relationship with DSS. It was clearly valuable to have the department's support for Ms. Biaggi. The relationship with DSS, however, did not prove to be quite so easy.

---

18. Mass. Regs. Code tit. 110, § 7.101 (1993), provides that the department shall consider placement resources in the following order: placement in the child's own home, placement in family foster care with relatives, and lastly placement in foster care with nonrelatives. The regulations further require that all out-of-home placement decisions take into consideration the close proximity to the home of the child's family and the ability for frequent visits between the child and his or her family.

19. Chambers and Wald, supra note 27, at 73, state that "[f]rom the biologic par-ents' perspective, the foster-care system often operates in a manner that impedes rather than facilitates their regaining custody of their children."

20. See discussion supra at 62–64.

Foster Care Review: I have hope of getting Gina in the summer. All white panel. Tony brings a priest. Only attended church for two weeks. Tony is always up to something. And he will use anyone to get what he wants. Why can't they see it? Gina is using drugs and drinking. Acting out. She needs me more now. I'm clean and sober and plan to stay that way. I can help her.

Verdict: Another year in foster care. I feel hopeless.

—Mary Biaggi

On January 2, 1990, a foster care review panel met to hear the progress of Gina's service plan and the department's future placement goals. Foster care reviews are conducted under the auspices of the Foster Care Review Unit, an independent unit within the Department of Social Services.[21] Members of this unit devote their time exclusively to case reviews of children in foster care. Administrative case reviews of the status of each child in the care of the department are required to be conducted at least once every six months. The reviews are performed by panels consisting of a member of the unit and two other people, at least one of whom is not an employee of the department but a member of the community. The purpose of the case review is to determine the necessity and appropriateness of the child's continued placement, the extent of the parties' compliance with the service plan, the extent of progress made toward alleviating the need for placement in foster care, and a projected date by which the child should be returned to her parents or placed for adoption.[22]

Based on conversations I had with the DSS social worker and area director, I believed that the department's goal was to return Gina to her home at the end of the school year, and that the department had decided that Gina should return to her mother's, not her father's home. At the foster care review, however, the social worker did not state these goals. The social worker had not prepared a current service plan and had not set a projected return home date. The panel, without guidance from the case worker, arbitrarily set a return date a year later, January 1991. When I objected, and questioned why Gina should not return to live with Ms. Biaggi sooner, the only reason given was that the child still felt anger toward her mother that she was not able to express. This explanation came from Gina's therapist, who said that the child fre-

---

21. Mass. Gen. L. ch. 18B, § 6A (supp. 1995); Mass. Regs. Code tit. 110, § 6.12 (1993).
22. Id.

quently expressed anger toward her father but did not often speak about feeling angry toward her mother. The therapist inferred that Gina did *feel* anger but was not able to express it. The therapist did not consider that Gina might not feel anger toward her mother.

The panel determined that Gina should remain in foster care another year. Panel members seemed unconcerned that Gina was separated from her family and placed in a foster home unnecessarily. The panel barely considered the fact that the child's foster home was 60 miles away from her mother's home, or that this placement made visitation very difficult. Indeed, the only thing the panel seemed troubled by was the exclusion of any visits between Gina and her father.

At the review, the panel was not presented with complete evidence of the actual circumstances of the family members. The caseworker had not done a thorough investigation and did not report on Ms. Biaggi's home life and strengths as a mother. Although the case worker had been assigned to the case for six months, she knew very little about Ms. Biaggi and could not provide the panel with information upon which to base its determinations.

A few weeks later, the social worker sent the new service plan adopting the January 1991 return date, with no indication of the home to which Gina would return. The service plan also failed to set forth any new goals for strengthening the family unit, including increased visitation or joint counseling for Ms. Biaggi and Gina, as Ms. Biaggi had requested. Most significantly, the service plan left blank the last page, which requests information about relatives who were considered for placement and the reasons these relatives were rejected.

Ms. Biaggi and I met with the social worker and expressed our concerns about the inadequacy of the service plan. At first, our complaints seemed to have no effect. Soon, however, a meeting was scheduled with the service plan team. At this meeting, several of our concerns were addressed and the area director announced that she had made a number of decisions that were in accordance with Ms. Biaggi's requests. The most important of these decisions was that the department's long-term goal was to return Gina to her mother's home.

In the two years of its involvement with the Biaggi family, DSS never made a determination that Ms. Biaggi was unfit to care for her daughter. DSS never articulated the reasons why Gina should not be living with her mother. Rather, DSS, like the court, operated from a wait and see position and maintained the status quo. The department began by placing Gina in foster care and then was reluctant to change this arrangement until the child showed improvement, until visits between the child and the mother increased, until the child resolved certain issues in therapy, or until the child was able to express her anger toward her mother. The department, however, did not begin at an appropriate starting point—a level playing field—from which to maintain the status quo. Had Gina been in her mother's home initially, DSS's decision to maintain the status quo might have been reasonable. Such a response would have accorded with the statutory and regulatory standards requiring the department to try to keep children in the family home.[23] But to maintain the status quo at a point when the child was living in a foster home 60 miles away from her mother's home was arbitrary and capricious. This is precisely what DSS did. The department thereby perpetuated Gina's separation from her mother, notwithstanding the child's and the mother's clearly articulated desires to be reunited.

The department defended its unwillingness to alter the status quo, and increase visits or place Gina with her mother, with claims of inability, or lack of power, to act. The case worker said: it is not up to me, it is up to my supervisor. The supervisor said: it is not up to me, it is up to the area director. The area director said: it is not up to DSS, it is up to the Family Court. The Family Court said: we can't determine custody until DSS recommends placement with one parent. This circularity continued with each bureaucrat and agency shirking full responsibility.

Initially, the department indicated that it wished to leave the custody decision to the Family Court. Once the department was awarded custody, however, DSS had an obligation to take a position in support of one parent over the other. For over a year, the department declined to do so. Finally, with constant pressing from Ms. Biaggi, DSS began to work with Ms. Biaggi and recommended to the Family Court that Gina return to live with her mother and that Ms. Biaggi be awarded custody.

Obstructionism as a Result of Multiple Players

Much of the delay in both the court system and DSS resulted from the number of people involved in the case at all levels of the bureaucracies. The Family Court and the Department of Social Services employ professionals to assess the family situation and report to the court or agency

---

23. Mass. Regs. Code tit. 110, § 7.101 (1993).

their findings and recommendations. These professionals, including guardians *ad litem*, Family Services officers, and DSS caseworkers, are sometimes regarded as independent investigators. In fact, however, they always remain arms of the state institutions. Judges and DSS administrators rely on the investigators' opinions, frequently rubber-stamping the recommendations, even when the governing statutes or regulations point toward an opposite result.

Judges and administrators adopt the recommendations without providing the parties an opportunity to testify or present their own evidence about the circumstances of their lives. Because of the investigative substructures, judges are able to abdicate both their fact-finding responsibilities and their decision-making duties. When the appointed investigator does not conduct a thorough evaluation or makes a recommendation based on personal prejudices, the family member has very little chance of persuading the court or agency to adopt a contrary position. These investigators, therefore, often limit rather than expand the decision maker's understanding of the parties' circumstances. The family member is, in effect, rendered remote from the arbiter's consideration.

In addition, courts and agencies often refuse to act or to take responsibility for a situation, passing such responsibility on to another office or official. Because the lower-level investigators, as well as the judges and administrators, fear recommending the *wrong* decision, they frequently opt for the wait and see approach, delaying action indefinitely while maintaining the status quo. The institutional preference for inaction is often traumatic for a child and onerous for a parent who applies to the court specifically for the purpose of obtaining some change.

Maintenance of the status quo, in many ways, rests on the false dichotomy between act and omission: as long as the court or the agency does not order a specific change, it cannot be faulted for its inaction. Yet, when a court refuses to transfer custody from an abusive father to a fit mother, or when the department remains unwilling to transfer a child from a foster home to her mother's home, these institutions *are* acting. When the starting point is an unsafe one, maintaining the status quo is action that harms the child.[24]

---

24. The Supreme Court in DeShaney v. Winnebago County Department of Social Services, 489 U.S. 189 (1989), relied upon this distinction between action and inaction to

Judges and administrators are able to maintain a sense of freedom from responsibility by relying on the institutional structures that have been established to provide them with factual assessments and recommendations. When a GAL argues that a judge should not remove a parent's legal custody until a report issues, the judge can maintain the status quo on the grounds that she is simply delaying decision, not deciding *for* custody to that parent. When a DSS caseworker has not gathered and provided complete information about a mother, an administrator can choose to wait until such information is available before determining whether the child should return home, without explicitly ruling that the child needs to remain in foster care.

Reliance on lower-level investigators also leads decision makers to issue judgments contrary to governing statutes and regulations. Notwithstanding well-prepared legal arguments and briefs in support of particular actions, judges and administrators may postpone decisions on an issue, maintaining the status quo until additional facts are supplied. Thus, while the law may look good on the books, in reality the system may impede rather than facilitate the espoused goal.

Arbiters maintain the status quo based on the belief that they do not have sufficient information upon which to act affirmatively. In reliance upon lower-level investigators, the decision makers do not, themselves, become familiar with the people whose lives they determine. Yet, the very institutional structures that are constructed to provide the decision makers with information operate to obscure the facts and circumstances of the parties. The system itself may make them feel constrained from acting. Their ignorance, in turn, breeds a false sense of security in inaction.

Concluding Thoughts

A first step in remedying the effective exclusion of family members from the institutional actors who determine their lives is to bring judges and administrators closer to the realities of the parties before them. Critical matters, such as child custody or visitation, should not be determined without providing the parties an opportunity to be heard

---

find that due process rights are not violated by the department's failure to act when the child was not in the custody of DSS. In Ms. Biaggi's case, because DSS had custody of Gina and the child had been placed in foster care, the department had intervened to an extent greater than that in *DeShaney,* and therefore unquestionably had a duty to protect the child.

directly by the decision makers. Notwithstanding investigators' recommendations, judges and administrators should consider the views presented by the parties themselves.

Both the Family Court and DSS, like most bureaucracies, operate with a continual changing of the guard. In the Family Court, litigants must present their cases to a new judge each time they appear. Although sometimes a new judge, who does not have strong allegiances to other players in the system or preset notions about the parties, can provide a fair hearing,[25] more often the rotation system results in decision makers drawing inaccurate conclusions about the parties based on insufficient information provided by "investigators" who do not investigate adequately and who wish to dispose of the case quickly. Assignment to a particular judge throughout the entire action could allow for greater familiarity with the people and circumstances involved.

Likewise, the high turnover of social workers and administrators at DSS leads to frequent regressions back to square one, while new social workers become acquainted with the family members and familiar with the case. The heavy caseload of both the court and DSS increases the difficulty of obtaining thorough investigations or well-supported determinations based on accurate information about the parties' circumstances.

Efforts must be made to restructure the institutions so that individuals who seek assistance from these institutions have greater access to the decision makers. The gap between those who issue determinations and those whose lives are determined must be bridged. Professionals designated as investigators should conduct in-depth investigations and base their recommendations on the fruits of these investigations.

Perhaps such a shift in priority would be facilitated by employing a wider range of experts rather than the current short list of repeat players. Perhaps less reliance on these intermediate-level professionals would bring the decision makers closer to the parties and closer to the truth, thereby better enabling them to render just decisions. In the end, what is critical is that the institutions shed some of their institutional armor—the layered structures that weigh down institutional actions and result in maintenance of the status quo—and remember the purpose for which they were created. Both the Family Court and the Department of Social Services were formed to serve families in crisis

---

25. See discussion supra at 63–64.

and to assist families in resolving disputes. Both institutions were created to ensure that children are placed in safe, loving homes that can foster healthy development. It is time for all the professional players—the investigators and the decision makers—to take responsibility for their roles in the system and to act affirmatively to serve the best interests of the child.

"We Are All We've Got": Building a Retiree Movement in Youngstown, Ohio

Alice and Staughton Lynd

Introduction

On July 17, 1986, LTV Steel Company, the second largest producer of steel in the United States, declared bankruptcy and immediately cut off health and life insurance benefits for approximately forty eight thou sand retirees. Within days, retirees of steel mills in and around Youngstown, Ohio, formed an organization called Solidarity USA to fight for promised pension and medical benefits.

LTV's decision to stop paying medical insurance claims when it filed for protection under Chapter 11 of the Bankruptcy Code had catastrophic results. Retiree Roy St. Clair came home from the hospital on July 17. He spent a day frantically seeking alternative medical insurance. When he experienced a recurrence of his heart symptoms, he did not seek hospitalization because he did not know how he could pay the bill. He died a few hours later.

Delores Hrycyk, a lector at her Catholic church and wife of a retiree with thirty-six years at Republic Steel, telephoned radio talk shows and called a rally in downtown Youngstown for Saturday, July 26. A thousand people attended.

Several days later, hundreds of Youngstown-area retirees, under Hrycyk's leadership, met in Poland, Ohio, a Youngstown suburb, to

---

For further reading on this issue, see S. and A. Lynd, "Labor in the Era of Multinationalism: The Crisis in Bargained-For Fringe Benefits," *W.Va.Law Rev.* 93 (1991): 907.

form an organization. The suggestion was made from the floor that the group resembled Polish Solidarity. That's right, Hrycyk responded. Thinking out loud, she added, "Let's call it Solidarity USA."

The Attorneys' Story

Our office was overwhelmed with clients coming in and phoning. One woman told us she had enough heart medicine for fifteen days, and when that ran out, she could not afford to buy more.

We are not bankruptcy lawyers. We could not get the help we needed from people who were bankruptcy lawyers. Many of the questions having to do with medical and life insurance were outside their experience. Our questions were not ones where there was already black-letter or established law.

Alice asked a bankruptcy attorney whether a hospital bill incurred after the bankruptcy by a person who retired before the bankruptcy was a postpetition or a prepetition debt. The obligation to pay arose prepetition, but there was no way to know prepetition whether or when the hospitalization would occur or what its cost would be. Whichever way she presented the argument, pre- or postpetition, the bankruptcy lawyer replied, "That's a good argument."[1]

> *Alice:*[2] During the early months after LTV declared bankruptcy, we would go to meetings with LTV retirees at which the level of anger was high. At times I was afraid the tension would erupt into violence. I did not know what to do or say. But as time went on, we

1. It was not until years later that Judge Duffy ruled, in the context of the LTV bankruptcy, that the Pension Benefit Guaranty Corporation's (PBGC) claims were prepetition for anyone who retired prepetition even if the money was not due to be contributed to the plan or paid to the pensioner until after the bankruptcy commenced. *In re Chateaugay Corp.,* 130 B.R. 690 (S.D.N.Y. 1991).

2. Individual remarks are from an edited transcript of a collective oral history by several members of Solidarity USA. It was recorded at a session of the Ed Mann Labor School in Youngstown, Ohio, in July 1992. The principal speakers are: Cora Sanchez, Jerry Morrison, and Jean Rider, officers of Solidarity USA; Jack Minear and Marian Fleps, members of the elected Ad Hoc Steering Committee for GF Retirees and Former Employees; and attorneys Alice and Staughton Lynd, counsel for both groups. Additional comments are drawn from notes taken during meetings or phone conversations when the actual words of retirees could be jotted down.

Attorneys did not speak first at the Labor School but are presented first here so that the reader will have a glimpse of the role played by attorneys in this saga.

knew Ralph would say, "It's time to get out the baseball bats." Some people would cheer and some would laugh. But, in a way, Ralph spoke for all of us: it's time we did something to make a change in the situation. After a time I realized that there were others in Solidarity who reacted as I did when violence against person or property was suggested.

Staughton: How do retirees have any clout, any power? They can't strike. They can't vote for officers of the union. The union will modify their benefits and not put it up to retirees for ratification. You think of those things and you think, this is a powerless group of people. But somehow, we stirred up a storm.

Alice: I think one thing the retiree movement has indicated is that if you are a retiree, one little voice can't do anything. But I think Solidarity experienced that when one, two, or three busloads of people arrived somewhere, we got a response. I felt, as a lawyer, if I were to call them up or send them a letter and say, "I want to talk to you," do you think they would take the trouble? No way. But if I come and there are three busloads of people outside, they are going to say, "Alice, won't you come in?" And I say, "Yes, and I'm not going in alone. I'm bringing these people with me." Then we begin to be able to grapple with them.

Staughton: Between the seventeenth of July, which I believe was a Thursday, and I think it was the second Saturday after that when the first rally took place downtown, Delores informed me that I was going to be her lawyer and she wanted me to be at that rally. I remember that on the day of the rally there was a little article in the Youngstown *Vindicator* which said that at the LTV plant in East Chicago, Indiana, there was a strike connected with the benefits. We were all trying to figure out what was going on. I was convinced that day, and I am convinced sitting here six years later, that some women—like Cora and Jean and Marian—went out and started picketing at the plant because LTV had taken away their medical insurance. I think the security guards roughed up the women or pushed them around and treated them disrespectfully. The whole mill walked out—that's my understanding. And a couple of days later the International said it was an official strike. Ever after the International claimed credit for calling the strike. I don't think they had a thing to do with it. I think it was first of all the women, the wives of retirees, and secondly the guys inside who felt ashamed when they saw how these women were being treated outside the plant.

I remember, at the rally, listening to Congressman Traficant and the Steelworkers Union sub-district director Joe Clark and other speakers. And I thought to myself, that's not going to get results. What's going to get results is the way they did it in Indiana. People just did it themselves. They hit the bricks and brought pressure on the company.

The Retirees' Tale

Cora Sanchez, Jerry Morrison, and Jean Rider became officers of Solidarity USA. None of them had ever done anything like this before.

> *Cora:* I was in bed. I never get up early. I always lie in bed and listen to the Dan Ryan talk show. It came over the air that LTV had gone bankrupt and there was no insurance, no hospitalization. That woke me up real fast!
>
> I ran all over the house looking for my husband, Augie, to tell him. He told me, "Calm down! Calm down, now. It's not true. That's just a rumor." And I said, "What's it on the radio for?"
>
> *Jerry:* I heard Delores Hrycyk on the radio saying, "We're going to have a rally downtown. Come down." I went down. She started talking. She was mad as hell and she wasn't going to take it any more. It was just how I felt. And I said to myself, it's time that people get off their duffs and, instead of reading about it and listening about it, start doing something about it. And I just dedicated my life right then and there to doing something about it, seeing what I possibly could do.
>
> I listened to her, and in the crowd there was a guy intermittently coming in with a bullhorn, whom I didn't know. It was Ed Mann. We had a few of the hustlers up there talking on the microphone, telling us not to worry. But Ed Mann wasn't like that. And neither was Delores. And I said, now these are the guys I want to be involved with.
>
> *Cora:* We went to the rally at Federal Plaza. All these big shots got up there and talked and we asked the union man, "What's going to happen to us?" And he said, "You have to wait and see." I'll never forget his words. It made me so mad, I thought, "I'm not going to

wait and see. What these people are going to do, I'm going to be right with them." So that's how I got involved with Solidarity.

Jean: I remember the first meeting we had. My husband stood up and said that he would sign up people to join Solidarity. It wasn't named yet. We divided up into sections. We were from Austintown, so he took Austintown and the West Side.

Cora: When Delores started her group, she told the women to come to these meetings. I'd never been to a meeting. I stayed home and scrubbed and baked cookies. Solidarity has really changed me. I don't do that any more.

Jean: My kids tell me, they can't believe all I'm doing. I used to stay home and bake pies and bread and all that stuff.

Petitioning the Court

By early August 1986, LTV, fearing that the East Chicago strike would spread to its other mills, had sought and received permission from the Bankruptcy Court to put retirees back on insurance for six months. But the future looked uncertain. The banks that were LTV's secured creditors appealed the decision. Solidarity USA organized a demonstration in front of the Bankruptcy Court in New York at which they presented a petition addressed to Judge Lifland.

The undersigned are retirees from LTV Steel, their spouses and supporters.

We are coming directly to you because we feel we have no one to speak for us in your Court. . . . Please consider the following:

1. *Promised payment of medical expenses, life insurance, and pensions, should be given priority over ordinary business debts.* A business debtor can declare a business loss, go into bankruptcy, etc. A retiree who must regularly take insulin for diabetes, who must go to the hospital for necessary treatment, cannot postpone or avoid expense in the same way. In the Youngstown area, at least one person died in the days following July 17 because he could not arrange for alternative coverage and was afraid to go to the hospital for his heart condition without insurance.
2. *Post-petition medical, life insurance, and pension payments deserve at least as much consideration as the fees of bankruptcy lawyers.* We

understand that medical, life insurance, and pension payments that fall due after July 17 can be given the same priority
as payments to bankruptcy lawyers if classified as "administrative expenses." We think it would be unfair, to pay lawyers 100 cents on the dollar and to give retirees and their
surviving spouses less.

3. *The company that encouraged us to plan our whole lives around the
expectation of a secure retirement should not be permitted to turn its
back on us now.* We are not asking for charity. The union, acting
on our behalf, bargained for fringe benefits instead of current
wages so our retirement could be peaceful and secure. These
benefits are therefore deferred compensation, taken in place
of current wages. Moreover, many of us as retirees pay part of
the cost of our major medical coverage in monthly out-of-
pocket payments deducted from our pension checks.

Getting Organized

There were bake sales and a lot of fund-raising activities going on. If
you're handling much money, you've got to think about taxes. You've
got to think about having not-for-profit incorporation.

Alice: Incorporation became a way to redistribute power, because
you don't have a corporation with just one person. You have to
have three incorporators, and then you have to have a president,
and a vice president, and a secretary, and a treasurer. And that did
not take in all of the people who were actually taking leadership so
we set up a steering committee. We had at least twelve people on
the steering committee, and it was the steering committee that
would meet together and make decisions, or would recommend
decisions to the membership meeting which would make the
decision.

We found that we could get a bus and it would cost so much
money. "Shall we take it?" And the membership would say, "Yes."
And Delores would say, "If there's anybody that doesn't have ten
dollars for the bus, tell them to come anyway. We'll have a bake
sale and we'll raise the money."

Then the committees were set up. The medical committee, that
Cora and Jean worked on, helped people when their insurance

wasn't paying. There was one man who would write articles for the newsletter every month giving his perspective on what was going on.

I remember trips to Washington when we would divide up into little teams and we'd each go to certain senators and congressmen. Some of them couldn't figure out what we were talking about. They had no conception: retirees? benefits? It was like, "Are you from the moon?" There was no response.

There were others who were responsive but who said, "You've got to stay within the framework of bankruptcy law. And in bankruptcy law, everybody gives."

There were a few people, like Senator Heinz's aide, who listened to the retirees. He took their medical bills and tried to figure out what the problem was and why they felt such anxiety.

City Council Resolutions

Busloads of Solidarity USA retirees and spouses went with LTV retirees from other groups to city councils in the region during the winter of 1986–1987. They asked the Pittsburgh City Council to support LTV retirees in demanding no compromise or concessions in their medical, life insurance, and pension benefits.

On a cold, wet December 2, 1986, Solidarity USA demonstrators joined a rally in Cleveland followed by a march to the Cleveland City Council.[3]

Many carried signs bearing such messages as "LTV Masters of Deceit," "LTV an Expert Employee Traitor," "Liars, Thieves, Vultures," "LTV Has Stolen Our Dreams," "LTV Screws Retirees," and "Steel Pension, Not Steal Pension."

Delores Hrycyk of Solidarity USA, an organization of LTV pensioners, described July 17 as a day of infamy for every worker in America. She said, "LTV committed fraud that day. They promised us a secure retirement, but we got the shaft." She described LTV's actions as murder since some retirees died because they had no medical benefits.

---

3. The following account (with minor changes in punctuation and spelling) is quoted from Local Union 2265 USWA, "Steelworkers Rally in Defense of LTV Pensioners," *Stripscript* 7, no. 9 (January 1987): 1, 6.

Chanting, "Justice: We fought for it; We struck for it; We earned it; We won't take anything less" the protestors marched to the Blue Cross Headquarters where they held a brief rally to protest Blue Cross's recent announcement of higher rates for senior citizens and its inhuman attitude toward the retirees on July 17.

Blue Cross employees met the demonstrators with free coffee and donuts.

SEIU Business Agent Mike Murphy spoke stating, " . . . If they take away our health care, we need nationalized medicine."

The protestors then marched to City Hall for a giant indoor rally at the City Council Chambers.

Hrycyk said, "We're not here to beg; we're just here to get what we earned. We built the country, paid the taxes, and are paying the pension of every politician in this country. . . . Give us what we bargained for. . . . I don't want to see this American dream destroyed. . . . Workers of this country have to unite, come to the grass roots and say we've had enough and want what's coming to us." She demanded a complete Congressional investigation of LTV's merger and bankruptcy, adding, "They're telling me I'm a creditor. No, they stole my pension money. That's why they wanted these mills—to get my pension money. I'm no creditor, they're thieves."

Emergency Legislation

The first governmental response to the plight of LTV retirees came in the form of temporary emergency legislation passed by Congress in October 1986. The law required a company reorganizing in bankruptcy that had not yet filed a reorganization plan to continue to pay retiree health and life insurance benefits until May 15, 1987.

The emergency legislation was extended several times. In June 1988, Congress passed a retiree benefits protection act known in the Mahoning Valley as the Metzenbaum bill. The new law did not protect pension supplements and, as it turned out, offered little protection to medical and life insurance benefits.[4]

---

4. The Metzenbaum bill referred to in the following discussion is the Retiree Benefits Bankruptcy Protection Act of 1988, 11 U.S.C. § 1114, sponsored by Senator Metzenbaum of Ohio.

Jean: I remember Metzenbaum. He told us, "Don't worry. You won't lose a thing. You will not lose one penny." I remember him saying that at least four times to our face.

Cora: When we had the big rally down at Powers Auditorium in January 1987 . . .

Jean: And in Washington twice.

Cora: He wasn't going to come to the rally in Youngstown but we kept after him. He even got up and said he came because it's the squeaky wheel that gets greased.

Staughton: In March 1987, there was a meeting in Washington with Metzenbaum and Traficant.[5] Traficant took the position that you should simply pass a law saying companies have to pay retiree benefits no matter what. Period.

Everybody else explained to us that it was absolutely impossible for that law to pass. We would also have preferred such a law. But there are going to be some companies that actually don't have any money. What were they going to do if we passed that law? We had a choice between fighting the good fight for something that wasn't going to go anywhere, or settling for something that you, Marian and Jack, have found completely useless.

Cora: The union backed Metzenbaum's bill too. When we went to Washington, they almost put me in jail, because I passed out a leaflet supporting the Traficant bill. I made a mistake and gave one to Tony Rainaldi who is a district director of the Steelworkers.

Rainaldi came along and I gave him a leaflet. Pretty soon this guy came back and said, "You two better go upstairs to that room." I said, "I'm not going to no room!" He said, "Well, we're going to bring the police." And I said, "Well, make sure you bring enough because there's two old ladies here!" That made them mad.

They got the police and we were told to either leave or we would go to jail. So we just stopped. We put our leaflets away and we stayed. It was in the Shoreham Hotel.

The union had all these papers. The union had this long table. Before the union came in we stole all their papers and we hid them under the table and then they had nothing to pass out to us. We took all their badges. We had our pockets full of badges. The union took the microphone down so Solidarity couldn't talk.

---

5. Jim Traficant represented much of the Youngstown area in the U.S. Congress.

Mike: Now if your kids had done that, you would have whipped their butts!

Cora: Oh, yeah. If we'd have done that, we would have been grounded for a month!

Jack: They got smarter since then to make sure that nobody gets anything under the Metzenbaum bill.

Cora: But we're trying to get him to amend it because of what happened to you guys at GF especially.[6]

Marian: We were stuck because GF had no money. LTV had money. We didn't. Still don't.

Cora: I got threatening calls after this. Augie was in Puerto Rico and I was living here by myself. I was scared to death but I said, "You better say or do what you want now, because I don't run scared." Well, I never got a call after that.

Marian: You did right to tell them you weren't scared.

Cora: I was scared. I kept everybody's telephone number right by the phone.

$26.82

In August 1987, the United Steelworkers of America (USWA) negotiated a new labor agreement. The agreement provided that early retirees would receive from LTV approximately 90 percent of the pension supplement that had been negotiated for steelworkers forced into early retirement by mill shutdowns. (The supplement was $400 a month for the typical early retiree. Ninety percent came to $360 a month.) In addition, the new agreement provided that all employees and retirees would have to pay $26.82 per month toward the cost of basic hospitalization insurance. Current employees would have the money taken out of a profit-sharing pool, not out of their paychecks. But in the case of retirees, the $26.82 was deducted from their pension checks. If the company made sufficient profit, retirees would be reimbursed in April for the amounts they contributed during the previous year.

Retirees received checks in April 1988, reimbursing the $26.82 per month deducted from their monthly checks at the end of 1987. But

---

6. Notwithstanding previous enactment of the Metzenbaum bill, 11 U.S.C. § 1114, the GF Corporation of Youngstown filed for Chapter 11 protection in April 1990 and simply stopped paying medical benefits. See S. and A. Lynd, "The Crisis in Fringe Benefits," 25–31.

when LTV published its third quarter report in the fall of 1988, it appeared that LTV was taking advantage of a new accounting rule to wipe profits off their books for 1988. Retirees notified LTV that if they did not receive satisfactory assurances that the $26.82 for 1988 would be returned, Solidarity USA would stage a demonstration outside LTV's headquarters in Cleveland.

A busload of retirees from Retirees Against Greed and Exploitation (RAGE) arrived from Canton, Ohio, to swell the ranks of Solidarity USA demonstrators in front of the LTV Steel building in Cleveland. LTV got the message. Retirees were reimbursed by LTV in April 1989.

Porky: But there was no interest when we got the $26.82 back.

Confrontation with Blue Cross

For reasons not known to LTV retirees, their major medical insurance coverage was transferred from the Metropolitan Life Insurance Company to Blue Cross Blue Shield of Ohio. Blue Cross was already administering the basic hospitalization coverage and it continued to do so. LTV was self-insured for the basic hospitalization coverage—that is, LTV paid Blue Cross the amounts paid out in claims plus an administrative fee—but retirees paid the entire cost of the major medical program through premiums deducted from their pension checks.

Soon after Blue Cross took over the major medical, retirees began to notice that claims were not being paid as they had been before. In April 1989, someone reported to the steering committee of Solidarity USA, "Lab work used to be covered while in the hospital. Now they are only paying 80 percent after the deductible." But LTV had said in a letter in December 1988 that there would be no change in benefits.

At the membership meeting in June, Jerry Morrison exclaimed:

Blue Cross Blue Shield is deciding how sick you are and is saying how long you can stay in the hospital. They should expedite payment of medical insurance and pay more of the bills, and not tell doctors what care your insurance will pay for. We're going to go up and protest in front of their building. The last time we went to Cleveland, we got our $325 back [return of $26.82 for twelve months of 1988]!

And at the July meeting, Jerry said, "The dignity of a person is paying his bills."

After some correspondence and phone calls, Blue Cross was notified that Solidarity USA would appear at their Cleveland office on October 18, 1989. In the meantime, bills and "explanation of benefits" forms had been collected and numerous examples identified where items previously covered 100 percent by the basic hospitalization program were being paid 80 percent under major medical. Not only did retirees have to pay the premiums for the major medical coverage, but there was a lifetime cap of $50,000 per person as well as an annual cap on major medical benefits.

Blue Cross said that it would not meet with Solidarity USA. Solidarity said that it was coming anyway. Blue Cross then said that it would meet with only three representatives; but rather than endure a picket line outside their building, Blue Cross relented and met with the two dozen or so members of Solidarity USA who appeared at the designated time. Solidarity's agenda included the following questions and demands:

> Why is Blue Cross not paying 100 percent of what used to be paid under the basic plan? How can items that used to be paid 100 percent under the basic policy now be paid 80 percent under major medical? Put what the lifetime limit is and how much of it has been used on each major medical statement. Have a person at the Blue Cross office in Youngstown that people can go to with their papers to get problems resolved or effectively appealed or payment expedited.

A representative of Blue Cross explained that they service what LTV bought. The benefits are set out in the benefits booklet.

A retiree complained about Blue Cross's telephone service:

"The 800 number stays busy. You can't get through. An 800 number is not adequate for a person with a stack of papers. We need a person to answer claims problems."

Porky produced papers showing that when he had a stress test in the hospital in 1988, everything was covered; but when he had a stress test in the doctor's office in 1989, they took off the $100 deductible and then paid a percentage under major medical. "What difference does it make whether the test is done in the doctor's office or in a hospital?"

Porky later reported that Blue Cross told his doctor, "If the hospital sent the bill they would pay 100 percent; but if [the test is] done in the hospital but billed by a doctor who has an office in the hospital, they pay 80 percent."

Murph asked, when testing is done as an outpatient and surgery is done as an inpatient, why don't you pay for these tests when it saves money to have the tests done outside the hospital? Solidarity urged that the same rules should apply for everybody, whether or not they are in the hospital.

Cora had her papers showing that an "EKG was covered in one place but not in another. But the LTV letter says no change in coverage." Murph added: "You're being paid to provide the same coverage as Metropolitan."

"We're representing folks who are hurting," said Ed Mann. "I negotiated these [benefits] with the company. We gave up wages." And speaking about bills that "before were not major medical," Ed asked, "why are they major medical now? There is a lifetime cap on major medical benefits."

Two days after the meeting with Blue Cross in Cleveland, Cora told Solidarity that Blue Cross had taken her EKG off major medical and was paying 100 percent under basic. But, she said, "satisfying a few individuals does not take care of thousands of others." At the next meeting of Solidarity USA at the end of October, Cora reported as cochairperson of the medical committee:

> Blue Cross says, "We are doing what LTV tells us to do." Each [LTV and Blue Cross] puts the blame on the other. Individuals are being taken care of, but are we satisfied? No. We want [the same] for everybody. What they used to pay under basic is now major medical and there's a limit on major medical. . . . How can two companies use the same book and get different answers?

> *Jean:* We just went over to LTV. We had a picket in front of LTV's Youngstown office about our benefits. Finally they let a group of us go in and we said, "We want these bills settled." There was one man that had $17,000 that hadn't been paid. They were just holding him up. We went in and Bruce Mateer, LTV's benefits man, looked at each one of the bills with us. After that, whenever we had any trouble, we went over and saw them.

Cora: At first they were going to let only the people who had the problems go in and talk. And we said a representative of Solidarity would go in with each one. They said, "No, we can't do that." So I said, "Then we'll just stay here." Then they got used to us and they let us bring anybody. Now, all we have to do is tell people to say, "Solidarity sent me," or "Cora sent me."

The first time we went to LTV, there were all these policemen there. I walked in and shook the cop's hand because I grew up with him. That night I got a telephone call and they said, "Cora, we were told to watch for you and to arrest you if you misbehaved."

Health Benefit Guaranty Corporation or Universal
Health Care?

In the fall of 1988, the Tunnel Rats for Workers Solidarity (A Group of LTV Steel Retirees) in Aliquippa, Pennsylvania, circulated a petition that stated:

We the People demand that health and pension benefits of active workers and retirees of LTV and other companies in bankruptcy *can not* be modified or reduced *unless necessary* to avoid a company's full bankruptcy (Chapter 7).

Since some companies do go fully bankrupt (Chapter 7), We the People demand that a Health Benefit Guaranty Corporation (HBGC) be established to guarantee transitional health care benefits for unemployed workers, and permanent health care benefits for retirees of bankrupt companies like LTV.

Solidarity USA lent its support to this proposal, as did RAGE in Canton, but Solidarity USA did not feel that a Health Benefit Guaranty Corporation (HBGC) would take care of enough people. The Solidarity USA steering committee debated: If you want to extend government medical insurance to people who don't have it, who should be included?

The Tunnel Rats' answer was, "Guarantee insurance if you earned it." As Carole McMahon of the Tunnel Rats put it, "These are people that *earned* this health care. They were promised it and they should get it."

But what about the employee who isn't retired and is unemployed, or works but never had insurance? During a meeting of Solidarity USA in February 1989, Delores Hrycyk expressed her views:

> I am a firm believer that we need medical care for all. Service jobs can't afford it. Some people stay on welfare from generation to generation to keep their medical card. That discourages work. They never had a chance to earn it. Every man, woman and child should have the medical care they need. Put all the money together—Medicare, Medicaid—that route excites me.

A consensus formed within Solidarity USA to endorse the principle of health care for all, not just for one group, because that expresses solidarity. RAGE concurred. Bob Burns of RAGE told Carole that the HBGC "doesn't cover enough people. RAGE is for national health care insurance."

Collective Bargaining Demands

In August 1988, Solidarity USA asked the Steelworkers district director Coyle to come to the September meeting of Solidarity USA and to answer some of the retirees' questions:

> What is going on? What is being done about taxation of [supplements]? What is the union going to do for retirees? What will the union be raising in the next negotiations—specifically what does the union intend to do about the $26.82 charge for basic medical insurance? And, especially, how can retirees have input into the process of formulating bargaining demands?

The union declined to send a representative to meet with Solidarity USA. But the September 1988 issue of the Solidarity USA *Newsletter* carried a list of ten "collective bargaining demands":[7]

> The following bargaining demands for the next round of negotiations between LTV and the USWA were moved, seconded, and approved at the Solidarity USA meeting on Aug. 28:
>
> 1. Retirees must have a voice in contract negotiations that vitally affect them. The USWA should offer retiree groups a seat at

---

7. No. 2, pp. 1–2.

the negotiating table. . . . After a contract has been negotiated, the USWA should take an advisory poll of retirees before
submitting the contract to a ratification vote by active
employees.

2. The $26.82 per month contribution by retirees to the cost of
their basic medical coverage should be abolished. When this
insurance was negotiated it was supposed to be without
charge. LTV has plenty of money to pay what it promised to
pay. Also, with regard to 1988 we want a written accounting
as to LTV's ability to refund the $26.82 per month contribu-
tions for this year.

3. The pension supplement should be restored to $400. If this is
impossible, the Social Security and state income tax deductions on pension supplement payments should be abolished.
If these deductions cannot be abolished, the payments themselves should be increased so that the company (not the retiree) pays any taxes of this kind.

Other demands had to do with benefits for surviving spouses,
retirees on disability, an automatic cost-of-living increase, and other
benefits changes.

These demands were sent to the union. There was no response. In
December 1988, a retiree in Indiana Harbor called with information
about a meeting of union officials in Florida. He said he was "afraid the
union would go to the judge as to what they'll do before going to
retirees." Solidarity USA wrote to the president of the union, Lynn
Williams, and asked him to permit retirees to attend the meeting of the
basic steel industry conference. The union was reached by phone and
the message to Solidarity USA was that retirees could not participate,
not even as observers.

Meeting with the Union

"The contract is up in 1990," said Jerry Morrison, who had recently
become president of Solidarity USA. "They're squeezing us on medical
and on the $400. We will go back and fight if we have to." "And not go
to Pittsburgh and be docile like before," added Bob Burns. "If we're
going, we're going in. We built that hall!" responded Jerry, referring to
the Steelworkers' headquarters. "We sent letters to Rainaldi and Coyle

and Williams [international union officials] and we've had no answer for a year. They act as if we didn't exist," said another voice. Drawing on the tactic that worked with Blue Cross, the speaker added: "Tell the union we're coming on a certain day."

That certain day when buses rolled into Pittsburgh from Youngstown, Canton, and Aliquippa was December 7, 1989.

During the latter part of November 1989, LTV notified retirees that the premiums for major medical insurance were to be sharply increased. This added fuel to the fire. Cora wrote a report saying that when her husband retired in 1985, the major medical premium for a married couple not yet on Medicare was $41.74 per month; by January 1989, it was $86.66; and it was going to be raised in January 1990 to $141.32, an increase of $54.66.

> This is in addition to $26.82 we pay for hospital benefits. This will raise us to $168.14 a month that they are taking from our checks for medical benefits, and don't forget the $40.00 we lost and on top of that we have to pay FICA taxes on our supplement and then we pay state and federal taxes. Some retirees are getting a little over $300.00 now. How are they going to live?
>
> We were in Cleveland three weeks ago for a meeting with Blue Cross Blue Shield. They never told us of a raise. It is like a slap in the face. We are paying more and more and getting less and less coverage. . . . We have a $50,000 limit on major medical and for some people they are reaching it. We have to fight to get universal health care for all. So I guess Solidarity USA hits the streets again.

Upon arriving at union headquarters in Pittsburgh, retirees were directed away from media cameras to a room at the nearby Hilton Hotel. Some went to the Hilton, but others set up a picket line outside Steelworker headquarters. At the Hilton retirees finally were able to voice their demands to union representatives.

> *Jerry:* There are no retirees on the union bargaining committees. They tell us we're not paying members.
> *Another Retiree:* I'm a Steelworker who brought in the CIO. I go downtown and ask the union a question. They say, "We don't represent retirees."

Another Retiree: Why can't retirees have a say at least as to retirement benefits? Why can't we retain our voting rights? We are
treated like second class citizens. Our retiree group has no say.
That's not democratic.

The discussion went in several directions before returning to the
question of input from retirees. "I've had experience on the wage policy
committee," said Ed Mann:

We want input in negotiations and not just as advisors. [If we
participate and] it's a bad deal, we can't put [the blame] on you. We
want a piece of the action—not to be told, "This is the best we can
do for you." We don't want to solve our problems one by one with
LTV. We want to solve them as a union for everyone. . . .
    There are people in the union that want us to be adversaries. We
support young workers. We want to help organize. But when we
hear that [active workers won't take any more hits] for retirees,
they're splitting us apart.

Before the morning was over, demonstrators who had been picketing at union headquarters were invited into the hotel room where the
meeting with Jim Smith and other union officials was taking place. Ed
Mann spoke again:

We want to be on a negotiating committee for retirees, not on an
advisory committee. . . . There is no one here who is not for the
union. If the union goes down, we're dead. We want the right to
ratify.

GF Corporation

In April 1990, the GF Corporation (formerly General Fireproofing) of
Youngstown filed for bankruptcy protection and stopped paying negotiated benefits.

Jack: We had a shutdown agreement at GF. I was on the negotiating
committee. We sat down for a period of two and a half or three
months, agreeing what we were going to do. Being a nice bunch of

union people who are kind and thoughtful and speak nicely to each other, we agreed that GF could stretch out the money that was due in retirement and shutdown benefits and in vacations. We agreed they could stretch this out over a period of a year so it would not hurt them. They said we were great union people to do this.

Then, lo and behold, my daughter called me and told me, "GF just filed for bankruptcy." Real nice bunch of people! They informed us that the shutdown agreement meant nothing.

They sent me a letter saying I could pick up my insurance. All I had to do was to pay $384 a month. Now we had no money coming in. All of our money has been canceled. GF paid none of the severance, none of the hospital coverage, so I go back to my union and scream and holler, and do you know who shows up? About 25 people. And do you know what they said to me? "Don't worry about that, Jack. The union's going to take care of us." Does that sound familiar?

We've been paid zero. The estate now has over a million dollars.

Alice: What does the Metzenbaum bill say?

Jack: The Metzenbaum bill says the retirees are to be taken care of. Their benefits are to be paid. There is also a little part of the Metzenbaum bill that says the union, the company and the court can get together and decide to cut off the benefits if there is no money left.[8] GF made sure there was no money left. They made a deal to end the contract and the shutdown agreement in 1990 instead of in 1991 when the contract expired. By this little piece of paper they signed, it took 35 men who could have crept into retirement benefits out of the picture.

Where was the union? Sitting next to the bankruptcy judge. Where were we, over 1,300 former employees of GF? We were home. We didn't bother. If it wasn't for Solidarity, we would have nothing going, and that's only a small group of GFers who have gone to Solidarity to ask for help.

---

8. 11 U.S.C. § 1114(e)(1) states: "Notwithstanding any other provision of this title, the debtor in possession . . . shall timely pay and shall not modify any retiree benefits, except. . . ." See n.4 supra.

11 U.S.C. § 1114(e)(1)(A) states that "the court, on motion of the trustee or authorized representative, . . . may order modification of such payments." GF stopped paying medical benefits without seeking court approval.

At least they know we are here. We hope that Solidarity and groups like Solidarity will be around for a long time to come.

Are We Radicals?

Retirees who built the union agonize that the union has lost the vision it used to have. They are broken-hearted lovers.

Porky: Years ago, when I was a griever at Truscon, I was always considered a radical even though I was a part of the union. I was a radical because I never agreed with a lot of the things that the local union wanted.

Marian: But you're not really a radical to me. You're not way out. You're just standing up for your beliefs and trying to get across, and because you do that you're a radical.

Jerry: I can remember the first time I got up. I never got up and made speeches. All these dignitaries were sitting there. "We have a representative here from Solidarity USA. He'd like to say a few words." The minister was there. One politician said, "What do you think they're doing now, Mr. Morrison?" I said, "They're pissing in your face and telling you it's raining." I mean, the crowd roared: "That's it! You're telling it like it is." I talked right to the mill people that were there.

Alice: I'm reminded of a song that was sung at the memorial service for Ed Mann: "Oh, you ain't done nothing if you ain't been called a Red."

I think there is a question, are you within bounds or are you out-of-bounds? When you stand up and fight for your rights, some people are going to say you are out-of-bounds.

Jean: This country was started by people who, most people would say, were out-of-bounds.

Jack: The union was too. Don't forget that. The union was started by people that were out-of-bounds.

Jean: Don't you think that the union has now become like a big corporation? It is not run by ordinary people any more. You have people running our union that aren't even from our country. Lynn Williams, president of the Steelworkers, can go back to Canada and have his national health care. He doesn't have to worry.

And they don't have conferences in Youngstown. They go to Hawaii or places like that to have their conferences. They don't go first class. They go up-upper class.

The Legal System

Alice asked the retirees about what they had experienced from the legal system as the result of these bankruptcies.

Jerry: It's going to take a revolution to straighten it out, right back to where our values were when this country first began.

Marium: I believe we're being cheated by the legal system.

Cora: We brought our kids up to believe in the law and you listen to this and you do that. We went to New York to one of the hearings. The union and the judge and everybody was talking and the judge decided for the union. We walked outside the door. The union man had told the judge inside, "This is the best contract." When we got outside we asked the union man about some new provisions in the contract. And he said, "I never read the contract." He buffaloed that judge. So we are teaching our kids to listen to these people?

John: What kind of people are these people who do this kind of thing? Steelworkers are men who worked hard all their lives, who took heat, layoffs, strikes, and dirt. Part of us is still down there in some of those mills. Then some little jerk attorney who was born after we put half our lives in those mills and made America great, comes along with a ballpoint pen and takes away all our peace of mind.

Jerry: We need to show compassion for each other. Things can be done if we want to. *We* are all we've got!

The Struggle Continues

1990 brought apparent victories to LTV retirees. In April, the union, under pressure from groups like Solidarity USA and RAGE, negotiated an end to the hated $26.82 monthly payment for hospitalization insurance and obtained agreement by the company to pay half of the monthly premium for major medical. In June, the Supreme Court of the United States affirmed the Pension Benefit Guaranty Corporation's authority to restore to LTV the pension plans terminated in 1987. When the plans were restored, LTV not only resumed payment of the full $400 a month supplement to early retirees but made a lump sum payment compensating early retirees for most of the money lost from their supplement checks since January 1987.

However, bargaining agreements and court decisions do not change the underlying contradiction that threatens the pension and medical benefits of LTV retirees. LTV Steel has slimmed down to a leaner and no less mean company employing between ten and fifteen thousand active workers. These current employees must somehow produce the cash flow or surplus value to pay promised retiree benefits to approximately four times as many retirees. They cannot do it.

Retiree expectations of a stable and serene retirement have long since gone by the board. Instead of receiving unchanging vested pension and medical insurance benefits, paid for long ago by wage increases foregone, retirees find that they must engage in daily battle to keep even a significant part of what they were previously promised.

Judges, lawyers, and the law have not fared well in the perception of these retirees. Retirees feel at the mercy of Judge Burton Lifland, sitting hundreds of miles away in a bankruptcy court near Wall Street. When Youngstown retirees traveled by chartered bus to Judge Lifland's court for hearings, the bailiff told them on one occasion that they would be permitted in the courtroom only if there was room after all the lawyers were seated, and on another occasion directed them to move from the front seats to the back of the courtroom.

As for lawyers, under the very Metzenbaum amendment that they worked so hard to enact retirees must accept the union as their "authorized representative" in bankruptcy proceedings. Retirees are no longer members of the Steelworkers Union. They do not vote for union officers. They have no way to hold union lawyers accountable and no voice in what is negotiated on their behalf. The lawyers hired by the Steelworkers to speak in bankruptcy court, and to negotiate modifications of retiree benefits with other parties in interest, do not consult with Youngstown retirees before they cut such deals; they take orders from their union employers at Pittsburgh headquarters. The Solidarity USA *Newsletter* reports occasionally the amount of money paid out to bankruptcy court lawyers (more than $150 million at this writing) by an estate that claims it must cut retiree benefits in order to survive.[9]

Retirees' experiences have strengthened their conviction that the law is not on the side of the working man or woman. The chairman of the board of LTV Steel receives three-quarters of a million dollars annually in cash and other company executives are compensated in like manner. Yet when LTV Steel sought to increase executive compensation in the midst of bankruptcy proceedings, for the purported purpose of safeguarding the reorganizing company from management flight, Judge Lifland approved. He himself, like other federal judges, receives a salary more than ten times the annual pensions of the retirees who petition him for help. He is, retirees think, "one of them": that is, he is part of the social world inhabited by the company executives and corporate lawyers who practice before him in their dark suits and ties, and he has no experiential basis for understanding the quiet, orderly men in their clean, short-sleeved, open-necked shirts who occasionally come into his presence like visitors from another planet.

The law itself is "for them," retirees have concluded, not "for us." Men and women who consider that they always paid their bills, always held up their end of the contracts they undertook for buying homes or making steel, watch in increasing anger as companies break their promises and violate their contracts. "How can they get away with it?" retirees ask. They feel betrayed, and not only by their former employers and unions. They are disillusioned with the law itself because the law has failed to make the companies live up to their side of the bargain.

---

9. See, for example, *Newsletter*, No. 42 (Mar. 1992), p. 5; No. 47 (Aug. 1992), p. 2.

What's Wrong with These Pictures? The Story of the Hammer Museum Litigation

Nell Minow

"Unbelievable!" I held the phone away from my ear. "This is the most outrageous thing I have ever seen! Armand Hammer is stealing our money!"

The person on the other end of the line was Amy Falvy (name changed at her request), who worked in a tiny office at one of the largest banks in the world. She was responsible for voting the bank's proxies. Her job was low on the organization chart, and the scope of her duties was narrow. Yet she was one of the most powerful people in corporate America. If she did not agree with what the management of any of thousands of big publicly held corporations was doing, she could vote the bank's proxies against them. And she had just found something she did not agree with, when she read in the 1989 proxy statement from Occidental Petroleum that the board of directors had approved expenditure of more than $375,000 in corporate funds for an autobiography of CEO Dr. Armand Hammer covering the years 1987–89, and at least $74 million for a museum for his art collection.

On behalf of corporate and public pension funds and other institutional investors, Amy Falvy's bank held hundreds of millions of dollars worth of stock in America's largest corporations. And the institutional investors themselves held these stocks on behalf of workers who were participating in a pension plan, workers who had no idea what stocks were held for them, much less who held them or how they voted the proxies. Once a year, the bank would receive a proxy card from the companies issuing the stock, and the bank would be asked to vote, usually to approve the company's nominees for the board of directors and auditors. Occasionally, and then more frequently after the mid-1980s, there would be other items on the proxy card as well. Shareholder resolutions raising social policy concerns (infant formula sales, loans to Chile, investment in South Africa) appeared on proxy cards, along with proposals by management to adopt antitakeover provisions and proposals by shareholder groups to prevent or rescind them. It was all but unheard of for a proposal by management to fail or for a proposal by shareholders to pass. Votes according to the recommendation of management were routinely well above 90 percent.

Falvy's position, when it was first created, was thought of by some in the bank as almost entirely clerical in nature. She was to record the receipt of the proxies, vote them, record the votes, and mail them in. The assumption that she would vote according to management's recommendation was so implicit that it never occurred to anyone that there was an alternative. Indeed, her superiors were occasionally surprised that she even read the statements accompanying the proxies, not in itself surprising as proxy statements consist of mind-numbing lawyer jargon printed on tissue paper. The requirements of the Securities and Exchange Commission account for some of the density of the prose, but corporate counsel gets the credit for much of it—it seems that if the SEC would require them to disclose certain information, they would bury it in boilerplate. Most of her counterparts in other banks, investment firms, and brokerage houses never even read the endless legalese that accompanied the proxy cards, but Amy was different. She read every word. If she didn't like what she read, she voted against it.

In this case, however, Amy did not have a chance. The proxy statement included a brief, bland description of the book and museum deal and disclosed conflicts of interest—because they had to be disclosed—as "transactions with management," but it did not ask for shareholder approval.

So, all she could do was call me to complain about it. This is what the company said in the 1989 Occidental proxy she received:

> Occidental has undertaken to finance the costs of production of a book chronicling the recent personal and business activities of Dr. Hammer and his involvement with Occidental. This book will be a sequel to the autobiography of Dr. Hammer published in 1987, and it will describe Dr. Hammer's worldwide endeavors since then in

international affairs, art, and other philanthropic concerns, as well as significant domestic and international business activities of Occidental during such period. Occidental has expended approximately $255,000 for this purpose, principally in payment for services being performed by third parties and for their expenses, especially those expenses in traveling with Dr. Hammer to record such endeavors. Occidental is currently committed to pay an additional amount of approximately $120,000 plus expenses to such third parties. As with the 1987 book, which figured for 18 weeks on the *New York Times* list of best sellers and was a number one best seller in many countries around the world, Occidental will be entitled to reimbursement of its expenditures for this book from the net proceeds, if any, from its publication. To date, royalty payments from Dr. Hammer's 1987 autobiography in excess of $600,000 have been reimbursed to Occidental. Any remaining profits from the book now in preparation will be donated to The Armand Hammer United World College of the American West ("the College"), in Montezuma, New Mexico.

Mr. Krim (a director of Occidental and one of its subsidiaries) is Chairman of the Board of Directors, and Dr. Hammer, Dr. Irani, Mr. Groman, Mr. Kluge, Mr. Moss, and Ms. Tomich (all directors of Occidental) are directors of the College. Substantially all of the funds used to operate the College are provided by Dr. Hammer, the Armand Hammer United World College Trust, the Armand Hammer Foundation, and Occidental.

In February, 1989, a special committee of Occidental's Board of Directors, consisting entirely of outside, disinterested directors, approved a proposal to provide financial support for the Armand Hammer Museum of Art and Cultural Center ("the Museum"), which will be located adjacent to and physically integrated with Occidental's Los Angeles headquarters building, the Occidental Petroleum Center. The Museum will provide a permanent facility for the exhibition of three art collections to be contributed by The Armand Hammer Foundation and Dr. Hammer. Occidental's Board of Directors believes that the financial support of the Museum will promote the continuation of goodwill which has inured to Occidental from its long-standing past association with and support of the collections.

Dr. Hammer, as Chairman, Mr. Hammer [Hammer's grandson],

and Dr. Irani [Hammer's subordinate and successor], as well as
Alec P. Courtelis, a director of IBP [a subsidiary of Occidental], will
be members of the nine-member board of directors of the Museum.
Dr. Hammer, as President, together with Mr. Groman and Mr.
Moss, is also a director of the Armand Hammer Foundation.

Occidental will fund the cost of constructing the new Museum
building and renovating portions of four floors of the Occidental
Petroleum Center for use by the Museum under a 30-year rent-free
lease, as well as the cost of constructing an expanded parking
facility beneath the Museum Building and other improvements to
the Occidental Petroleum Center. These costs are estimated to be
approximately $50 million.

Occidental will provide additional financial support to the Museum through the funding of an annuity, at an estimated after-tax
cost of approximately $24 million, which is intended to provide
annual payments to the Museum over 30 years and a lump sum
payment at the end of such period. Occidental will also grant the
Museum an option to purchase the Museum complex and the Occidental Petroleum Center at the end of the 30-year lease for $55
million, their currently estimated fair market value at that time. If
the option is exercised, Occidental will have the right, subject to
certain conditions, to lease back space in the Occidental Petroleum
Center for a fair market rental as determined by an independent
appraiser.

Occidental expects to receive appropriate public acknowledge-
ment of its role in forming the Museum and will be entitled to
corporate sponsorship rights available to other corporate contributors, which are expected to include the use of the Museum facilities
at times that do not conflict with public access.

The issue here is not whether corporations should make charitable
contributions; it is that corporate charity illustrates the disconnection
between the directors and the people to whom they owe the duties of
care and loyalty. Some level of charity by corporations is not only acceptable, it should be encouraged. Companies should recognize their
obligations to the community through charitable contributions. And
these contributions provide important benefits to long-term shareholders, both directly and indirectly. Directly, shareholders benefit from
the favorable tax treatment of charitable contributions. Indirectly, they

benefit from the goodwill, support, and name recognition they inspire. Almost everyone knows that Mobil sponsored *Masterpiece Theatre* for twenty-five years. The official sponsors of the Olympics get four years of positive publicity. Public corporations have contributed to museum exhibitions, tennis tournaments, scholarships and other prizes, even local Little League teams. This makes their employees and customers happy, both important aspects of making shareholders happy. Companies do well by doing good.

But some charitable contributions are controversial. When AT&T responded to pressure from antiabortion groups and withdrew its support for Planned Parenthood, the controversy only increased, with a shareholder resolution calling for the support to be reinstated. Virginia Slims' sponsorship of a women's tennis tournament also led to controversy, when objections were raised to the connection of an unhealthy product to an athletic event. In the Hammer case, Occidental's contribution was so enormous, and the benefit to Occidental as a corporation so tenuous, that it is impossible to justify as a legitimate corporate contribution.

Charitable contributions also raise more direct conflict of interest issues. There have been opportunities for corporate officers to direct the company's contributions to beneficiaries closer to their own interests than the company's. Perhaps the most extreme example is when a president of the university that receives large contributions from a company sits on the board of that corporation. In at least one such case, the company's CEO also sits on the university's board, a nice, cozy situation. Charitable contributions to entities affiliated with directors can present conflicts of interest.

Another recent development is corporate charitable contributions as part of a director's pay package. While many aspects of corporate activity should bring "some tangible benefit to the community," director's pay should bring some tangible benefit to the shareholders. If the company does well, they will be able to make a very substantial contribution to any school or other good cause that appeals to them. There is simply no reason for the corporation to reward its directors this way. (One advantage from the corporate perspective is that it can be structured in such a way that it does not have to be disclosed in the proxy statement, so the shareholders will never know about it.)

Warren Buffett, chairman of the legendary Berkshire Hathaway, has a simple approach that makes a good deal of sense. Each shareholder designates a charity, and Buffett contributes to that charity, proportionate to the shareholder's holdings of stock. "Just as I wouldn't want you to implement your personal judgments by writing checks on my bank account for charities of your choice, I feel it inappropriate to write checks on your corporate 'bank account' for charities of my choice," he wrote in his 1989 annual report. "I am pleased that Berkshire donations can become owner-directed. It is ironic, but understandable, that a large and growing number of major corporations have charitable policies pursuant to which they will match gifts made by employees (and—brace yourself for this one—many even match gifts made by directors) but none, to my knowledge, has a plan matching charitable gifts by owners." If only the directors of Occidental had done it this way. But, knowing how they were picked, how they got their information, and who determined their pay, it is not hard to understand why they did not.

So, if the directors could not evelute the museum proposal objectively, who else had the authority to do so? The museum proposal was not put to a shareholder vote; it was in the proxy statement for information only. What about a lawsuit? It is important to make clear at this point that neither Amy Falvy nor I had what could in legal terms be considered standing to challenge this action. We do not allow people to bring cases, in our legal system, unless they have what the law considers an "interest." For one reason, it would create a huge burden on the system if we allowed anyone to bring a lawsuit about just about anything. But there is another, more important reason. One of the most basic assumptions of our legal system is that the best way for us to find the right answer is to have an objective judge or jury, not in any way connected to the case, listen to the opposing arguments of people who are vitally concerned with the outcome, and only people who are vitally concerned. Whether it is a question of fact ("Was the light red or green when the car went through the intersection and hit another car?") or law ("Do the apples from your tree that fall into my yard belong to you or to me?"), our view is that only those who are most interested in the results have both the knowledge and the focus that an objective reviewer needs to hear in order to decide.

Neither Amy nor I, as individuals, had standing. Neither of us held any stock in Occidental (at least none that we knew of, which is part of the problem). Amy Falvy's bank did not own the stock; they held it on behalf of beneficial owners, working people who were participating in a pension plan through their employer and who had no idea what investments were being used to fund that plan. The utterly sensible rules governing standing work well when we are ruling on who has the right to bring the lawsuit over the car accident or the apple tree. But they do not work very well when there are so many people involved that it is difficult to say who does indeed own the stock. The key to understanding the obstacles to justice in this kind of case is this: those who know about the problem have no standing to sue and thus no access to court, while those who do have standing to sue have no access to the information. And the structure established by our legal system to bridge that gap has made the problem worse.

I have already described how Amy Falvy got involved, so I had better explain why I was the person she called. I was then the general counsel of what was at that time a tiny consulting firm called Institutional Shareholder Services (ISS). ISS had been established four years earlier by Robert A. G. Monks. He was one of the first people to see that the world of corporate governance was about to be transformed by the growth of the institutional investors. Traditional corporate theory was that shareholders had a range of effective mechanisms for communicating with management. But all of those mechanisms became ineffective as corporations issued millions of shares and share ownership became too widely dispersed for shareholders to work together. The connection between ownership and control was little more than vestigial.

That was, until two forces collided in the 1980s. One was the unprecedented rise of the institutional investors: banks like Amy's, corporate pension funds, endowments, insurance companies, pension funds for unions and government officials, mutual funds, and others began to grow so quickly that they now hold half of all stock in American companies, much more than half in many of them. The other was the takeover era, which demonstrated forcefully that the system was permitting abuses of shareholders by both raiders and management, both of whom made and broke up companies with little concern for the impact on shareholder value. Like the crazed broadcaster in *Network*, shareholders were mad as hell and weren't going to take it any more. There was a whole new category of issues to respond to, and there was a whole new category of shareholders to respond to them. The easiest and most obvious way to respond was through voting proxies (ballots sent by mail, to be voted and counted at the company's annual meeting). It was in the statement accompanying Occidental Petroleum's proxy that Amy Falvy read of the book and the museum.

So Robert Monks at ISS was trying to build a business out of helping institutional investors to use their share ownership rights more effectively. This primarily meant preparing analyses of proxy issues for people like Amy Falvy, who had to decide how to vote them. In fact, I was about to start writing an analysis of the Occidental Petroleum proxy when she called. But the book and the museum were not being put to a shareholder vote, so I felt there was nothing much I could do. It did not seem that there was any way to stop it. So, I listened to her, and agreed with her, shook my head at the unfairness of it all, and put down the phone.

Then I saw the supplement to the proxy statement, sent out by Occidental, explaining that two lawsuits had been filed on behalf of the shareholders. I had no standing because I had no stock, but thanks to Amy Falvy I did have information, and I knew how to get it to the people who did have stock in Occidental, lots of it, my institutional investor clients.

I was thrilled. This was just the way the system was supposed to work. Someone had seen the wrong and was going to court to get it fixed. For a moment there, I was proud to be a lawyer. It was a brief moment. I called the lawyer in charge of the class action suit to ask about it. He had to get court approval to represent the entire class of Occidental shareholders, so I figured he would be glad to be in touch with someone who had contacts with a lot of them. I told him that I knew a number of large institutional investors with a lot of stock in Occidental, and I wanted to know how we could help with the lawsuit. He said that the best help we could give was to support the settlement he had negotiated, and he assured me that it had been a tough fight, with substantial results. "Does that mean that they are not going to fund the museum? Did we win?" I asked. "No, no, no," he said. He explained that under Delaware law it was all but impossible to overturn a board's decision to make a charitable contribution. But he had, he assured me, elicited significant concessions from the Occidental lawyers, including their agreement to send out the supplement to the proxy statement, which described the lawsuits and gave a few additional facts about the museum plans and expenditures. The proposed settlement he described was this:

1. The museum would be called the Armand Hammer Museum of Art and Cultural Center, but the building will be called the Occidental Petroleum Cultural Center Building. This was signif-

icant because of all the goodwill for the company that visits to the museum would generate. I never heard of anyone who made a decision about oil based on an afternoon looking at art, but the value of this concession was stressed throughout the case, including testimony from an expert witness that it was worth $10 million to the shareholders.

2. Occidental will have the right to appoint designees to the museum's board.

3. Dr. Hammer will execute a legally binding agreement to donate his collection. In other words, Armand Hammer would really give the artwork to the museum. This was significant because he had originally promised the same pieces to the Los Angeles County Museum, which had created a special wing for them, but he had rescinded his gift when they refused to meet his conditions. These conditions were inconsistent with worldwide curatorial standards. For example, he insisted that his collection be separated from everything else in the museum, that all plaques from other donors be removed from the wing with his collection, that the curator report to him or his foundation and not to the museum's director, that a life-size portrait of him be hung at the gallery's main entrance, and that nothing ever be added or sold from the collection. Forever.

4. Future charitable outlays ("Hey!" I interrupted him. "You mean not only are we getting no money back, but we are actually agreeing to pay more?") would be limited to 1.33 percent of dividends, unless the shareholders approved. The amount could be paid out early, based on anticipated dividends, or late, if the entire amount is not paid out in any year. As far as our records showed, Occidental had never come near that level in past charitable contributions, so it was hard to make a case that this represented any diminution of future outlays.

5. The 1.33 percent ceiling would include payments to Dr. Hammer under his then-current compensation agreement, which guaranteed his foundation a payment of seven times his annual salary after his death.

6. Occidental would limit the amount it will pay for overruns of construction costs to an additional $10 million, paid before 1990.

7. In the event that the museum should decide to sell the building within 30 years, the company will receive half of the sale price

over $55 million. I am not sure what the market is these days for museum buildings, but I suppose this was a useful provision, just in case.

8. The attorneys would be paid $1.4 million by Occidental.

I told the lawyer I would think about the settlement, and hung up the phone. The company would be spending at least 50 percent more on the museum than originally planned, the lawyers were going to collect huge fees, and the shareholders were going to get nothing. This was worse in every way than it was when Amy Falvy called me. The shareholders had been mistreated by the directors, who in theory owed them a fiduciary duty. But they had also been mistreated by the lawyers who were supposed to represent them, an even stronger obligation. This settlement not only added insult to injury, it added some more injury too.

My father has many gifts and many accomplishments, but I sometimes think that the thing he does best is clip news articles. Everyone close to him gets envelopes filled with articles relating to any subject he or she has ever mentioned (or may someday mention). Shortly after my conversation with this lawyer, my father sent me a clipping from the *New York Times,* a brief article about the prospective settlement of the lawsuit. The article quoted the plaintiff in another suit on the same subject, a man named Alan Kahn, who was as angry about the settlement as I was.

So, I called him. Alan Kahn turned out to be a money manager of great charm, humor, and integrity. He had a quixotic streak, but his windmills were corporate managers and his Sancho Panza was a sole practitioner who specialized in shareholder litigation. Together, they had filed a number of suits and had some successes. They had also called the class action suit lawyer I had spoken with, who told them that he would cut them in for part of the fee if they would support the settlement. Kahn said he would settle for no money at all, if Occidental would put the book and museum expenditures to a shareholder vote. Needless to say, they refused; and he was going to try to stop the settlement. He was the one I wanted to help, but by that time we only had ten days before the hearing.

All Occidental shareholders were members of the class of plaintiffs, though most of them did not know it. In most cases of a class action (where one party represents all those with similar interests), all members of the class are notified that the action has been filed and given a chance to opt out of the class and file their own case. But the Federal Rules of Civil Procedure exempt shareholder class actions from the notice requirement, on the theory that since they are all shareholders they all have identical interests. I knew that if any of the institutional shareholders were going to respond, I had to let them know what was going on.

I called two of my favorite clients, the California Public Employees' Retirement System and the Pennsylvania Public School Employees' Retirement System. Like Amy Falvy, they held billions of dollars worth of stock on behalf of employees participating in pension plans. But unlike Amy Falvy, their ability to take on corporate management was not constrained by commercial relationships (see discussion below), and both had been active and vocal on issues of shareholder rights although, except for their role as ex officio members of the equity committee in the Texaco bankruptcy, not in any matter involving litigation or court filings.

I told them that this was not a protest of a legitimate charitable contribution. As noted above, there are many justifications, both social and commercial, for corporate charitable gifts. But this museum was not justified in either category. As a matter of public relations and public policy, Occidental's museum failed. The art collection was originally promised to the Los Angeles County Art Museum. It could not create goodwill for the company to assist in permitting Dr. Hammer to take his collection away from the county museum and to insist that it be displayed and maintained in a manner inconsistent with the standards applied universally by art museums. This was not charity; it was a hostile takeover of the arts. As a commercial matter, it failed as well. According to the complaint filed by Kahn, Occidental's previous year's loss carryforward of approximately $825 million was so large that Occidental might not realize any tax benefit at all. Charitable donations in excess of the amount deductible for purposes of the Internal Revenue code may be considered unreasonable under the law of Delaware, which is where Occidental is incorporated. This expenditure exceeded that limit, and therefore could not be justified in business terms. Kahn's complaint called Occidental's contributions to the Hammer Museum, the Hammer Foundation, and the Hammer College (as well as Hammer's compensation) "gifts to defendant Hammer."

As for the book about Dr. Hammer's life from 1987 through 1989, while the amount to be paid was a tiny fraction of that allocated for the museum, the issue was the same. The directors had approved the expenditure of $375,000 to write the story of his life from 1987 through 1989. Unarguably, Dr. Hammer had led an extremely interesting life, and, as the proxy pointed out, the first volume of his autobiography had been a best-seller. However, its very success should have made it possible for Dr. Hammer to negotiate a contract for a sequel with a commercial publisher. Instead, money was simply scooped out of the corporate till and given to someone to fly all over the world with Dr. Hammer while writing the story of the past two years. While that money was to have been reimbursed, out of the profits (if any) from the book, that just makes it an interest-free nonrecourse loan to Hammer, whose $2,454,637 cash compensation was already more than generous, given the company's performance.

I told the two funds that this litigation presented exactly the kind of issues we wrote about in our analyses of proxies and in contests for control. Shareholders could go along with the settlement here and permit more than $120 million of their money to be spent on something that would give them no benefits. Or, for the price of a postage stamp, they could object and insist on a better deal. In this case, it seemed clear to me that shareholders could accomplish a great deal by simply objecting to the proposed settlement. I recommended that they sign an affidavit and submit it to the court, registering an objection to the proposed settlement and asking the court to permit discovery to continue. It could also ask that any settlement be put to a shareholder vote. I felt they had nothing to lose, and a real chance to do better than the terms of the proposed settlement.

Traditional trust law provides that a legitimate legal claim is considered an asset of the trust, and failure to protect and pursue that claim is wasting assets. These two funds were not about to let that happen. They did file affidavits. The judge did not grant Kahn's request for an injunction, for procedural reasons, but he did express concerns about "troublesome issues," including "the lack of any direct substantial benefit to the stockholders" and the size of the attorney's fees. The settlement was stalled, and discovery was allowed to go forward. I was proud to be a lawyer—for a longer moment this time.

In discovery, many additional new facts came out, including the fact that some of the artwork in Dr. Hammer's personal collection was paid for by the corporation. This included the more than $5 million paid for a Leonardo da Vinci notebook, originally called the *Leicester Codex* but renamed by Hammer the *Hammer Codex*. (In my talks with institutional shareholders I suggested that, since they paid for it, it should be renamed the *California Public Employees' Retirement System Codex*.) Furthermore, depositions revealed that Albert Gore, Sr., the chairman of the committee of "independent" directors who approved the museum expenditures, had no understanding of the financial consequences of the deal.

It seemed as though we could not lose. The California Public Employees' Retirement System, with two million shares one of Occidental's largest holders, was granted permission to intervene. I was again proud to be a lawyer. But that moment, too, came to an end. Despite all our progress, and despite the filing of another lawsuit by the beneficiary of Dr. Hammer's late wife's will, claiming that half of the art collection belonged to her, construction of the museum continued, and a curator was hired. It is perhaps worth mentioning that the curator was a young woman who had no museum background, and that she met Dr. Hammer when she interviewed him for an airline magazine. Her name at that time was Martha Kaufman, but after meeting Dr. Hammer she changed it to Hillary Gibson, left her husband, and became curator of a museum that, at that time, still did not have any art. (At this writing, she is suing the Hammer estate for moneys due her for services as "his confidante, consultant, and partner.")

Despite the additional evidence, a year later the same lawyers came forward with the same settlement, only it was now up to $120 million. This included seven years' worth of Dr. Hammer's salary to be paid directly to the museum after his death, a sort of "coffin parachute."

With more time than before to gather opposition to the settlement, I wrote to 200 of the company's largest shareholders, asking them to file an objection with the court. In my letter dated March 12, 1990, I said,

> The settlement preserves and perpetuates the power of the Board of Directors of Occidental Petroleum to spend corporate funds on a construction project that serves only the company's Chairman of the Board, Dr. Armand Hammer, with little, if any, benefit to the shareholders or the corporation. . . . The settlement by its own terms is excessive, but more importantly, it should not be approved because it is premature for the court to allow a settlement of this case at this time. The preliminary stages have already raised ques-

tions about the museum's business plan, the allocation of costs for construction so far, and even the ownership of some of the artwork, which was apparently purchased for Dr. Hammer's personal collection but paid for by corporate funds. This settlement makes no effort to resolve—or even address—these issues.

Several of the people I wrote to did file objections with the court. The State of New York pointed out that, unlike the nominal plaintiff's few shares, its investment in Occidental alone was nearly as much as the $120 million of the settlement. The State of California sent its counsel to make its case in person. Despite the protests of many major shareholders, and the court's finding that the benefits to shareholders were "meager," the Chancery Court approved that settlement.

While the judge expressed strong reservations about its terms, he said that the likelihood that the museum expenditures would be approved under the business judgment rule made it impossible for him to do anything else. The judge took the unusual step of expressing his concerns about the outcome by cutting the attorney's fees nearly in half. He also said, "If the Court was a stockholder of Occidental it might vote for new directors, if it was on the Board, it might vote for new management, and if it was a member of the Special Committee, it might vote against the Museum project." But he said that, because the expenditures would likely be upheld under the business judgment rule, the case had to be settled. An appeal was unsuccessful, and it was settled on those terms.

The business judgment rule sensibly provides that the courts will not intervene or second-guess informed decisions by the directors and officers of a corporation regarding its planning and operation. Anyone challenging the decision must persuade the court that no person of ordinary, sound business judgment could possibly have made that decision. The effect is to place the burden on the shareholders to prove fraud, bad faith, or self-dealing. In one well-known case, the court upheld the decision of the Wrigley Company directors not to install lights in Wrigley Field, where the Chicago Cubs play baseball, despite the fact that the ability to play night games would almost certainly improve the returns to shareholders. During the takeover era, a series of legal challenges to hostile takeovers led to court decisions that deferred more and more to the discretion of the directors (with one significant exception, the all-but-overruled or -overtaken by events Trans Union case). The result was that the business judgment rule has now been extended so broadly that it can bar a trial on the merits in a challenge like this one, despite evidence that corporate funds were used for personal acquisitions. If a clerk did that, it would be called embezzlement. If Armand Hammer does it, it is business judgment.

In the Occidental case, even the protests of shareholders with millions of dollars invested in the company were not enough to stop an outrageous settlement. What's wrong with this picture? Or, perhaps more appropriately, what's wrong with these pictures?

This story illustrates the unintended consequence of the corporate structure. The very aspects of its design that made it so robust, so able to survive changes in leadership, in the economy, in technology, were the aspects that led to this result—in the classic law school terms, a right without a remedy.

The story, in its outline, is a simple one. Millions of people invested money in Occidental Petroleum on the explicit assurance that the people entrusted with that money, the corporate managers, would use their best efforts to maximize long-term returns, and with the assurance that those "elected" by the investors to oversee the overall direction of the company would represent their interests in doing so. Indeed, these representatives, the board of directors, must in theory meet the highest standard developed by our legal system, the fiduciary standard, in protecting the interests of the shareholders. Somehow, in this case, that was found to include spending $120 million of investors' money to house a museum for the chief executive officer's art collection, some of which they apparently also purchased for him. Once that decision was made, the shareholders, in theory, had the right to communicate their disapproval. As the Chancery Court judge said, they could just vote for new directors. Or they could challenge the decision in court, with a class action on behalf of all shareholders, or a derivative action, literally deriving the right to sue the directors on behalf of the corporation itself. Again, in theory, a legitimate claim would easily find legal representation, and the class action/derivative action procedures would eliminate any collective choice obstacles.

Well, that is the theory. Let's look at the players again, to find out about the reality, to ask who had the right and what happened to the remedy. The players fall into three major categories: (1) the directors, who committed the wrong by approving the expenditures for the book and the museum; (2) the shareholders, particularly the institutional shareholders, who should have had the right to challenge those decisions; and (3) the plaintiff's lawyers, who crafted and advocated the settlement.

1. Where was the board in all of this? Let's begin with the chairman of the board, the legendary Dr. Armand Hammer himself. His career is the subject of hundreds of articles and several books (some not his own). His career as an industrialist, philanthropist, and unofficial diplomat spanned the twentieth century. He was the first to do business with the Soviet Union and with many third world countries. He was the friend of world leaders. He was also a convicted felon, due to his violation of federal campaign contribution provisions in 1976. (He was officially pardoned by Ronald Reagan.) At the sentencing proceeding, held in Los Angeles because he was too weak to travel to Washington, he appeared in a wheelchair, hooked up to monitoring devices that were checked by a team of cardiologists. His lawyers told the court that he was "a sick old man (who) lives four blocks from the office, goes in late, goes home for lunch, and takes a nap in the afternoon." (The Kahn complaint noted that, "Despite the fact that Hammer is too old and sick to work," Occidental paid him over $6 million from 1985 to 1988. Furthermore, his employment contract, which provided for a minimum of $1,420,000 in annual compensation, extended to 1998, when he would be 99 years old, and was then automatically extendable for an additional seven years.)

Contrary to the testimony provided at the sentencing hearing, Dr. Hammer was a most energetic CEO, who ran the company in many ways as though it was his kingdom. Wall Street recognized his deep (and sometimes eccentric) involvement in every aspect of the company with sharp increases in the stock price every time he got sick. Hammer repeatedly designated successors, only to become dissatisfied and throw them out. He insisted on holding all of the stockholders' meetings on his birthday, to drown out business with festivities. And he picked his board members very carefully.

While the textbooks and judicial decisions speak of the shareholders "electing" directors, the reality is that directors are selected by management, and in more than 99 percent of the cases they run unopposed. Edward Jay Epstein says in *Who Owns the Corporation?* (New York: Priority Press Publications, 1986, p. 13) that director elections are "procedurally much more akin to the elections held by the Communist Party of North Korea than those held in Western democracies."

Hammer not only picked his directors, he set their pay, and often put them on boards of Occidental subsidiaries, where he paid them again. Perhaps the Occidental directors were unusually malleable, but it is a fact of corporate America that directors are not picked for their ability to challenge management. On the contrary, they are more often chosen for their business or personal ties, or for their ability to add symbolic lustre. Compensation expert Graef Crystal describes boards as "Ten friends of the CEO, a woman and a black."

Directors are picked because the CEO knows them and knows that they are likely to be on his side. Many of them, even those termed "outside" directors by the New York Stock Exchange's rather liberal definition, have some business or personal relationship with the CEO. At Occidental, for example, more than half of the directors were either insiders or outsiders with these kinds of ties. More than half of the directors were over 72 years old, including most of the "outside directors." Hammer himself was 91, and Louis Nizer was 87. Nizer is a partner and Arthur B. Krim (age 79) is counsel to a law firm that received $5 million from Occidental in the year they served on the "independent" committee that approved the museum. Another member of this "independent" directors' committee was Rosemary Tomich, a director of an Occidental subsidiary. And the CEO has both a carrot and a stick in "persuading" his directors. A widespread rumor in the financial community was that Hammer possessed signed, undated letters of resignation from each director in his desk drawer. True or not, this is consistent with the unnamed CEO quoted in the *New York Times*, who said, "I always tell my directors they have two choices—vote 'yes' or 'I resign.'"

In my letter to the Occidental shareholders about the settlement, I said that the board's "willingness to rubber-stamp Dr. Hammer's attempts to use the corporate treasury for his own purposes is a serious concern for shareholders. Directors have two duties, a duty of care and a duty of loyalty. The Occidental directors violated the duty of loyalty in approving these expenditures, which benefit Dr. Hammer as an individual, rather than the company and its shareholders." The committee did not retain its own counsel before considering the museum. Instead, the chief counsel of Occidental retained a firm that had previously represented Hammer to advise them. It did not retain its own account-ing firm. This is another indication of its lack of genuine independence. (After the litigation was filed, they did retain their own counsel.)

I added that Senator Gore's deposition testimony showing his ig-norance of the tax consequences of the museum when he voted to approve it showed that the board also violated its duty of care. "And, despite evidence that the corporation paid for some of the artwork and what were supposed to be Dr. Hammer's personal contributions to the Los Angeles County Museum (the original designated recipient of the art collection), the directors have made no attempt to investigate or pursue any remedies from Dr. Hammer."

The "dance with the one who brought you" mentality is prevalent in boardrooms. Bryan Burrough and John Helyar's *Barbarians at the Gate* (New York: Harper and Row, 1990) documents in devastating fashion the way that RJR Nabisco CEO Ross Johnson handled his boards, with a combination of lavish perquisites and meager information. His tech-niques for the care and feeding of his directors included everything from arranging for them to rub shoulders with celebrities to endowing chairs at their alma maters. Perquisites like use of the corporate planes and apartments made it hard for directors to push him on tough ques-tions. While he was dazzling his hand-picked directors, who could expect them to complain about his jets, his household help (on the company's payroll), and his 24 country club memberships, all paid for by the shareholders?

The controversy over executive pay is just one more symptom. The CEO of Coca-Cola, whose performance was, by any measure, spectacu-lar, was awarded 81 million dollars worth of stock by his grateful board in 1992. Those who thought that was too much pointed out that his compensation committee included a consultant whose firm was paid $225,000 in 1991. More troubling are the other cases where CEOs were rewarded for performance that was, by any measure, anything but spectacular. The Securities and Exchange Commission issued revised rules in late 1992, partly in response to the outcry over executive pay. The new rules require companies to provide information about execu-tive pay plans that is not only more clear but also more consistent, enabling shareholders to compare apples and apples. Furthermore, the new rules give shareholders much more flexibility in communicating with each other about these and other issues, which should make it easier to get support for initiatives like shareholder resolutions. Majority support for these initiatives, even unanimous support, does not guarantee change, however, as under federal and state law virtually all shareholder proposals are advisory only. And the revised rules are unlikely to have much impact on the most important issue for shareholders, the selection of directors.

Since they are selected by management, paid by management, and, perhaps most importantly, informed by management, it is easy for directors to become captive to management's perspective. Information is the key, and it is often frustrating to directors to have such limited access. Former Supreme Court Justice Arthur Goldberg, a member of the board of TWA, suggested that the board form a committee to make periodic reports on the company's operations, and that it should have its own staff of experts, including a scientist, an economist, a public relations expert, an auditor, and, perhaps, a financial expert. The proposal was turned down, and Goldberg resigned from the board. When Ross Perot, brought on to the board of General Motors to make a difference, tried to make a difference that management did not like, the company paid him $747 million to get him off the board.

The reality is that directors are merely the parsley on the fish or the ornaments on a corporate Christmas tree. As Peter Drucker (1981, 110) put it many years ago: "Whenever an institution malfunctions as consistently as boards of directors have in nearly every major fiasco of the last forty or fifty years, it is futile to blame men. It is the institution that malfunctions."

The law is of little help in keeping the focus of the directors on the interests of the shareholders. The fiduciary standard for directors has all but vanished under the broad reach of the business judgment rule. State law governing corporations has been, in former SEC Chairman William Cary's famous phrase, a "race to the bottom." At the very bottom is Delaware, the second smallest state in size, but the largest in terms of the number of corporations chartered there. Corporations have been very profitable for Delaware, and Delaware has been very accommodating in order to keep it that way. Incorporation in Delaware is convenient for a number of reasons, and one of them is its broad protection for corporate directors. This explains the court's finding that a trial on the issue of the Hammer Museum was unlikely to end in a decision for the plaintiffs, despite the questions about the ownership of the paintings and the deliberations of the directors.

The classic description of the fiduciary as above the morals of the marketplace simply does not apply to directors. The business judgment rule reasonably provides that directors should not be judged in hindsight. So the courts will not second-guess the merits of business decisions made by directors even if, in retrospect, they turn out to have been wrong. But takeover-era decisions and amendments to state legislation have given corporate directors a scope of protection far broader than in any other profession. Even if the shareholders have the information and have counsel who are genuine advocates for their interests (both unlikely, as discussed below), their chances of winning a claim against the directors, absent out-and-out fraud or self-dealing, are all but nonexistent. Delaware's Chancellor William Allen, who presides over more of these cases than almost anyone else, said that a director has more of a chance of being hit by lightning than of paying a penny out of his own pocket as the result of a shareholder lawsuit.

2. Where were the shareholders in all of this? The textbook theory on corporations is that one group contributes the capital and another contributes the labor, for the benefit of both of them and of society as a whole. In order to prevent agency costs—misuse of the capital by the management, the agents of the investors—the system is designed with a series of checks and balances. Shareholders, the theory continues, have three avenues for keeping management acting in their interests. They can vote their proxies, file a lawsuit, or sell their stock.

But this theory is based on a model of share ownership that is decades out of date. That model assumes that a single investor studies the market and selects a stock to purchase, then follows that company and uses his or her ownership rights (voting proxies, filing a lawsuit, selling the shares) to establish and enforce limits on self-dealing behavior. But it ignores the reality of a marketplace so large, diffuse, and diverse that the problem of collective choice overwhelms any effective action by individual investors. And it ignores the majority shareholder in today's capital markets, the institutional investor.

Because the markets are so big, complicated, and diverse, natural selection of the financial markets has replaced individual investors with large, sophisticated institutions. These days, instead of buying 100 shares of General Motors, investors buy 100 shares of the Fidelity Magellan Fund. They do not have to follow the market; they can invest their savings with those of thousands of others and enjoy the benefit of the money managers with the best records on Wall Street. Investing this way is safe and easy; you are automatically diversified according to the provisions of whatever fund you select, whether what you are looking for is a mix of companies that are high-tech, politically correct, or both. But what that means is that at any given moment the investor has no idea what the underlying stocks are in the portfolio. If you ask whether the portfolio contains Occidental, the answer will be, "No, but I have Kemper." These people do not get their proxies; those go to the money manager (who, until a few years ago, probably voted with management without reading them, or just threw them away).

And if you ask the investor what he or she holds through a pension fund, you will get a blank stare. Above, I stated that neither Amy Falvy nor I knew whether we had any Occidental stock. What I meant was that it was quite possible that we were indeed investors, through our employers' retirement plans, but that there was no way of finding out, and nothing we could do to change it.

The most significant development in corporate governance over the past 20 years has been the emergence of large institutional investors, who are expected to hold half the stock in American companies by the year 2000. They already hold a majority of the stock of many of the nation's largest companies.

Institutional investors include public and private pension funds, endowments, mutual funds, insurance companies, and others. The people who were wronged by the decision to pay for the book and the museum with corporate funds are precisely the same people who were wronged in many of the other cases in this book—working people. factory workers, state government employees, teachers, firemen, police officers, union members the people whose interests are supposed to be protected by prudent experts. The five largest groups of institutional shareholders had the following equity holdings (in billions of dollars) in 1994:

Private pension funds	$1,251.4
State/local pension funds	$ 507.4
Open-end/investment companies	$ 648.1
Life insurance companies	$ 60.1
Other insurance companies	$ 112.0

The holdings were skewed toward the larger capitalization companies, with the result that by 1989, institutional ownership of the top 50 corporations had reached 50 percent. Clearly, concerns of institutional investors should be of the utmost importance to corporate management. But, as Carolyn Kay Brancato (1990, 1–2) has noted, "institutional investors are by no means a monolithic group." While they are all governed by different statutes, they have one overriding obligation in common; like the directors of the companies they invest in, all are fiduciaries, obligated to act with the most scrupulous care in guarding the assets held on behalf of others. Unlike the individual investors, whose ineffectual role in governance has been documented since the days of Berle and Means, the institutional investors are sophisticated enough to understand governance issues and big enough so that their response is meaningful. Most importantly, though, as fiduciaries, when action is meaningful (when the benefits outweigh the costs), they must take it.

But for a variety of reasons, including the collective choice problem and the risks of commercial retaliation, institutional investors have not been as active as they can be. The problem they face is this one: Can it be prudent for them to expend resources, knowing that, without the ability to communicate with other shareholders, any positive results are unlikely? Even if the results are positive, any returns to the active shareholder will only be proportionate to its holdings, all of the other shareholders getting a free ride. Furthermore, to the extent that a money manager or a company's pension department adopts an activist posture with respect to portfolio companies, it risks retribution: retaliation in the marketplace. From the point of view of all institutions, then, it is simplest to do nothing, to try to maximize value by trading, despite the fact that all evidence indicates that the majority of those who do so fail to outperform the market. This is slowly changing, as proxy voting is considered another aspect of asset management, both by the market and by the government agencies with responsibility for enforcing the fiduciary standard for institutional investors.

But there has been almost no change in their activism with regard to shareholder litigation. For one reason, as noted above, they are not notified that the case has been filed and given the chance to opt out. Even when they do get notices, as with proxies (until recently), many institutional investors ignore notices relating to shareholder litigation. Indeed, one major financial institution ignored repeated notices of its right to claim $900,000 under the terms of a settlement of one such case. The deadline was extended three times, in order to permit it to file. Despite repeated calls from the plaintiff's counsel, the institution missed all three deadlines, and its final payment reflected a substantial penalty for late filing.

Even if the institutional shareholders all understood the actions by the Occidental directors and all wanted to stop them, what could they do? In this case, voting proxies made no difference, because the book and the museum were not put to a shareholder vote and there was no competing slate of directors to vote into office to protest the actions of the board. In my analysis of the Occidental proxy, I did recommend that our clients cast a "withhold" vote for the "independent" directors who served on the museum committee, but I knew it was a symbolic gesture, without much meaning. If every shareholder withheld their vote from the director candidates, they would still be elected, as long as they got a single vote, even their own.

Even if the book and museum had been put to a shareholder vote, it would have been all but impossible to stop them. Management has access to the corporate treasury to disseminate its side of the story. After the initial litigation forced the company to send out the supplement to the proxy statement, the costs of the mailing were borne by the company (meaning the shareholders). Anyone wanting to solicit a vote against management's recommendation would have to spend at least half a million dollars to get the shareholder list, write solicitation material, get it cleared by the Securities and Exchange Commission, mail it out to millions of shareholders, and hire a proxy solicitation firm to collect the votes. I know of only one time when shareholders were able to vote against a management proposal. In that case a shareholder with three percent of the stock was willing to pay for all of the expenses of a solicitation, despite the fact that he got only three percent of the returns when the vote caused the price of the stock to rise (in this case, fortunately, more than enough to pay his expenses).

Keep in mind that management not only counts the votes, they know who voted for and against them, and they know in time to call and talk to them about it. Amy Falvy, for example, once voted against management on a proxy, only to receive a furious call from another part of her bank. The company's management had received her proxy and called the bank to explain that it would reconsider its long-term commercial relationship with the bank (which handled its payroll and line of credit) if the bank did not reconsider its proxy votes. How can any investor, much less an institutional investor, risk-averse by law and nature, justify such an initiative?

3. Where were the lawyers? This case is just one example of the shareholders' utter helplessness under Delaware law in suits for breach of directors' duty. A small group of lawyers, representing "shareholders" with token investments, file almost daily lawsuits, with complaints that are photocopies of yesterday's suits against other companies, based on whatever is reported in the financial press. Then they settle, quickly, for small awards and high attorney's fees.

It wasn't supposed to happen this way. The procedures for class actions and derivative actions were set up just to overcome the problems of collective choice. No one shareholder can possibly justify the time and expense necessary to bring a lawsuit for only a pro rata share of the rewards. So these avenues were established to remove the obstacles, indeed to create incentives for participation in these suits. The rules pertaining to notice and approval of counsel and the provisions allowing class members to opt out are also designed to make it easier to litigate legitimate cases.

But there are two factors that the system fails to deal with. The first is the shareholder community, as described above. It is too diffuse and too diverse to be communicated with in a meaningful way. And the disincentives for participation are strong. Can we see the IBM pension fund as the plaintiff in a shareholder action against the management of General Motors? The second factor is the ineffectual nature of the law governing the directors' duty. As long as the overbroad reach of the business judgment rule makes the likelihood of success of these lawsuits so small, there is little incentive for anyone to file one.

That is, except for the tiny but highly prosperous community of the "Wilmington (Delaware) filers." The ambulance chasers of corporate law, these are the people who have made an industry out of nuisance suits. They were described in *The American Lawyer* like this:

> Welcome to the plush and intimate confines of the Delaware chancery court, home turf of the Wilmington filers, the shareholder lawyers who sue any deal that moves. They are the bottom scrapers of the M&A world, the *Wall Street Journal* clippers with the mysterious professional plaintiffs. Racing to the courthouse on the merest rumor of a deal, they file triplicate copies of one another's suits—complaints that themselves read like duplicates from every other case. They are "rapacious jackals," in the memorable words of Chicago federal judge Charles Kocoras in 1982, "whose declared

concern for the corporate well-being camouflages their unwholesome appetite for corporate dollars." And they are the "pilgrims"—early settlers—litigators who never have to prove their mettle in a trial.

In the Occidental case, counsel for the California Public Employees' Retirement System noted that in negotiating the settlement, counsel for the plaintiffs "took no depositions, propounded no interrogatories and requested no production of documents" and could not therefore have sufficient knowledge of the merits of the case to negotiate an arms-length settlement. Yet they did manage to negotiate a $1.4 million fee for themselves. And it makes no difference to have a real plaintiff file a real suit with these guys around. Alan Kahn's lawyer told me that despite the fact that their suit was filed first, they were excluded from the settlement process because the other lawyers called Occidental, right after filing, to offer to settle.

In other cases, the lawyers manage to find something to keep them busy, whether it is justified by the merits of the case or not. As Chancellor Allen said to one attorney, who was attempting to justify his fees, "I have no reason to doubt that you proceeded as an advocate with energy and skill. What is causing me some obvious concern is (whether) you, in fact, got anything." Toward the end of the takeover era, the filers got around this uncomfortable question by filing as soon as an offer was made, so that they could claim credit (and a piece of the action) for any increase between the initial offer and the final deal.

These lawsuits are brought by a small group of people, who hold a small group of shares, working with a small group of law firms, and the conclusions are generally favorable only to them. For example, in the settlement of a shareholder lawsuit against CBS, the plaintiff, who held 12 shares, received $15,000, or $1,250 per share. (This was justified as fair payment for having to endure a "nasty deposition.") The attorneys got $1.5 million. CBS got about $4.5 million from its own insurer; it is not clear whether that sum covered more than its expenses. In another suit, where the judge called the complaints "helium weight," he awarded attorney's fees of $350,000. In a suit concerning the acquisition of MGM/UA Entertainment Company by Turner Broadcasting System, the return to the shareholders negotiated by "their" representative was the shareholder's choice of a videotape (*Poltergeist III, Moonstruck, Betrayed, Child's Play,* or *Spaceballs*). When the judge objected, the lawyer said he didn't appreciate the value of the offer because he probably didn't own a VCR. The lawyers were to get $1.2 million, despite the fact that one reason the case had to be settled instead of litigated was that its plaintiff repudiated one of the suit's claims in his deposition.

In a heartening development in the summer of 1992, however, the Federal District Court in Maine refused to approve a $2 million payment to 16 law firms, in settlement of litigation against Georgia-Pacific. The lawyers had filed the suit on behalf of the shareholders of Great Northern Nekoosa, the takeover target of Georgia-Pacific. Since the ultimate deal was better for shareholders than the proposal at the time the lawsuit was filed, the attorneys argued that they had made a contribution for which they deserved to be paid. Georgia-Pacific agreed to pay the attorneys $2 million, subject to what was expected to be routine approval by the court. In this case, however, the federal district court in Maine decided not to approve the payment, or indeed any payment at all. In an unusual move, designed to make it difficult for the law firms to overturn his decision on appeal, the judge also listed detailed objections to almost every item and calculation put forward to support the $2 million payment.

Responding to an amicus (friend of the court) brief filed by the State of Maine itself, the judge ruled that even had the law firms justified their involvement, they had overbilled by 80 percent: "Exaggeration, rather than restraint, has been the watchword of the plaintiffs' counsel's entire exercise. . . . [Even] a Michelangelo should not charge Sistine Chapel rates for painting a farmer's barn."

But this case is still very much an exception and is not expected to influence the Delaware Chancery Court, which has jurisdiction over most of these cases. The problem is that the defendants in these suits have no incentive to contest them. The filers' world would not be so plush and comfortable if the companies they sued would fight back aggressively. But to make things worse, corporations welcome these suits, because they can be settled quickly and cheaply, extinguishing the claims of all shareholders. According to a letter I received from CBS in response to questions about the settlement, "neither CBS nor the individual defendants participated in those (settlement) negotiations." Buying off the "Delaware regulars" is a small price for directors to pay to protect themselves from a serious lawsuit. Even if they do not think so, their insurers do. One disadvantage of indemnifying directors is that decisions like these are then made by the insurance companies. That is where it all ends, in the hands of the insurance companies. In a way, they play the role here that the courts have not been able to. And the results are, predictably, based on many considerations, but justice is not on the list.

What's wrong with this picture is that the people who had the right never knew about the wrong. The working people who want nothing more than a secure retirement income have no way of knowing that they have an investment in Occidental Petroleum, much less that their money is being used as though it was in Dr. Armand Hammer's personal piggy bank. The people whose job it is to protect the interests of these workers are prevented, through lack of information, through intimidation, and through the simple economics of the collective choice problem, from doing so. The corporate directors have less risk of accountability for the consequences of their actions in the boardroom than they do in any other aspect of their personal or professional lives. And the lawyers, in my opinion, are the worst of all. They tell the court they are there to be advocates for the shareholders, and then they take them again.

In order to cope with the complexities of modern life, both shareholders and corporations have established a series of structures that have diminished the vital connection between ownership and control almost to the vanishing point. Once the shareholder was an individual who selected a company and made a genuine commitment, with responsibilities on both sides, establishing a genuine connection. Now the shareholder is a worker who has a pension fund, overseen by his employer, who contracts with a money manager, who invests in a mutual fund, who buys and sells stocks on a daily basis (sometimes to other money managers investing money for the same worker), some of which may comprise a tiny fraction of the millions of shares issued by a huge conglomerate like Occidental Petroleum, and it is to somewhere in this litany that the directors, selected by the CEO, owe a poorly defined duty to exercise a very broadly defined business judgment. If that sounds like the house that Jack built, it is easy to imagine Jack's house as the Armand Hammer Museum.

What we need is a stronger connection between the shareholders and the corporate managers and directors. I do not want or expect it to come from the pension plan participants, despite the fact that they are the beneficial holders of the stock. The reason we established a system for pension funds, rather than expecting workers to take care of their own retirement, is that our experience has given us some respect for expertise and specialization. What I want is for that expertise and specialization to be as focused on managing the ownership rights of the stock as on managing the right to buy and sell. Pension fund managers and other institutional investors must make a commitment to making sure that the directors they elect do their job, and to putting in better ones if they don't. They must also make a commitment to recognizing their right to litigate as an asset, which must be managed with the "care, skill, prudence, and diligence" that the Employees' Retirement Income Security Act (ERISA) requires for all pension assets. Real plaintiffs, with significant investments, will be able to find lawyers who will be genuine advocates for all the shareholders, and will be able to get better results.

One final note. As noted previously, at the settlement hearing, the lawyers arguing on behalf of the settlement presented testimony that the value to shareholders of having the Occidental Petroleum name on the museum building was $10 million. It is worth pointing out that once the museum was opened, the museum directors then forgot to put up the sign. The company that was to gain so much goodwill from the museum was barely mentioned in any of the museum materials or press releases. The final ironic twist was that in 1992, after excoriating reviews and internal turmoil, the museum was taken over by the University of California at Los Angeles.

REFERENCES

Borden, Anthony. "The Shareholder Suit Charade." *The American Lawyer,* December 1989, 67.

Brancato, Carolyn Kay. "Patterns of Institutional Investment and Control in the USA." The Victoria Group Incorporated and Riverside Economic Research (Virginia, 1996).

Brancato, Carolyn Kay. "The Pivotal Role of Institutional Investors in Capital Markets: A Summary of Research at the Columbia Institutional Investor Project." Center for Law and Economic Studies, Institutional Investor Project, Columbia University, New York, June 4, 1990.

Drucker, Peter. "The Bored Board." In *Toward the Next Economics, and Other Essays.* New York: Harper & Row, 1981.

Johnson, Teresa L. "The Armand Hammer Museum of Art and Cultural Center: The Vanity of Human Wishes." Unpublished paper, Stanford Law School 1991.

Kirsch, Jonathan L. "Art, Law and Ego." *California Lawyer,* September 1990, 30.

Monks, Robert A. G., and Nell Minow. *Power and Accountability.* New York: HarperBusiness, 1991.

O'Toole, Patricia. "The House that Hammer Built." *Lear's,* October 1991, 21.

Various litigation documents and rulings filed in Sullivan and Brody v. Hammer Civil Action No. 10823.

Public Defender, Public Friend: Searching for the "Best Interests" of Juvenile Offenders

Charles Ogletree

Sammy rubbed his knuckles nervously as he waited for me to begin the interview. He was sixteen years old, but the scars on his face made him look a weathered thirty. I noticed that he scraped at his knuckles as we talked, scraping them sore. Those sore knuckles would turn out to be an important part of his case: Sammy was charged with bludgeoning to death a counselor at TRY House, a group home for juvenile delinquents in the District of Columbia. The police who arrested Sammy had noticed his knuckles too; they had assumed Sammy's hands were bruised from having beaten the counselor to death.

Sammy was a typical juvenile client: young, impressionable, African American, and from a single parent family. Many of my juvenile clients were functionally illiterate; most had difficulty in school and some exposure to drugs. If Sammy were convicted of this homicide, he would almost certainly be set on an irreversible course of criminal behavior and incarceration. Confined at Oak Hill or at Cedar Knoll, Sammy would probably be subjected to verbal, physical, and psychological abuse. He would also learn how to become a first-class, professional adult criminal—places like Oak Hill and Cedar Knoll separate kids from any positive adult role models and surround them with other, often older kids who are happy to teach them the tricks of the criminal trade. Juvenile commitment facilities are one of our nation's most effective job training programs for underprivileged youth—unfortunately, the job is that of career criminal.

Sammy was originally charged in juvenile court with the murder of the counselor (he was later transferred to adult court). The case would be difficult: on the weekend of the murder, only Sammy and three other children had been at TRY House. TRY stood for Teaching Responsibility to Youth. The idea behind the ironic acronym was that TRY House, a shelter home, would be an environment where juvenile delinquents were taught important lessons about life and steered away from crime.

TRY House was only one of the juvenile justice system's many grim euphemisms. Juveniles charged with crimes were not called defendants, but respondents. Moreover, they were prosecuted not in the criminal division but in the family division. They were not charged with a complaint, but with a "petition"; previous arrests or convictions are called "contacts with the court." Judges made the decision to detain juveniles awaiting trial at a "fact-finding hearing," held not in an arraignment court but in a new referrals court. Juveniles detained before trial were held in the "Children's Center," where they were monitored not by guards, but by "counselors." They were reviewed not by court officials, but by social workers. If they were found to have committed a crime, they were not labeled "guilty" but only "involved," and judges imposed penalties at "disposition hearings," not sentencing hearings.[1] One of the real benefits of juvenile court proceedings is that, as their special nomenclature suggests, they are considered noncriminal proceedings. Because juvenile proceedings are confidential, neither the names of the defendants nor any details about the cases can be reported to the public. Although juveniles are charged with the same crimes, such as rape, murder, armed robbery, burglary, and kidnapping, the possible penalties for involvement in a crime are quite different. When a child is first brought before the court, a judge either releases the child to a parent or other responsible adult, places the child in a temporary shelter house (a city-run facility that operates like an adult halfway house), or detains the child at the Children's Center.

If a juvenile has been found involved in an offense, he or she is not automatically sentenced to any period of incarceration. The juvenile court rules require a disposition hearing, a two-step process. First the judge must determine that the juvenile has committed a "delinquent act," that is, a crime punishable by the laws of the District of Columbia.

---

1. As this brief comparison demonstrates, the nomenclature used by the juvenile court reflects a desire not to label, often at very young ages, a child as a "criminal," and it reflects a conscious effort to distinguish his transgressions from those of adult criminals.

If so, the judge must then determine whether the juvenile "is in need of care and rehabilitation." If the court does not find that the juvenile needs care or rehabilitation—regardless of the nature of the offense—the court cannot detain or commit the juvenile. In practice, this two-step process is often muddled. If a judge determines that a juvenile has committed an armed robbery, he or she still may commit the juvenile to a detention facility, despite strong parental support for the juvenile, any mitigating circumstances, or care available in a community setting.

The maximum penalty that a judge can impose on a juvenile for any crime—including rape, murder, or armed robbery—is two years of confinement. Moreover, anyone charged and confined as a juvenile will be released on his or her eighteenth birthday, even if the delinquent act was committed the week before his or her birthday and regardless of the nature of the crime. The only exception to this rule is when a judge determines that a juvenile who has already been incarcerated at the Children's Center has not been rehabilitated. There are then special provisions to hold the child until his or her twenty-first birthday, although these provisions are rarely employed.

While these penalties seem extraordinarily lenient when a juvenile commits serious crimes, they can also be extraordinarily harsh when the offense is relatively minor. For example, a court may sentence a juvenile to two years if the juvenile fails to pay a proper fare while entering a bus, is truant from school, or steals lunch money. Minor acts punishable with a mere fine for an adult can and have resulted in significant periods of incarceration for juveniles.

It is very difficult to describe the juvenile court experience adequately. We were expected to report to the courthouse at 8 A.M. daily to check our case assignments. New Public Defender Service (PDS) lawyers (as opposed to "Fifth Streeters")[2] were routinely assigned to handle the juveniles charged with the most serious offenses.

One of the first issues we faced was whether the prosecutor would try our clients as juveniles or adults. When a defendant is fifteen years old or younger, prosecutors have to petition the court to remove the juvenile from juvenile court so that he may be tried as an adult. This requires an adversarial hearing, in which the burden is on the government to show that there are no services available in juvenile court that

---

2. *Fifth Streeters* refers to the lawyers with offices near the D.C. superior court and who are appointed by the court to handle criminal cases. Clients often complained that some Fifth Streeters did not spend adequate time on their cases.

could aid the juvenile and that the juvenile is beyond rehabilitation in the juvenile court system. Prosecutors rarely use this provision, and courts rarely grant prosecutors' motions to try juveniles younger than sixteen as adults.

However, when a juvenile between sixteen and eighteen is charged with certain felonies, such as rape, murder, armed robbery, or kidnapping, the U.S. attorney can automatically waive the juvenile to adult court and prosecute him as an adult. Neither the defense attorney nor the judge has any discretion to prevent such a waiver, although our public defender office sometimes dissuaded the prosecutor from waiving juveniles in certain cases. For example, when a prosecutor contemplates charging a sixteen-year-old as an adult for an armed robbery, the juvenile defense attorney approaches the U.S. attorney and offers mitigating evidence, such as that the child has no juvenile record or that he played only a modest role in the incident.

In cases involving juvenile and adult codefendants, prosecutors are less likely to try juveniles in adult court, since the U.S. attorney might need the juvenile's testimony to convict the adult codefendant. A juvenile facing only juvenile court charges is likely to be released pending trial and thus be more cooperative with the prosecutor. Juvenile witnesses are especially effective against adult defendants because a juvenile's convictions are not ordinarily available to impeach his testimony. Furthermore, a jury's tendency to believe that the adult codefendant adversely influenced the juvenile leads them to give greater credit to the juvenile defendant's testimony. Armed with the right information in cases involving adult codefendants, a good juvenile defense lawyer should always be able to persuade a prosecutor not to try his or her client in adult court.

In almost every case, the juvenile clients come from single-parent families, usually headed by women. When we met with the mothers to discuss the case, they typically reacted with disbelief at the juvenile's arrest. At the same time, they often felt that the child should be sent to a detention center to punish him for his actions. In such cases, my first responsibility was to persuade the mother to take her child home— often a very delicate operation. I had to describe to parents some of the horrible experiences that a child, particularly an unsophisticated one, would encounter if sent to a juvenile detention facility. Assaults and rapes in juvenile detention are not uncommon. Parents generally accepted custody when they realized that confinement would interfere with or destroy their child's ability to go to school or keep a job. If these arguments failed, I would grit my teeth and push for release anyway, hoping the court would place the child with another relative or guardian. A hostile exchange between parents and lawyers often ensued when the lawyer urged the court to release the child to the custody of another responsible adult. Public defenders in the District of Columbia would often see their role as representing the child's, rather than the parent's, interests. On occasion, judges would take the view that defense lawyers who attempt to have a child placed outside the home because a parent refuses to accept the child are violating the acceptable limit of representation; in this view, judges believe that defense lawyers are morally obliged to defer to the natural parent-child bond. As public defenders appointed to represent the best interests of the child, we would argue that when a parent refuses to accept a child, under circumstances where the child is entitled to and would benefit from release and would likely suffer disastrously if detained, it is beyond question that an advocate should argue for the least restrictive placement for the child. I have taken different positions on the issue at different times.

I believed that the best option for Sammy was placement in a shelter home for his previous offense, because he would have a chance at a normal life later. As judges aptly claim, a shelter home is a halfway house: residents were halfway home if they did well, and halfway to prison if they didn't. TRY House, however, had not been much of a home for Sammy, nor was it a shelter from the streets. The kids in TRY House had a host of problems. They had been placed there rather than in Oak Hill or Cedar Knoll mostly because they had good advocates fighting for them. Effective advocates get their clients admitted to shelter homes, special programs, or perhaps even sent home with restrictions such as curfews or house arrest, sometimes even if they have been found involved in serious offenses.

Sammy was therefore in TRY House with young rapists, burglars, and robbers. Many of the residents were also hyperactive, functionally illiterate, mentally retarded, antisocial, and in some cases, suffering from depression. Residents were as young as thirteen and as old as seventeen. The only common element among them was that they had all been accused of crimes in the District of Columbia and had all ended up in a place that both kept them out of prison and denied them the freedom to go home.

As a public defender at a very good office, I had at my disposal considerable resources to help Sammy. I had an investigator to talk to witnesses, and a secretary to type up motions, letters, notes on my discovery conferences with prosecutors, and other documents that might be useful in his behalf. I also had a budget that allowed me to retain psychologists and psychiatrists to examine clients, and access to experts who could tell me how a gun could be fired properly or whether a semen sample came from a particular suspect. I also had the advantage, unlike so many other public defenders, of formal restrictions on my caseload, which allowed me to give the necessary time to each client whose case was pending. By statute, the District of Columbia Public Defender Service had limited case loads, access to investigators and expert witnesses, and a training program that prepared us for all the nuances that would occur in juvenile court practice.

My role in representing Sammy and others presented complications, however; some were the result of institutional practices, others were self-imposed. While I was his lawyer, not only did I play many roles as his legal representative, but I also served as counselor, spiritual advisor, father, brother, and friend.[3] Sammy called upon me to provide lunch money and rides to court, to convey messages to his mother, to bring his girlfriend to see him at TRY House, to litigate on his behalf, to talk the counselor into letting him go home on a weekend visit, and to be his sounding board when he needed to talk about his frustrations.

Although I chose this multifaceted role in representing Sammy, it posed difficulties for me as a lawyer. I had been taught that to be effective, an advocate must be independent and detached. In fact, the prevailing view was that getting too close to a client would compromise a lawyer and, in the long run, work to the client's detriment. Although these views had been well taught in law school and made plenty of sense there, they were totally irrelevant to my ability to represent Sammy. In law school and in the legal profession, law students and lawyers are taught to be detached from their clients to insure independent judgment on legal issues. My view is that detachment is often not in the clients' best interests and that a closer relationship insures greater protection of the clients' best interests.

The effectiveness of my relationship with Sammy depended on his sense that I was a true friend and that I was committed to his case and to

<hr/>

3. For a more detailed explication of this special relationship with clients, see Charles J. Ogletree, Jr., "Beyond Justifications: Seeking Motivations to Sustain Public Defenders," *Harvard L.Rev.* 106 (1993): 1239.

his interests. I did not want to merely represent juvenile defendants like Sammy, I wanted to represent them well. I also had another agenda: as his lawyer, I wanted more than just the best possible *legal* outcome for him, I also wanted to steer Sammy, who was one of my younger clients, away from a life of crime and toward more positive goals. The young people we dealt with were the troublemakers in school—they were frequently truant, socially active in school, often the center of attention (for good and bad reasons), and needed adult supervision. I felt it was my role, as did other public defenders, to help people like Sammy through difficult times. And I felt a special duty—as an African American male—to be there for these young people who may have no other role model or advisor truly on their side.

I used multiple strategies toward the prosecutors and judges in juvenile court. Prosecutors were typically unsympathetic and overworked. Sometimes I took a highly legalistic position, informing the prosecutor that he or she would have to file every form and meet every deadline in order to really pursue my client. On other days, I was conciliatory, suggesting to the prosecutor that certain formalities— procedures that made life harder for my clients, but also meant more work for the government—could be ignored. It often worked, and I was able to use the incredible flexibility in juvenile court to my advantage.

I was also willing to take contradictory positions on behalf of clients like Sammy. One day I would insist that my client could not go to the Children's Center because it had been condemned by the court years before, and my client should therefore be allowed to go home. On other days, when the choice was between the Children's Center and an adult confinement facility, I would argue that since the Children's Center was still open and some young people were still placed there, my client should be allowed to stay there. My life was filled with contradictions, all designed to try to navigate young men and women safely through the shoals of the juvenile justice system.

Sammy's murder trial started out as an uphill battle. Because he was already in a shelter house when charged with murder, we couldn't keep him from being moved to the Children's Center. Furthermore, he was prosecuted as an adult. The government had no difficulty getting him transferred to adult court, where their strategy promptly backfired. There we argued that he had no adult record, was no risk of flight, and at worst, should be released subject to a money bond. (The option of a money bond was not available in juvenile court.) In adult court, we were also able to delay the trial because of the crowded criminal docket, and our chances of finding witnesses, obtaining discovery, and preparing adequately for trial were greatly increased.

At trial, we would be able to cross-examine the government's witnesses, including residents of TRY House whose own problems would make it easy for us to demolish their credibility. Given the poor relations between the counselors and the residents of TRY House and the dead counselor's reputation as an unpleasant bully, everyone who lived in the house had a motive to commit the murder. Equally important, the records of the counselor's work shifts and the records of who had left the house, and on what type of pass and when, were in such poor condition that it was impossible for the prosecutor to prove who was actually in the house at the relevant times.

My cocounsel and I decided to put Sammy on the stand. He refused to confess to the murder, denied that he committed it, and seemed sympathetic. Sammy looked young and innocent—unlikely to bludgeon anyone to death. We finessed his knuckles by calling several witnesses, including other residents of TRY House, who testified that he often scraped or chewed on his hands.

Sammy was acquitted. I don't think he ever dreamed that he would be convicted. If he did, he kept his fears from us. We, on the other hand, were worried and were relieved when the acquittal was announced. Afterward, he occasionally dropped by the office—he seemed to be getting his life together. Having been tried as an adult had somehow made him feel like one: his maturity after the trial was amazing. We were pleased that Sammy was one of the clients who did not "graduate" to adult court.

I represented many other juveniles like Sammy. Sometimes my commitment to be there as a friend to the young client did not work out as well. The problem was not the demands on my time, although the many late-night calls from juvenile clients crossed the boundary between my work and my private life. But sometimes, being there for a juvenile carried bad as well as good consequences. For example, when I represented Paul Ricks, who was charged with unlawful use of a vehicle, although I helped him as both friend and lawyer, I eventually reached a point at which I had to restrict my role in order to avoid undermining the authority of his mother.

As a friend, I spent time not only trying to help Paul find a job that would keep him from stealing cars, but also working with his mother to show her that using the criminal justice system was not the only way to address his problems. Paul's mother was a single parent and he gave her nothing but trouble. His behavior made it difficult for her to control his six siblings. Paul was the oldest; if he got away with things in the house, she had difficulty keeping the others from doing the same. By taking the time to listen to Paul, I discovered that he was a slow learner; that he had a great deal of discomfort because he didn't know his father, making him often feel embarrassed, unloved, and depressed; and that as a large kid, his size and limited intellectual capacities made him the constant target of jokes, teasing, and humiliation. By convincing Paul that he was an important person and that people cared about him, and by giving him responsibilities that lay within his means, I tried to build his self-esteem and turn him away from crime, toward more socially useful goals.

The difficulty arose, however, when Paul began to draw me into his battles with his mother, trying to use my advice to override or undermine the rules his mother had set for him. I had to modify my relationship with Paul so that he knew that his mother was in charge. Although Paul believed I was trying to help him and listened to my advice, he did not like my dual role—representing him and defending his mother's right to set conditions on his conduct—and let me know of his disapproval. Yet his willingness to complain was a sign that he was listening; in some respects, my message was getting through.

One of the special qualities of the District of Columbia Public Defender Service is its carefully orchestrated, step-by-step approach to attorney training. Although many public defenders around the country are assigned to handle adult criminal cases within a few days of their arrival at the office, PDS is different: almost every attorney must spend a year in juvenile court before handling any adult criminal case. PDS is convinced that recent law students are not properly equipped to handle criminal cases and that the risks to clients are too great to allow them to learn on the job. Most of the case law relevant to adult cases also applies to juvenile proceedings, although there is a special body of juvenile law. Additionally, since all juvenile trials in the District of Columbia are nonjury trials (bench trials), young lawyers will also learn more from the automatic supervision and occasional advice given by the judges.

On my first "pick-up" day in court, where I was appointed to represent clients, I was given four clients, three of whose cases were small matters disposed of without a full initial hearing. The fourth client was K. W., a juvenile charged with burglary. I grappled with this case for most of the time I was working in juvenile court. K. W. had been arrested on a custody order (the juvenile equivalent of an arrest warrant). The complainant told the police that K. W. had entered her home and stolen some items. She was on her way home and happened to see K. W., whom she knew from previous escapades in the neighborhood, leaving her house with some luggage. Several days after the burglary, the police brought her photographs, and she positively identified K. W. as the burglar.

Before the initial hearing, I met with K. W.'s mother, who was very upset. I tried to convince her that it was not so bad, telling her that there was a chance that K. W. could be released to her custody if she were willing. She seemed reluctant and told me that this was not K. W.'s first contact with the court; I wondered how serious a record he had. The social worker and the assistant corporation counsel quickly cleared up my ignorance. K. W. had quite a record of burglaries. In fact he had been committed to the juvenile detention facility on prior occasions. To cap off the bad news, I found out that K. W. was "in abscondence" (had escaped) from the juvenile detention facility.

When K. W.'s case was called, we began the initial hearing. If the court intends to detain the respondent, a probable cause hearing, at which the prosecution must demonstrate that there is probable cause to believe that the respondent committed the offense, must be held. Judges are often undecided about whether or not to release the child at the beginning of the initial hearing. The judge in this case wanted to have a probable cause hearing before deciding what should be done with K. W. until his fact-finding hearing date. I argued against having a probable cause hearing, on the grounds that K. W.'s mother was in court and prepared to take him home, that she had made arrangements for him to return to school where he had dropped out, and that he absconded from the Children's Center because he learned that one of his siblings was ill and wanted to be helpful in her time of need. Although such displays of empathy toward family members and other important figures in their lives are common among our clients, this rarely had any impact on judges or prosecutors. If judges, prosecutors, and police better understood the affection our clients hold for their loved ones, I think they would be less quick to see punishment as the only response to crime.

I thought my arguments on behalf of K. W. had been eloquent, forceful, and persuasive. The prosecutor, the social services representative, and the judge were not impressed, however. In fact, the prosecutor deemed my argument "ridiculous," in light of the fact that my client had many contacts with the court, had escaped from a juvenile detention facility, and was charged with a serious felony. Although I felt resentful, I was beginning to understand the nature of the adversary system. The social services worker also questioned the accuracy of my report about K. W.'s home setting and his mother's willingness to take him home. The discrepancy in our impressions was the difference in when we had talked to K. W.'s mother. As is normal social services practice, the social worker had called her at 7 A.M., before an attorney had been assigned to the case.

K. W.'s mother had told *me* that she was willing to allow him to return home if he was released in court, but she had told the social services worker that K. W. had not been staying at home since his abscondence and that he had spent his nights on the street. Under the auspices of helping the family, social workers' reports can often convince judges to lock up a child. It was clear in this case that K. W.'s mother had changed her mind because I had adamantly insisted that K. W. would be much better off at home than at the children's center.

Parents like K. W.'s mother are victims of conflicting pressures from various components of the criminal justice system. We all thought that we were doing what was best for K. W. in urging his mother to follow our advice. The social services worker clearly believed that K. W. would be a problem for his mother, would not stay at home, and would not return to school. His recommendation was based on his view that K. W. would be better off in a secure facility in which he would theoretically be able to attend school and get the supervision that he needed. I, on the other hand, believed that K. W. would not receive any effective education, vocational training, or therapy in confinement. I thought he would benefit more from the nurturing and affection from his mother than from the hostility and indifference of the counselors in the Children's Center. We put his mother in an untenable position, telling her what was best for her.

After hearing this disagreement about what to do with K. W., the judge decided to hold the probable cause hearing. The officer who took K. W. into custody was the prosecutor's only witness. The officer provided a very skeletal sketch of the burglary. I cross-examined the officer for what seemed like an eternity but actually was 15 minutes. I was abusive, arrogant, and disorganized. I made some points, but they were of little significance to the probable cause hearing. I was able to browbeat the officer into conceding that he was not present at the burglary, so he did not know who did it. Although an interesting concession, it was of no consequence as to whether the eyewitness had observed the burglary. I was also able to force the officer to admit that he was not present when the complainant identified my client's photograph. That point was also of no importance, however, since he received the information from an officer who was present. I pressed the officer about the victim's opportunity to observe my client—the distance between the eyewitness and my client, any obstructions to her view, the length of time and the time of day. The officer patiently answered all my questions, giving me some information that might be of use later in the case, but every time I asked a question, the prosecutor objected, claiming that the hearing was not the proper forum in which to conduct my "discovery" of their case. He was right, and the judge sustained many objections.

I asked if my client had made any statements to the police, and the prosecutor again objected. The court admonished me that the existence of any statements was irrelevant, since the government was not relying on the statements in order to establish probable cause for the burglary. I tried to question the officer about whether any of the items had been recovered when my client was arrested. The prosecutor objected, and, again, the court admonished me that this information was irrelevant. The court went further, to tell me that it would be foolhardy to expect my client to have stolen items in his possession several weeks after the burglary had been committed.

After the officer completed his testimony, I forcefully argued that probable cause had not been established and urged the court to release the client. The court listened patiently and firmly denied my request. K. W. was to be committed.

The battle was not over, however, since the court still had the choice of detaining my client either in minimum security at Cedar Knoll or in maximum security at Oak Hill. I argued that although K. W. was tall for fifteen years old, he was slightly built and could be a victim of abuse or assaults at Oak Hill. The corporation counsel scoffed, noting that my client was nearly six feet tall and probably as big, if not as heavy, as any juvenile detained at Oak Hill. The prosecutor also observed that my client had been placed at Cedar Knoll and had escaped from that facility.

I shifted to a constitutional argument, arguing both that it would be cruel and unusual punishment to place K. W. at Oak Hill because he might be abused there and because conditions at Oak Hill were inadequate under the constitution. We had been trained to make these constitutional arguments whenever they were appropriate, with the hope of protecting our clients' immediate interests, but also (and more realistically) to build a record for a future lawsuit that might force D.C. to change these conditions. The judge referred to these points as "PDS arguments," meaning that he heard them in every case we handled and did not feel obliged to take them seriously here.

After finding my constitutional arguments unpersuasive, the judge repeated K. W.'s record of prior contacts with the court, his history of abscondences from Cedar Knoll, and his failure to attend school or cooperate with his mother. The judge even said K. W. would benefit from a secure detention facility. K. W. was going to Oak Hill.

I was devastated. My first case and my client was being detained. How could I be considered a sentinel of liberty when I had just failed in my maiden effort to prevent a juvenile from being detained? I was convinced that I would never be a successful public defender and that I had entered the wrong line of work. Compared to my earlier mock hearings, the real judges seemed tougher, the prosecutors more relentless, and the social services workers dispassionate. Furthermore, my client seemed totally unimpressed; I just knew he believed a proper lawyer would have gotten him released.

I met with my supervisors who had observed the hearing, hoping for reassurance. Although they did offer some encouraging words, they also gave me some realistic critiques. First, they told me that I did not appear to listen closely to the detective's answers. In my zeal to control his testimony, I missed several opportunities to explore areas that could have been useful in preparation for the trial. Additionally, they thought that I did not have a response to social services' arguments. I should have called his mother as a witness in order to show her willingness to accept K. W.

I left juvenile court that day without my client, contemplating updating my resume and reconsidering my decision not to join a corporate law firm. My classmates were more supportive. They commiserated with me. We had been encouraged to think that if we made an eloquent and forceful argument, citing the proper statutes and case law, we would prevail in any case. Now we wondered if our trainers and supervisors had been overly optimistic or had misled us about the realities of juvenile court.

I might have lost the battle with K. W., but I was *not* going to lose the war. I went back to my office and dictated a memo to my client case file about the probable cause hearing and the affidavit supporting the custody order. I was going to prove that K. W. had not committed this burglary. We visited the neighborhood where the burglary occurred. We met the complainant on our first visit; only later did I discover how unusual it was for an investigative interview to take place on schedule.

The complainant was an attractive black woman who politely invited us in to discuss the case. As was the custom, I asked the questions, and my investigator wrote a statement for her to sign. She gave a very thorough account of the burglary, including the items that had been stolen and never recovered, and the suspect she described bore a remarkable resemblance to K. W., including his slight build and his prominent "elephant ears."

When I asked how she was able to identify these features from such a distance, she corrected me: she had been much closer than I had been led to believe. The detective's vague description of the distance was misleading: she had been only a few feet away from the culprit when she saw him leaving her apartment. It had been in the middle of the day with bright lighting and no obstructions to her vision. Moreover, she knew my client because she had seen him in the neighborhood.

What surprised me most was that she was able to describe articles of clothing that the burglar was wearing—and her description matched the clothing that K. W. had on when he was arrested. Apparently the police officers did not notice this, since they did not try to seize his clothes when he was arrested. The complainant gave me some room for hope, however, because she described the burglar as three or four inches shorter and as slightly darker-complected than K. W., a factor I felt would be crucial at trial. Although she was absolutely confident of her identification, I thought I had some useful lines of cross-examination.

After we interviewed the complainant, we took photographs of the area and walked around the neighborhood to see if we could find any other witnesses. When we returned to the area near the complainant's apartment, she began asking me questions about the trial: Did I have a subpoena for her or would I be getting one to her? Did I think the case would go to trial? When was the trial date? I told her again, as I had at the beginning of the interview, that I was not representing her, but K. W., the person charged with the crime. She said that no one had been in touch with her about the case, and she didn't really seem to know the difference between defense attorneys and prosecutors. When my investigator was taking a statement from her, she assumed he was associated with the prosecution, since all of the statements she made clearly identified K. W. as the burglar. Although I was clearly aware of the trial date and time, I chose not to give her any other information about the trial. One of the things we learned in training was the importance of separating the obligations we have as public defenders and the obligations of general public servants. It was not my responsibility to inform the witness of the trial date. I had heard that the corporation counsel was sloppy in preparing cases for trial and that witnesses often were not contacted until the night before trial. Green though I was, I knew that K. W.'s best prospect of success at trial was for the complainant not to appear. I left confident that we had a chance of success if she showed up, and a good chance of dismissal if she didn't.

Next I had to "get discovery" from the prosecutor. I received information about K. W.'s prior criminal record and some information about his arrests. I then learned that K. W. had made a statement at the time of his arrest, but the prosecutor claimed not to have a copy. I insisted that he give it to me as soon as possible. The prosecutor said that I would have it before trial, but that it did not really pertain to this case. As I pressed further, he became vague and evasive, saying only that it would be presented before trial.

I visited the prosecutor on two additional occasions, requesting the statement and other information to which I was entitled under discovery rules. The prosecutor turned over everything but my client's statement. The prosecutor made a vague excuse about the detective being unavailable at the time and said that I would receive it by the day of the trial. I told the prosecutor that I would move for dismissal if the statement was not turned over promptly; he seemed unmoved.

Finally, the day of trial arrived. On the first call of the calendar of case list for that trial day, I announced we were ready for trial. K. W. was ready to go forward, my investigator was prepared to impeach the complainant on some minor discrepancies, and I thought we had a decent misidentification defense. The prosecutors said they were not ready. When the case came up again (the second call), the prosecutor again said that he was not ready. I moved for dismissal, and the court denied it, on the prosecutor's representation that he would have further information on third call. Finally, on the third call, the prosecutors admitted that they were unable to find the complainant and moved to dismiss the charges against K. W.

I was elated. I had won my first juvenile case. As I was preparing to leave the courtroom with K. W., the prosecutor told me that they were bringing new charges against K. W. Apparently at the time of his arrest for this burglary, K. W. had confessed to 66 other burglaries, taken the detective to the locations, and pointed out each burglary. I was devastated by the new charges. My success was a Pyrrhic victory. Even more distressing, both the prosecutor and the judge seemed to smirk as my expression changed from elation to disappointment.

I was disappointed in myself, disappointed in the process, and disappointed in K. W. We had discussed his case on several occasions, and he never acknowledged making the statement to the police. In fact, he insisted that he had made no such statement and that my assertions to the contrary were ridiculous. Not only had K. W. lied about making a statement, he completely ignored the fact that he had confessed to 66 different burglaries.

After my miserable experience at K. W.'s bail hearing, I had felt that matters could not get any worse. But after getting a dismissal along with 66 new charges I did indeed feel worse. Alone in the PDS class of 1978, I had been appointed to represent a 15-year-old, one-person crime wave. It was an honor I would gladly have declined, but that option was not available. For the second time in my young career as a public defender, I was convinced that I was not cut out for this kind of work.

A long and emotional conversation with Harry Flint, my training director, saved me from utter despair. Harry was very philosophical about the incident, saying that I should be pleased with the dismissal, since an acquittal would have been hard to win. He also told me that I should not assume that K. W.'s fate had been determined, since there might be grounds to suppress the statement. I was so overwhelmed by the 66 new charges against K. W. that it had never occurred to me that a motion to suppress the confession could result in up to 66 dismissals. Harry told me to think about the particulars of the confession. First of all, K. W. had been detained for a long time before he had signed it. The detective, in an effort to clear up all the burglaries in the area, had included some burglaries that K. W. could not have committed because he was confined at those times. Harry also told me I should think about whether the statement reflected the 15-year-old K. W.'s vocabulary or sounded more like something written by a police officer.

These suggestions intrigued me and convinced me there was some life after my first failure in court. I left Harry's office with a renewed sense of hope and began investigating the case. And I learned another important lesson: never accept at face value any inculpatory evidence offered by the government.

Harry's advice was accurate and powerful—each of his three suggestions turned out to be fruitful. Although I was not convinced that a motion to suppress would be granted, I finally discussed the statement with K. W., trying to find out whether he had been adequately advised of his rights. He admitted that he could not read well enough to have read the form himself. The inquiry at the hearing on the motion to suppress would be whether K. W. had understood his rights, and if so, whether the statement was voluntary.

During the investigation, I had determined that some of the burglaries could not have been committed by K. W. because he was detained. Moreover, the prosecutor had difficulty finding the police reports for 66 burglaries, another ground for dismissal. The prosecutor seemed unfazed, however; he would be happy, he told me, to go forward on just 30 or 40 counts of burglary.

Just as Harry had told me, some of the language in the "confession" sounded nothing like K. W.'s speech and a lot like law enforcement argot. When K. W.'s statement had him saying that he "proceeded" to a certain area or "responded" to a certain action, it was clear to me that those words had been the detective's. After investigation, I was convinced that we could dismiss a significant number of the burglary charges but also was aware of the fact that many of them were valid and would stick.

At this point, my focus changed from a trial in a clearly hopeless case to trying to arrange an appropriate disposition for K. W. After some negotiation with the prosecutor, we agreed that K. W. would plead guilty to some of the burglary charges, and the vast majority would be dismissed.

Based on K. W.'s psychological tests and other evaluations, he was clearly learning-disabled and would benefit from a structured program.

Before the disposition hearing, I reviewed the literature and visited facilities for juveniles with learning disabilities. K. W. had fallen so far behind in the public school system that it was not likely he would be able to return, nor would it be in his best interest to put him in an environment where he would surely fail again. At the disposition hearing, I persuaded the judge to place K. W. in a special residential program in the district, which included counseling and vocational training. Although K. W. wanted to go home rather than into the program, the residential program was clearly preferable to Oak Hill. What had seemed like a hopeless case turned out quite well for K. W.

It was also an important learning experience for me. First and foremost, the primary role of a lawyer in juvenile court is that of a social worker. There are important motions to litigate and legal arguments to make, but the critical focus is the disposition of the case and placement of your client. As much time must be spent on coming up with dispositional alternatives and appropriate placements as on litigating motions, investigating factual issues, and preparing a defense.

In my efforts to dissuade my juvenile clients from further delinquency, I failed more often than I succeeded. Some of the young delinquents apparently took my advice to heart. Others, unfortunately, graduated to adult court where I would in time see them again.

After nearly nine months in juvenile court, I moved on to adult court. Although I eagerly anticipated my upcoming appearances before some of the most notorious judges in superior court and the opportunity to handle some jury trials, my time in juvenile court had been a wonderful experience. I would not have many future opportunities to represent youthful offenders who were more likely to follow my advice about life after the case was over. At the point when it seemed that I knew all there was to know about juvenile court, it was time to leave. Yet whatever my regrets about shifting to adult clients, I should not have worried about missing contact with my juvenile clients. It was not long before many of my former juvenile clients appeared in adult court and sought me out for legal representation. Was my approach to client-centered advocacy a failure? Did my juvenile clients simply learn to become more sophisticated adult criminals? Was my effort at a multifaceted role counterproductive? I have no ultimate answers to these questions. I only know that exploring them is a necessary part of the job for those who are committed to the juveniles in the juvenile justice system.

On Representing a Victim of Crime

Abbe Smith

Rebecca Wight and Claudia Brenner fell in love in graduate school. In May 1988, when Rebecca was still in school in Virginia and Claudia was living and working in upstate New York, they decided to meet for a weekend of hiking and camping. They picked a halfway spot, on the Appalachian Trail in the Michaux State Forest, in central Pennsylvania. They both loved the outdoors and were avid hikers.

They met at a prearranged outpost, parked their cars, donned their packs, and set off. They spent the day hiking, at times arm in arm, ambling leisurely, and at times covering serious ground. The weather was unusually warm for that time of year. The trail was serene and untrammelled; it was still early in the season.

They shared a sleeping bag and spent the first night tucked close together. The air outside the tent was clean and crisp and cool. The only sound was the night.

The next morning, after breakfast, Rebecca headed for the outhouse, which was next to a lean-to. She was naked, believing no one else was near. She and Claudia had encountered no other hikers there. She was startled to find a man, ragged and haggard, standing in the lean-to. "D'ya have any cigarettes on you?" he asked. "No," Rebecca replied, annoyed by both his presence and his question. She was naked. Of course she had no cigarettes "on" her.

She swiftly headed back to the tent to tell Claudia that there was a strange man lurking around, and they'd better pack up and go. They collected their things and departed, passing the man on their way out.

They walked for about a mile before stopping at a crossroads to consult the map and consider their options. As they studied the map, the strange man appeared again. This time he had a rifle across his shoulders, his arms slung over each end. He mocked the women with his posture and his words. "What, are you lost already?" he sneered.

"No, we're not lost," Claudia replied, intending to end the conversation. "Are *you?*" She and Rebecca went back to their map, ignoring the man. They picked a route that would take them far off the main trail, to regain their seclusion. They wanted to be left alone.

They hiked three and a half circuitous miles into the wild, far off the well-traveled paths, far from other human contact. They found an ideal spot to set up camp, near a stream. They made camp and a cold jug of iced tea, which they drank as they lounged by the stream. Believing they were completely alone, they made love.

They were resting near the stream when the shots came. Claudia thought the earth was exploding. She felt herself hit first in the arm, and then, as she looked up in wonder, in the neck, in the other side of her neck, in the face, in the head.[1] She was hit again and again and again, five bullets in steady succession. Blood was everywhere. Someone's terrified scream accompanied the sound of the shots. Only when Rebecca grabbed ahold of her did Claudia realize it was her own.

Rebecca said, "It's him, he's back, we have to run for cover." As they rose to flee the attack, Rebecca was hit twice, in the head and in the back. She made it to a patch of trees before crumpling to the ground.

It was late afternoon when they were sure the shooting had stopped. Claudia and Rebecca knew they had to get out of there, they had to get help. Rebecca directed Claudia to get a towel from the tent to tie around her neck like a tourniquet in order to stop the bleeding.

Rebecca could not have known that she was slowly bleeding to death from a bullet lodged in her liver. As she prepared to flee with Claudia, she realized she could not put her shoes on. She couldn't see her shoes. She couldn't stand. Claudia put Rebecca's shoes on her. She pulled Rebecca's arm around her shoulder to help support her weight, but Rebecca's legs gave way. Rebecca was wheezing, gasping for air. She was losing vision, losing speech, losing consciousness. "It hurts," she said to Claudia, who cradled her in her arms. "Oh God, it hurts."

---

1. See generally Claudia Brenner, *Eight Bullets: One Woman's Story of Surviving Anti-Gay Violence* (Firebrand Books, 1995). *See also* Claudia Brenner, "Survivor's Story: Eight Bullets," in Gregory M. Herek and Kevin T. Berrill, *Hate Crimes: Confronting Violence Against Lesbians and Gay Men* (Newbury Park: Sage Publications, 1992), 11.

Claudia had to pull herself together. She knew that she had to leave Rebecca, now unconscious, and go for help. She put on a sweatshirt and sweatpants and covered Rebecca with warm things. The approaching dusk would soon become darkness. Clutching the homemade tourniquet tightly, armed with only a flashlight and a map, Claudia made her way out of the woods. She traveled nearly four miles alone, in the dark, in pain, in terror. Might her assailant be stalking her still? She didn't know.[2]

Somehow, she reached the road. She tried to flag down a car. She looked frightened and frightening: her clothes were rumpled and bloodstained; her face was streaked with tears and dirt and blood. One car passed her by. She was determined to stop the next one. Finally, two teenaged boys stopped and carried her to the nearest town. She was then flown by helicopter to the Hershey Medical Center, where she had emergency surgery.

It was late when the telephone rang in my Brooklyn apartment. The only time a late-night phone call is anything other than bad news is when I'm in the midst of some sort of courtship ritual. On this night, there was no sign of romance. I shoved the student exams I was grading out of the way and picked up the receiver.

The caller asked for me by name and said someone who knew me through the National Lawyers Guild suggested she contact me. She was looking for a feminist criminal lawyer who had practiced law in Pennsylvania. A close friend was in serious trouble in central Pennsylvania, near Hershey.

I was nearly finished with my first year of law teaching. Though teaching had come naturally—I liked the performance part, I liked the students, I liked the time to think—in many ways I considered myself a public defender in academic clothing. I had been a defender for five years before I took a teaching job. I took the job because it was an interesting opportunity, not because I was a burned-out defender. I loved my work and brought that enthusiasm to my teaching. My first scholarly article was on public defenders. That summer, I was going to handle a few cases for the public defender office in Philadelphia, my alma mater, and teach an evening criminal law class at a local law school.

---

2. See Brenner, "Survivor's Story: Eight Bullets," supra note 1, at 14.

Now, I get a fair number of calls from people in criminal trouble. The calls are usually terribly urgent and not terribly serious: someone's brother arrested for drunk driving; someone's son charged with assaulting a guy outside a bar; someone's daughter locked up on a drug charge. Though I am firmly on the defense side of criminal law practice, every now and then I get calls on behalf of victims of crime: someone's friend needs a restraining order to get an abusive husband or boyfriend out of the house; someone's sister was raped; someone's child shows signs of sexual assault.

This call was about a victim and was both urgent and serious. There had been a shooting on the Appalachian Trail. One woman was dead and another was in critical condition in a trauma unit in central Pennsylvania, about to be questioned by a team of Pennsylvania state police officers. The women were lovers; the surviving woman was a lesbian. The police were certain to ask questions about the women's sexual identity and what they were doing before the attack. What should the surviving woman do? Should she answer the police officers' questions forthrightly? Should she leave certain things out? Should she not answer at all until she could speak to a lawyer?

I had this instinctive response from my years as a public defender: "Say nothing to the police. Tell them you're asserting your rights under *Miranda*. Tell them I'm your lawyer." There is a plainer version: "Keep your mouth shut. Wuddaya think, you're gonna talk your way outa them charging you? Jeez, and you wonder why you're always getting locked up."

But this call was not about someone being accused of committing a crime. This was a *victim*. This was someone who had been hurt. This was someone who had almost been killed. Her lover had been killed. What was she worried about? What was I worried about? Was my instinct to advise silence really about my old familiar role or was it about what it means to be a lesbian, victim or not, in central Pennsylvania, in the criminal justice system, in the world? The worry was personal.

The good lawyer in me, kind of a superego, kicked in. It was not my role to play criminal defense lawyer here, though it was my role to use the experience I had as a criminal defense lawyer to give sound advice. It was not my role to play feminist critical legal scholar here, though it was my role to use those insights to give sound advice.

The advice I gave was to tell the truth to the police, to tell it all. I told her this because when witnesses lie or distort or omit, those lies, distortions, and omissions inevitably hurt them later. Good trial lawyers live for the smallest inconsistencies in police statements, defense investigative statements, pretrial testimony, and trial testimony in order to argue that the witness should not be believed. If a witness doesn't tell all, the lawyer for the other side will say she's not telling still.

The caller thanked me for the advice, and said she was looking for one more thing. She wanted to obtain a lawyer for her friend, someone who would look out for her friend's interests, not just those of the prosecution. The lawyer would be retained by the surviving victim with money raised by her friends and by the feminist and alternative communities in Ithaca, New York, where she lived. She asked me whether I was interested.

I said probably not, because, first, I wasn't sure that hiring a lawyer was such a good idea for the surviving victim, and second, if they decided to hire a lawyer, I wasn't sure it ought to be me. Lawyers representing victims in criminal court were a relatively new phenomenon.[3] Jennifer Levin's family had one—Jennifer Levin was the young woman who was killed in Central Park by Robert Chambers, the "Preppie Murderer," who eventually pleaded guilty to manslaughter—but all that lawyer seemed to do was hold the family's hand and appear at press conferences.[4]

On the other hand, I had to admit that, if ever there were a case that called out for independent counsel for a victim, this was it. Who knew what the prosecutor might be like? Who knew what political pressure might influence the handling of the case in central Pennsylvania, hardly a bedrock of social liberalism? Who knew what evidentiary issues might arise? Who knew what the jury pool was like, and what strategies might be devised by the defense to play upon a jury's homophobia and misogyny?

---

3. See, generally, Ellen Yaroshefsky, "Balancing Victim's Rights and Vigorous Advocacy for the Defendant," *Annual Survey of American Law,* 1989, 135.

4. See, for example, Vivian Berger, "It's the State, Not the Family, vs. Chambers," *Newsday,* March 9, 1988, 62. It is interesting to note that the recent spate of highly publicized cases where criminal complainants hired their own lawyers almost always involved women and sex. After Jennifer Levin, there was Patricia Bowman, who accused William Kennedy Smith of raping her in Palm Beach in 1991, and Desiree Washington, who accused Mike Tyson of raping her in Indianapolis the same year. Both had private lawyers representing them throughout the course of the criminal proceedings.

Still, as a criminal defense lawyer, the idea of private counsel for criminal complainants was vexing. The cards are already stacked against most criminal defendants. The last thing they need is more lawyers on the other side. Victims are witnesses for the prosecution, that's all. They are not a party in the case. These private lawyers just hover in the courtroom, constantly underfoot and in the way. They aren't a part of the record; they don't officially "appear" as counsel in the case. They're just looking for a civil case to grow out of the criminal litigation. They're looking for publicity. They're looking for money.

But if the surviving victim had made up her mind to hire someone, I understood why. So then the question was whom to hire. My view was that it would be best to hire someone local, someone who had practiced criminal law in central Pennsylvania, someone who knew the players in the court where the case would be tried. Criminal law is very parochial. Knowledge of local practice is often more important than knowledge of law.

I said I'd make some phone calls and see what names I came up with. I'd be in touch. I hoped for a speedy recovery for her friend in Hershey.

Despite some diligent phone calling, I came up with few names. Apparently, there were very few feminist lawyers who practiced criminal law in central Pennsylvania. One prospective lawyer burst into tears upon seeing the surviving victim in her hospital room. This behavior was not helpful. It did not engender confidence.

The original caller called back. What about you, she said. It's you we want. I said okay, let's arrange for a meeting and we'll see what your friend says. If she wants me to be her lawyer, I'll do it. I was going to be in Philadelphia that summer, teaching. The case was certainly interesting. Homicides are always interesting.

In the time since the original call, the Pennsylvania police had apprehended Stephen Roy Carr and charged him with murder in the first degree of Rebecca Wight and attempted murder for the shooting of Claudia Brenner. The prosecution was seeking the death penalty.

When I met Claudia Brenner in June 1988, she reminded me of me. She was around my age, Jewish, Ivy League educated, energetic. We both talked a lot. We wore the same Patagonia jacket.

I didn't cry when I saw her, or even when I heard her story. I listened. I asked questions. I wanted to know everything there was to know. I was there as a lawyer; that's the only reason I was there. I came with a legal pad, a pen, an appointments book. I told her about my background and what I envisioned my role to be in the case, painting both the worst-case scenario and the best. I could be a glorified hand-holder, part tour guide, part soothsayer. I could play an active, consultative role in the prosecution.

But I was moved by Claudia, moved by the horror of her experience, moved by her courage. As a public defender, I had heard a lot of stories, a lot of terrible stories. I had questioned people who had both committed and endured acts of violence that are unimaginable to most of us. I'm also something of a criminal law junkie: I seek out crime stories in the news, in movies, on television. I figured I had pretty much heard it all.

But I hadn't. I hadn't heard this. I hadn't heard about two people innocently hiking in the woods, two people who loved each other, gunned down for no reason at all. I hadn't heard about two people hanging out by a stream in the aftermath of lovemaking, who suddenly found themselves in a war zone. I hadn't sat before a woman who told me how she held her lover in her arms as she slowly and painfully bled to death.

Claudia and I got along well. We established the parameters of the lawyer-client relationship and we agreed upon a fee, something I'd never done before. Part of me felt like an imposter: What's a poverty lawyer doing charging money for legal services? Part of me felt guilty: What's a feminist lawyer doing charging money in a case like this, after all Claudia has been through? The guilty part was noisy: I can't believe you're charging poor Claudia; the honor of being asked to participate in such an important case should be compensation enough. But I also knew that the case would require an enormous amount of time and energy, and that I make my living by being a lawyer. So we settled on an amount that seemed fair to both of us.

I still wasn't sure how I felt about representing a victim, though I felt pretty good about representing Claudia. This dynamic felt familiar. I'm often more comfortable with the concrete than the abstract. I may not feel good about representing "rapists," but I almost never feel bad about representing individual clients charged with rape. I like my criminal clients, though I don't like crime. I like the sandwich, but I don't like the ecological agony that produced the ingredients.

I was a lifelong criminal defense lawyer, and more, a public defender. I defended everyone, no matter who they were, no matter what they'd done. So long as they couldn't afford a lawyer, they had me. I became a public defender because I believed in taking sides. I believed that, especially in the criminal justice system, there were clear sides. I believed it was critically important for skilled lawyers to defend poor criminal defendants against the power of the state.

I became a public defender for all of the reasons that have ever been offered by anyone else,[5] and for some of my own.[6] Being a public defender suited me. It combined irreverence and commitment, cynicism and idealism, the lure of the good fight and the sweetness of victory. Becoming a prosecutor never occurred to me. Between my politics, which started out liberal and moved steadily left through college and law school, and my personality, which aimed to please for most of my childhood and became increasingly smart-alecky as time went on, I just wasn't the type. I could speak on behalf of people but not on behalf of The People.

I had to figure out what bothered me most about being on the other side. Was it that my role was new and different and uncertain? Was it that I felt like a traitor to the criminal defense cause? Was it that I worried I would feel for the defendant, notwithstanding the crime, and feel that my place was with him?

I had to acknowledge ego. No matter what I did here—no matter how many strategies I devised, arguments I authored, witness examinations I crafted—I would be no more than a supporting player. Someone else was going to try the case. And I'm not a natural silent partner. No doubt, that's one of the reasons I decided to become a trial lawyer instead of something quieter. I worried that representing the victim was

---

5. See Barbara Babcock, "Defending the Guilty," *Cleveland State Law Review* 32 (1983–84): 177–79 (citing the "garbage collector's reason," the "legalistic or positivist's reason," the "political activist's reason," the "social worker's reason," the "egotist's reason"). Also see Seymour Wishman, "A Criminal Lawyer's Inner Damage," *Minneapolis Tribune* (July 23, 1977): 6A ("everyone is entitled to the best defense, . . . ego gratification, the joys of good craftsmanship, the need to make a living, the desire to minimize the length of inhumane treatment of those convicted, and, after all, some of my clients may be innocent").

6. See Abbe Smith, "Rosie O'Neill Goes to Law School: The Clinical Education of a Sensitive, New Age Public Defender," *Harvard Civil Rights-Civil Liberties Law Review* 28 (1993): 1 ("I like my clients, I like the work, something funny happens everyday, something poignant happens everyday, and I saw *To Kill a Mockingbird* too many times as an impressionable child. As far as I'm concerned, there are no two more joyful words in the English language than the words 'not guilty'").

too removed a role for me. I worried that, while some of my insights might find expression in the way the case was tried, my instincts would not. Good trial lawyering involves both preparation and instinct, reading and reacting to the moment. This is nearly impossible from the sidelines.

Still, the newness was challenging. The client was appealing. The case was important. I thought I could help.

Stephen Roy Carr was nobody from nowhere. Though he was 28 years old at the time of the shooting, he looked both younger and older, like discarded people do. Some people who kill look evil. There is a meanness in them.[7] Other people look like sick puppies. They've been hit too many times "upside the head" to think straight anymore. Something just snaps in them. Carr was in the second group. He had been sexually and physically abused as a child. He had been on his own since he was a teenager; he was kicked out of the house or ran away. He had lived here and there.

The crime just didn't figure. Carr didn't have much of a record, and no prior violent crimes to speak of. He had spent some time in a Florida prison for grand larceny; he had stolen. He was a loner who had taken to living in the woods near the Michaux State Forest in Adams County, Pennsylvania, where the shooting occurred. He stayed on and off with old family friends, mostly going there to shower. He was closest to a teenage boy in the household, someone considerably younger than he. But he wasn't much of a talker.

After the shooting, Carr broke his rifle down, put it in a plastic garbage bag, and buried it in the ground. He also buried a knit cap he was wearing. Then he fled.

He managed to elude capture for nearly two weeks. He briefly visited the home of a family he sometimes stayed with. He told a friend that he had done a bad thing and that his rifle had been stolen. He then departed the area. He found cover and work on a farm owned by a Mennonite family; they gave him a pair of boots, and he was working to repay them. But he was apprehended because a Mennonite woman saw a composite drawing of Carr in the local newspaper, a composite Claudia had helped to construct. She called the police and told them

7. See, generally, Norman Mailer, *The Executioner's Song* (Boston: Little, Brown, 1979). See also Bruce Springsteen, "Nebraska," on *Nebraska* (Columbia Records, 1980).

that she believed the man they were seeking had attended her church the past Sunday.

The arrest was dramatic. Troops of armed police officers in both uniform and camouflage descended upon Carr in a barn where he was working. During his transportation to the Carlisle State Police Barracks, he talked. He talked about meeting two women on the Appalachian Trail. He said he had shot them accidentally. He thought they were deer. Then, he talked about how he didn't like the Mennonites very much. He didn't like it that the men kissed the men and the women kissed the women. Then he said he saw the two women kiss. He said he saw them have oral sex. He said if he told the truth about what happened he would be put away for a long time. Carr took the police to the dead stump under which he had hidden the murder weapon.

Claudia had a lot of support. When she was hospitalized, there was always a crowd of friends in her room, hanging out in the hall, having coffee in the cafeteria. Her parents came and went; her mother was loving and concerned, but her father couldn't seem to deal with who his daughter was or what had happened to her. Her previous lover, Anne, was now best friend and family.

Several people accompanied her on every trip to Gettysburg, the county seat of Adams County and the site of the trial. The first trip was to meet the prosecutor, attend a lineup, discuss Claudia's (and my) role in decision making, talk about scheduling, and talk about initial strategy.

The prosecutor, Roy Keefer, was a nice guy, open and nonterritorial. He was *the* prosecutor for the county; the only other prosecutor on staff was a part-time assistant. He took the case very seriously; this was a big case in a caseload that contained mostly small property crimes, domestic "disputes," and drunken brawls. He was remarkably unthreatened by either the case or the cast of characters. He was happy to have me participate actively in the case and to confer extensively with him; he figured two heads were better than one. This is unusual for trial lawyers, who tend to be very independent and protective of their turf. Though he didn't seem terribly worldly, he did not seem homophobic. He was a good, decent person.

We met the defense lawyer at the police station where the lineup was to be held. I had been the defense lawyer at so many lineups, it felt strange to be in this new role. I introduced myself. I wanted to say, hey,

I'm usually in your shoes. Hey, I know how it feels to be the one defense lawyer in a place filled with cops and DA's. He was awkward and kind. He told Claudia he was sorry about what had happened to her. There wasn't much more to say.

Actually, two lineups were held: a corporeal lineup, where the witness views a line of people who generally match the description of the perpetrator; and a voice lineup, where the witness listens to several out-of-view people uttering certain words. The question is whether the witness can identify the perpetrator of the crime either visually or auditorily. Claudia identified Stephen Roy Carr immediately upon seeing him in the line. The words the voice lineup participants said were "Are you lost already?" I doubt I could identify the voice of someone who spoke to me every day, if that person were concealed from me and uttered only those few words. Claudia picked out Carr with no hesitation.

By now, the group of police officers who had been involved in the investigation of the case and the apprehension of Carr were founding members of the Claudia Brenner Fan Club. She was something of a local hero. Not only had she taken five bullets in her face and body and survived, not only had she hiked several miles out of the woods in the dark in that broken and bloody condition, not only had she been able to describe Carr with enough specificity to yield a composite drawing that led to his apprehension, but she had confidently and quickly identified her assailant by both his face and his voice. She was also strong, articulate, and charming. No one seemed terribly bothered by her relationship with Rebecca. No one seemed to care that she was a lesbian.

The preliminary hearing was next, coupled with a hearing on a number of pretrial matters. These included a motion to suppress the defendant's statements and the murder weapon on the grounds that they were the product of improper police questioning. There was also a lengthy discovery motion that requested, among other things, evidence of Claudia and Rebecca's sexual relationship. Apparently, we had not overestimated the role of sexuality in the case. It was clear where the defense was going.

But no amount of notice could have prepared us for what happened at the preliminary hearing. When the direct examination was concluded, defense counsel confronted Claudia with a series of cross-examination questions suggesting "provocation." Defense counsel said, you knew he was watching you, you meant to tease him, you were putting on a show, you opened up your blouses and showed him your breasts, you meant to taunt him, didn't you, didn't you, didn't you. Claudia uttered no to every question, with disbelief but dignity. She and Rebecca believed themselves completely alone.

I couldn't believe Keefer wasn't objecting. How many preliminary hearings had I participated in where the prosecutor objected to nearly every question I posed? Of all times for a prosecutor to afford the defense a meaningful opportunity for discovery in a preliminary hearing. Of all times to allow wide scope. What happened to objection, relevance? How about objection, beyond the scope of the preliminary hearing? If nothing else, what about objection, asked and answered? How many times does defense counsel get to ask plainly irrelevant, highly inflammatory, and downright insulting questions before the prosecutor complains? Maybe Keefer wasn't quick on the draw when it came to evidentiary objections, but why didn't he feel protective of his witness?

I was beside myself, stuck in the front row behind the counsel table. I wrote frantic but polite notes, not wanting to alienate the prosecutor or shed light on my true, controlling personality. I crept up to Keefer and handed him the notes once, twice, three times. More than that seemed excessive. The notes seemed to have little effect anyway. "Object," I wrote. "These questions are irrelevant to whether there is sufficient evidence to establish a prima facie case," I added. "Roy, don't you think this is getting out of hand," I pleaded. Look, he said to me later, it's a capital prosecution. I think it's fair to give some scope.

I couldn't fight him there. How could I fight him there? This was a capital case; a prosecution for murder in the first degree could lead to the death penalty, a death case. Of course, fairness required letting the defense do what they needed to do to mount a defense. What was I thinking, what could I have been thinking? How did I let myself get involved in this case in the first place? If there is an issue about which I feel deeply, about which I have always felt strongly, it is the death penalty. My opposition is unwavering.

My defense lawyer identity suddenly burst forth, like a hungry person released from a diet farm. My allegiance to the defense surfaced and reminded me that criminal defendants and criminal defense lawyers need all the friends they can get. Suddenly, I felt I should have been passing notes to the defense lawyer: don't go for broke, take small steps, establish the prior contact with the defendant on the trail, establish the contact at the first camp site, get something from the witness to suggest the defendant had a peculiar affect, get something to suggest a mental disturbance, establish that there was some nudity, establish that the defendant may have observed some sexual conduct, get what you need to get to support defendant's alarm at seeing the women intimately engaged, maybe the defendant was screaming too. Some of this might be useful in negotiating a plea or in arguing for leniency at sentencing. Some of this might lead to something less than a murder one conviction.

But wait. I was Claudia's lawyer, not Stephen Roy Carr's.

Claudia and I had discussed the capital punishment question when we agreed to become lawyer and client. I told her I would do everything I could to help the prosecution obtain a conviction for murder in the first degree; this was a case of deliberate, premeditated murder. But I told her that I would not help the prosecution secure the death penalty. I could not support it and I could not participate in someone's execution.

Fortunately, Claudia had agreed. At the time, I mostly felt my own relief to hear that she, too, opposed the death penalty. As the case proceeded, I began to see her position as more and more remarkable. Her lover died in her arms. The guy who killed her was still walking around. Carr fired eight bullets at Claudia and Rebecca, with a single-action bolt rifle. He reloaded his weapon with each shot, and emptied his weapon after each shot. They had done nothing to him. He took his time. He fired and fired and fired. He aimed to kill.

No doubt, Claudia had conflicting thoughts about the question of punishment. Probably, there were moments when she thought Carr should pay for what he did with his life.[8] But she was always measured and reflective when she spoke about it. Execution was not the kind of vengeance she needed. She wanted Carr to understand the pain he had caused. She figured killing him wouldn't do that. She preferred that Carr be deprived of freedom for the rest of his life. She knew imprisonment would be a terrible punishment for someone who had lived out in the wild. She wanted Carr to be shunned and isolated and caged for the

---

8. See Susan Jacoby, *Wild Justice: The Evolution of Revenge* (New York: Harper and Row, 1983), 10 (quoting Albert Camus's essay, "Reflections on the Guillotine," in which he explained that his opposition to the death penalty was not based on an illusion about the natural goodness of human beings: "I do not believe . . . that there is no responsibility in this world and that we must give way to that modern tendency to absolve everyone, victim and murderer, in the same confusion").

rest of his days. She wanted him to understand the pain. She wanted him to have to live with himself.

Moreover, there were some serious questions about the *legal relevancy* of defense counsel's questions. What did Claudia's sexual orientation, her relationship with Rebecca, an afternoon's lovemaking have to do with the defendant's homicidal rage as a legal matter?

After the preliminary hearing, and after some lawyerly soul-searching, I became convinced that the prosecution should file a motion in limine, to exclude irrelevant evidence. This would prevent the defense from introducing evidence of the relationship between Claudia and Rebecca in order to argue that Carr's murderous act was the result of provocation. The motion would prevent the defendant from cross-examining Claudia about her sexual conduct with Rebecca before the shooting and from introducing other evidence about their sexuality. Under the facts of the case, there simply was no provocation as a matter of law.

Why did this motion require soul-searching? Because the part of me that was a defense lawyer felt as I had during the preliminary hearing when I remembered that this was a capital case: disloyal and disjointed. Stephen Roy Carr had no defenses at trial: he was not insane; he was not wrongly identified; he had not acted in self-defense; he did not stumble in the woods, accidentally pulling the trigger seven times. The only defense he could raise related to the lesbian sexual relationship. Assuming I would convince the prosecutor of the soundness of my strategy, I was going to prevent the defendant from raising this defense. I was going to prevent a defendant from raising his *only* defense in a prosecution where his life was on the line.

But this was not his "only defense." This was not a defense at all. The absence of viable defenses does not give a defendant license to create one that is contrary to established law. It does not give a defendant license to create a defense that serves only to exploit the victim and inflame the jury. Under Pennsylvania law, the sort of provocation that reduces murder to manslaughter must be "serious."[9] That does not apply to someone who intentionally kills a stranger because he doesn't like her choice of lover or is offended by her lawful sexual conduct.[10]

---

9. 18 Pa. Cons. Stat. Ann. § 2503(a)(1)(2).

10. See Commonwealth v. Cisneros, 381 Pa. 447, 451, 113 A.2d 293, 296 (1955) ("The law of Pennsylvania is clear that no words of provocation, reproach, abuse or slight assault are sufficient to free the party from guilt of murder"); Commonwealth v. Bonadio,

A criminal defendant's "rights" are not compromised by an insistence that the defense be based on more than deep-seated bigotry. No injustice is caused by prohibiting a defense that gives legitimacy to homophobic violence. Why was I doing so much hand-wringing about proceeding with the motion? Had I, a practitioner and teacher of zealous criminal defense advocacy, reached my limit? Was I jumping ship here?

And what if I'd been the public defender in town, appointed to represent Stephen Roy Carr? Would I do it? How would I feel about it? What defenses would I raise? Would I offer the women's sexuality as relevant to my client's culpability—or to his punishment? At what cost to criminal justice? At what personal cost?

The answer is yes, I would do it. If I were the only defender in town (or one of two, as was the case in Gettysburg), the question is an easy one. The role of a public defender is to defend poor people accused of crimes, not to judge them. In view of the public hostility most criminal defendants face, and their lack of choice in counsel if they are poor, public defenders ought to be steadfast. If our clients can't choose their lawyers, why should we be able to choose our clients? The accused criminal defendant should not have to face the charges alone, whatever the nature of the charge. Soon enough, if convicted, the defendant will have to serve the sentence alone. My answer is not simply intellectual, built on my belief in the Sixth Amendment. There is a defender in my soul.

How would I feel about it? I don't know. The hypothetical may be too hypothetical. During my years as a public defender, I never felt so conflicted about representing a client that I believed the client's representation would be compromised. I have represented many clients alleged to have committed acts of hate and violence. I have represented some clients accused of bias crimes. I have represented some clients who seemed to be almost heartless. I have never felt unable to provide zealous, even empathic advocacy.[11] I believe in a high standard of crim-

---

490 Pa. 91, 415 A.2d 47 (1980) (holding that it is not unlawful for consenting adults to engage in sexual conduct with a member of the same sex in Pennsylvania). See also Commonwealth v. Long, 460 Pa. 461, 333 A.2d 865 (1975); Commonwealth v. McCusker, 460 Pa. 382, 292 A.2d 286 (1972); and Commonwealth v. Colandro, 231 Pa. 343, 80 A. 571 (1911).

11. See, generally, Charles J. Ogletree, Jr., "Beyond Justifications: Seeking Motivations to Sustain Public Defenders," *Harvard Law Review* 106 (1993): 1239.

inal defense advocacy. Had I been unable to provide it, I would have withdrawn as counsel. This may be a case that pushes my personal and ideological limits. This may be a case that stirs up too much conflict for me. I don't know.

The truth is, no matter what crimes my clients are accused of committing, once I become their lawyer I feel a connection to them. No matter who they are, there is almost always something to like about them, or at least something redemptive. In this case, Claudia Brenner was my client, not Stephen Roy Carr. My allegiance was to Claudia. My heart was with her. Still, I must admit to feeling some sort of pull to the defendant here, to Claudia's attacker. I was fascinated by him. How could this skinny, woeful, barely-a-man have done this horrible, apparently deliberate act? While in jail, he had been drawing these childlike cartoons for the jail newsletter. He had drawn a Christmas card and sent it to the district attorney. I felt haunted by these pictures. I wondered who Stephen Roy Carr was. What was going on in his head? What had his life been like? What led him to the moment of the shooting?[12] I sometimes even worried about the quality of his representation.

I suppose the harder question is whether, if I were one of many public defenders or court-appointed counsel available, and I had a choice in the cases I took, I would represent Stephen Roy Carr. I probably would. I don't think I would go out of my way to get myself appointed to this case, but I don't think I'd turn it down either.

I would not use the victims' sexuality as part of any substantive defense, such as provocation; it is irrelevant. I admit that I also find this defense deeply offensive—but, more importantly, I believe that many jurors would share my reaction. My decision would be legal and tactical. If observing women engaging in lawful, consensual sexual conduct sparked some sort of mental impairment in the defendant, such as temporary insanity or diminished capacity, and I had the evidence to support this assertion, I would raise it. If there was something about encountering the women lovers that related to something in the defendant's background which mitigated his culpability, I would absolutely raise it at sentencing.

---

12. See, generally, Abbe Smith, "Criminal Responsibility, Social Responsibility, and Angry Young Men: Reflections of a Feminist Criminal Defense Lawyer," 21 *New York University Review of Law and Social Change* 433 (1994) (hereinafter Abbe Smith, "Reflections of a Feminist Criminal Defense Lawyer").

My view is that there would be a cost to criminal justice if lawyers like me refused as a group to represent defendants like Stephen Roy Carr. As to personal cost, I suppose there might be some if I *only* represented the Stephen Roy Carrs of the world. But I don't.

At the hearing on the motion in limine, which I wrote and the prosecutor argued, the defense added a novel argument to their opposition. They argued that the defendant ought to be able to introduce evidence of his personal history to support the defense of provocation. His offer of proof included the following: he had been sexually abused as a child; he had been sexually assaulted by a man in prison; his mother "may be involved in a lesbian relationship," he was ridiculed at school and made to take showers there; he had been rejected by women his entire life.[13]

The offer of proof defied both credibility and the reasonable person standard, which is at the core of legally adequate provocation. Carr was sexually abused and assaulted? He and how many others? His mother "may" be a lesbian? What are we talking about here? Is there a rumor in the neighborhood? Did someone see Carr's mother in a gay bar? And what if his mother *is* a lesbian? He had been rejected by women his whole life? Now, there's a frightening defense for murder.[14]

The motion in limine was successful. Who could have predicted that the presiding judge would understand the issue well enough to write the following:

> [The women] sought the solitudes of a location thought pristine. Many may frown upon what they did, but they broke no law and only pursued activities in which they had a right to engage.
>
> Defendant, on the other hand, brought an attitude and disposition that would be considered evil in any civilized circumstance.
>
> People seem to live constantly in eras when one group or another feel justified in ending human life for reasons thought to be sufficient. History is replete with examples of utmost cruelty being inflicted on those termed heretic, witches, sodomites and the like. . . .

---

13. See Commonwealth v. Stephen Roy Carr, no. CC-385–88, Court of Common Pleas, Adams County, Pennsylvania, *Opinion on Post-Verdict Motions,* Oscar F. Spicer, President Judge, at 3–4 (hereinafter *Opinion on Post-Verdict Motions*).

14. See, generally, Abbe Smith, "Reflections of a Feminist Criminal Defense Lawyer," supra note 12.

> [T]here was no relationship between the victims and Defendant.
> The victims . . . did not harm Defendant. . . . His murderous act
> cannot be mitigated by such trivial provocation.[15]

On the eve of trial, the defendant decided to plead guilty to murder in
the first degree in exchange for a sentence of life in prison without the
possibility of parole. The plea was the result of the motion in limine, the
absence of any meaningful defense to the charges, and the defendant's
fear of the death penalty.

Claudia was relieved; as she had hoped, Carr would be convicted
of nothing less than murder in the first degree. Carr had committed the
most serious crime under law, and nothing about her relationship with
Rebecca lessened his crime. Notwithstanding her experience at the preliminary hearing, she had mixed feelings about the loss of her day in
court. We had prepared well, and she was ready. The plea was, no
doubt, an anticlimax.

Rebecca's father was less accepting of the plea negotiation. He
wanted Carr executed. He did not mince words. He had no ambivalence about how Carr should be punished. He would not feel "whole" if
Carr was merely sent away forever.

Claudia never expected the criminal system to make her whole.
Something had been taken from her that could never be replaced. Nor
was the healing process going to take place in a criminal courtroom.

Today, Claudia is fully recovered from her physical injuries, lives with
friends in a house in the country, and practices architecture in Ithaca,
New York. She speaks frequently on hate crimes and violence against
lesbians and gays.

As for me, I have become a criminal lawyer and teacher who writes
and talks a lot about personal and professional conflict in the practice of

---

15. *Opinion on Post-Verdict Motions,* supra n. 13, at 13, 16. See also Commonwealth v.
Stephen Roy Carr, 398 Pa. Super. 306, 308, 310, 580 A.2d 1362, 1363, 1364 (1990) ("[T]he
principle issue is whether the trial court erred when it disallowed evidence of the defendant's psychosexual history to show the likelihood of a killing in the heat of passion
aroused by defendant's observation of two women engaged in . . . lovemaking. . . . The
sight of naked women engaged in lesbian lovemaking is not adequate provocation to
reduce an unlawful killing from murder to voluntary manslaughter. It is not an event
which is sufficient to cause a reasonable person to become so impassioned as to be
incapable of cool reflection. A reasonable person would simply have discontinued his
observation and left the scene; he would not kill the lovers."); Commonwealth v. Stephen
Roy Carr, 527 Pa. 621, 592 A.2d 42 (1991) (allocatur denied).

criminal law. I am interested in the complexities of professional roles, in the demands of personal conscience.

Life looks a little different to me now, more paradoxical, more gray. While I still believe in picking sides, and I remain convinced that there are sides to pick, the picking is tougher.

I know I met a hero back in the summer of 1988. I have never met anyone quite like Claudia. I know that I was profoundly affected by serving as her lawyer. There are some cases that spill out into life. Sometimes I think I get more from my clients than I give. More than anything else, this essay is a tribute to courage, to unbending belief in self, and to Claudia Brenner.

Daily Log of
Independent Fieldwork

Lynne Weaver

During the fall of 1991, Lynne Weaver, a third-year student at Harvard Law School, spent ten hours per week in a clinical program at Greater Boston Legal Services in downtown Boston. The author, who is hearing-impaired, worked with Cristy Barsky, a paralegal who had implemented a program of outreach to the deaf community in the area. Following are excerpts from Ms. Weaver's journal over the course of the semester.

Wednesday, September 11, 1991

Today was essentially an orientation to GBLS—meeting some of the staff, learning where things are located. However, Cristy and I spent several hours talking about my goals for the clinical and what I hoped to experience or achieve during the semester.

Some of the ideas we discussed included sign language classes (two hours per week) in addition to the ten-hour clinical; my participation in intake and case development; my meeting and becoming familiar with some important members of the deaf community, such as deaf attorneys, persons at D.E.A.F., Inc., and the Massachusetts Commission for the Deaf and Hard of Hearing; and becoming more familiar with the court system and the deaf litigant—what happens when a case involving a deaf person actually reaches the court stage? What particular problems does the deaf (or possibly hard of hearing, as well) person have?

Cristy also gave me numerous things to read: four case files (now closed) involving: a deaf client's encounter with the police, a deaf student's attempt to obtain readmission to college, a deaf printer denied a position he was entitled to based on his seniority, and a deaf aviation mechanic denied the opportunity to take his certification test. Some of these cases were "atypical," according to Cristy, in that GBLS took them on despite the fact that some were over GBLS's income guidelines. I read them in order to gain some understanding of several cases, GBLS's procedures, and some statutory knowledge. I also read a memo by the Developmental Disabilities Law Center (now the Disability Law Center) on Massachusetts Chapter 533 of the Acts of 1983; this statute prohibits an employer in Massachusetts from firing, refusing to hire or rehire or promote, or otherwise discriminating against a qualified handicapped person on account of that person's handicap.

Thursday, September 12, 1991

Today I learned to use the TTY in the office, and subsequently called a client who had been earlier referred out due to being over income; she had been denied an interpreter by Lesley College for graduate courses. The office (Cristy) was interested in whether the person had subsequently found legal assistance or whether she had decided to pursue legal action.

The referred client typed on the TTY that Cristy's initial suggestions (for her to write a letter to the administration demanding an interpreter and stating the basis of her legal rights, as well as demanding a meeting with administrators) had not worked; she had still been denied an interpreter. Cristy today suggested that she contact the Massachusetts Commission Against Discrimination to request a complaint, and that the commission would then investigate. However, the remedy would, from what I understood, be limited to damages. Cristy also suggested the name of an attorney in the private bar who might be interested in such a case (although there was the substantial possibility that the attorney might demand a considerable retainer) and, finally, Cristy suggested an attorney, Barbara Lybarger, who used to work at, I believe, the Massachusetts Office on Discrimination. One thing that I definitely need to do is to get Cristy to explain to me further the interworking of these offices and exactly what they do.

This use of the TTY was extremely informative, as I learned that there are various "cultural" ways of communicating on a TTY that are different than communicating by voice phone. For example, one might include expressions explaining one's emotions; i.e., "HaHaHa" to denote laughter, "smile" to denote amusement. In addition, punctuation is generally not used. Furthermore, I learned that one does not abruptly end a conversation; one makes sure that the other person has finished speaking before one terminates communication.

I sensed a particular willingness and inclusiveness in using the TTY, a mark of the presence of a special community. For example, Cristy noted that there is often a certain playfulness used in communicating by TTY, particularly when one knows the other individual. For instance, when I would make errors in typing, she suggested that I type "oops" and also admit to the client that this was my first time in using a TTY.

Cristy and I went to lunch and talked further about the clinical. We agreed to spend the next week or two exploring various things before setting a final agenda. She also discussed some additional background on the program at GBLS and how they just happened to do a program targeting the deaf community; a prior colleague had taken an interest in deaf issues, because of an aunt that was hearing-impaired, and thus began to do outreach and generate interest in the program. If this woman had not shown this interest (the project was later passed on to Cristy) would the program have been started?

Also, how should a deaf access program be structured? Should each unit have someone designated to handle deaf clients, rather than the present method, that is, all deaf clients coming in through Cristy? Cristy advocates the present system, as she feels that she has the knowledge, expertise, and dedication that is needed to handle the various clients or to make the proper referrals. She may be correct, but how much do other people know in the office? Are there limits to one person supposedly knowing everything? Again, one might want to refer to various models of Legal Services: a generalist neighborhood practice versus a specialist practice centered around various units. Presently, Cristy believes that the units are the only way to go so that one can have the expertise needed to handle the cases. This may very well be true, but how does this translate to deaf clients? Perhaps there should be a model after that of the National Center for the Law and the Deaf (at Gallaudet University in Washington, D.C.): that is, various local or state centers to serve deaf clients only. What would be the limits or benefits of this model? Something to think about.

Finally, Cristy pointed out the critical nature of client communications in dealing with deaf clients; even when one seemingly is doing everything right, things can very easily go awry. She used the example of a 17-year-old deaf woman who had just had a child and was living with her boyfriend, also deaf. The woman's mother decided to pursue custody of the newborn child. The woman came to Legal Services, asking about the complaint. Cristy and an experienced attorney in family law, as well as a certified interpreter, all met with the client and her boyfriend to discuss the case. The attorney began to ask the client questions, attempting to be extremely straightforward, as frequently legal terms do not translate well into sign language. She told the client, "You understand that your mother is seeking custody of your child?" This was signed to the client, who nodded as this was signed to her. (Incidentally, I learned that a deaf person often will nod as they are being signed to, to show that they understand the signs; this can present problems in court such as when an attorney asks, "Did you murder your wife?" and the defendant, when reaching the end of the question, may then vigorously sign "No!") Anyway, in this case, the interpreter used signed English (i.e., spelling in sign) to convey *custody*, as there is no sign in American Sign Language for *custody*. The client continued to nod and the attorney proceeded to go on with questioning. Cristy, however, intervened, and signed to the woman, "What is custody?" The woman then indicated that she had no idea.

While an incident of this sort can easily happen with a hearing client, it is probably much more likely to happen with a deaf one. Deaf persons often are not inculcated with the culture the same way that hearing persons are and often miss out on various aspects. Their native language frequently is not English, but American Sign Language, which can make reading comprehension difficult. Finally, in oral communication, that is, if hearing persons are communicating with one who is deaf as in this situation, there is much more likelihood that they will not recognize when the deaf person does not understand due to, I believe, cultural and communication barriers.

Wednesday, September 18, 1991

Today I observed a failure to give proper service to a deaf client and then an office conflict over this client. This client, who had an unemployment compensation problem, had been referred by Cristy (before my arrival) to a colleague in the Boston University (BU) clinical program. Apparently the client was to come in for a full intake. The client called Cristy today to let her know that an interpreter was not going to be provided for this meeting; he had been told by Cristy's colleague that an interpreter was not available and that they could communicate by writing notes, and that he should bring a friend if possible. Cristy commenced to contact this colleague and demand that, under section 504 of the Rehabilitation Act of 1973 and chapter 220, section 92A of Massachusetts law, the client was entitled to an interpreter. Evidently, in the past six months to a year, Cristy had had the same conversation with this same colleague, who, according to Cristy, was a conscientious advocate but was just not recognizing the rights of deaf clients. An earlier client (deaf) whom Cristy had referred to her had had his case stalled; an interpreter was not provided. Finally, the advocate went on vacation, and the case was assigned to someone else. When this happened, the client was accommodated and the case moved smoothly.

Today, Cristy attempted to retake this (present) client by telling the colleague that she wanted the case back; however, she is not senior to this colleague. The colleague, realizing that she had failed to do her job properly (Cristy also reported this incident to the colleague's superior), insisted that the client wanted her to represent him and then finally called (today, after some two-week delay) the Massachusetts Commission for the Deaf and Hard of Hearing. The commission was unable to provide an interpreter on such short notice (the appointment was scheduled for tomorrow).

Well, this shows, perhaps, the usual office infighting. However, in this case the client suffered. He has yet (as of today) to obtain an interpreter for his intake. Cristy backed down after the conflict, noting that the client was no longer hers and that we probably shouldn't intervene further. Supposedly, now, the client will receive an interpreter when the office is able to obtain one. This made me wonder, though, how many other advocates do what this particular one did? That is, although they have good intentions, they still fail to recognize the crucial need for a *qualified* interpreter? How good is the communication at GBLS, anyway?

Thursday, September 19, 1991

GBLS infighting continued over the deaf client who is not being represented adequately. He is a computer programmer who was fired due, he claims, to discrimination. Because he is presently unemployed, he falls under GBLS guidelines. He called in about two to three weeks ago because he was given Cristy's name by someone in the deaf community. Cristy did a preliminary intake by TTY and referred him to the BU clinical program, which is overseen by GBLS. This client was then given to a paralegal in the BU unit. The client, however, was frustrated and continued to contact Cristy, telling her that the paralegal stated that she could not obtain an interpreter and that they could write notes or communicate through a friend of the client's, both of which methods are extremely inadequate. Also, it appears that there was some reluctance on the part of the advocate to use the TTY to communicate with the client.

Cristy talked with the paralegal's supervisor and reminded everyone that part of her (Cristy's) job description is maintaining accessibility to the deaf community. The result: Cristy managed to retrieve the case for us to develop further. Thus, she and I will meet with this client as soon as we can obtain an interpreter (probably sometime next week). At this point we are not even sure if the client has a good case, as GBLS has not yet done a sufficient intake. Still, this will be a good opportunity for me to observe an intake and to learn about employment discrimination law and unemployment compensation.

I spoke this morning with an attorney who does mock interviews for public interest jobs on campus; we discussed the accessibility of the courtroom. She commented that as we spoke—I was "interviewing" for a job with the Civil Rights Division of the Justice Department—she thought to herself, "Why aren't courts more accessible to deaf and hard-of-hearing clients, as well as advocates, as it *can* be done?" Exactly—why not???

Wednesday, September 25, 1991

I got my first real client today, the client whose treatment prompted the in-house conflict described earlier; however, today was spent actively working on his case.

The client was fired in August from a job as a computer programmer; he was denied unemployment benefits as he was fired for cause, that is, misconduct. We are examining his case to ascertain: (*a*) whether we can win at a hearing to obtain unemployment benefits, and (*b*) whether he has an employment discrimination claim. Our meeting with him lasted about two hours. It appears that we may be able to obtain unemployment benefits; in order for benefits to be denied the employer must demonstrate willful misconduct on the part of the employee. The client states that he was not unwilling to do the particular task in question, but was merely putting it on hold in order to complete first what he felt was more important, based on the earlier instructions of his employer. He paints a picture of an employer who was willing to meet him halfway in providing reasonable accommodation. The employer provided an interpreter for his initial job interview and, later, for some meetings. However, for day-to-day interactions, the client relied upon writing notes and using lipreading skills and limited oral skills. According to him, he has never been fired before, has never received unsatisfactory ratings before, and thus when he was placed on probation and later fired, he was incredulous, as he thought he was doing a good job.

It seems that there were communication problems. The client stated that with a reorganization that occurred about two years ago, the problems escalated, as his supervisor was hostile to him and had very little patience with him.

Listening to him was an incredible experience for me. Even though I do not know sign language, I could lip-read him some, and in listening to his account from his interpreter, I could not help but feel a tremendous amount of empathy for him. Clearly, he is intelligent and articulate; however, he faces huge obstacles, as the world is a hearing one and does not particularly desire to accommodate a person who is not. In his account of various complaints he had about his supervisors, he mentions their refusal to repeat some things for him, his feeling that they discussed him behind his back, and his basic feeling that he was not treated as an equal.

I could not help but relate to personal experience. Although I have never signed, I very much know what it is like to have people unwilling to repeat things for you, to become impatient with you, to treat you as though you are stupid simply because you can't hear, and to make fun of you. This brought back many memories, for social situations have always been very difficult for me, and work situations may be, too. (I have not yet seen enough of legal practice to see how I am going to function—the phones are a major concern, as well as meetings, and possibly the courtroom, should I decide to litigate.) I could not help but become angry as he related his experience. Why can people not have just a little more patience? This man, according to him, was doing a job that he was qualified to do, and was working very hard, even coming in on weekends. However, the company refused to obtain even a part-time interpreter for a few hours a week (except for some meetings) in order to facilitate better communication. He seemed to feel that he was taking the fall for a supervisor who had little patience with him and who was getting a bad rap from her supervisor. Also, the company was facing budget cuts and may have felt that his recent requests for an interpreter were excessive.

One thing that makes this case even more egregious is that his employer was a very large company in the defense industry, that is, $$$. Also, as they receive federal contracts, they have even greater obliga-tions (at least this is my understanding at this point) under section 504 of the Rehabilitation Act of 1973.

It appears that I will be handling his unemployment hearing, and it seems we may have a strong case on this point. We have a lot to do to analyze the discrimination case; to better assess this and the unemploy-ment case, we have another meeting with him and the interpreter next week.

While speaking through an interpreter was more time-consuming than speaking directly to a hearing person, I felt that the time was not a tremendous hindrance. Indeed, it gave me more time to collect my thoughts and decide how next to proceed. (I conducted much of the interview and Cristy took notes as well as taped the meeting.) We could have communicated with the client without an interpreter, as he could speak (you had to make an effort to understand him, though) and he had excellent lipreading skills (however, as Cristy pointed out, studies have shown that the most effective and fluent lipreading is less than 50 percent accurate); but in order to really communicate, an interpreter was essential. Also, he was obviously much more comfortable with one.

Again, I could analogize. When the batteries fail on my hearing aids, I can hear nothing. So, I know what it is like to be in a room that is silent. I am very uncomfortable communicating, as it is very difficult for me to understand, even though I can, when I have to, depend solely upon lipreading. There are situations where I am inevitably without my hearing aids, such as when I am swimming, and someone tries to speak to me, or before or after a shower, and someone in the dorm tries to speak to me (you do not wear hearing aids in water). I then really have to strain to understand the person. So I can imagine the difficulties this client had to deal with at work.

Of course, he is completely deaf, and I am not, so I am sure he has learned to make some adjustments. However, the hearing world has to understand that lipreading and note-writing can only work to a limited degree. I've had a million professors think that just because I lip-read they could talk incredibly rapidly, or because I use a microphone and receiver in some classes, that they can turn their backs to me and walk all over the classroom. It simply doesn't work that way. While accommodation is not easy, it can be done. Indeed, I have had professors who, in addition to wearing a microphone, would walk backwards when they lectured, in order to avoid turning their backs to the classroom. Others would just try to remain stationary.

Accommodation can be made in the workplace if everyone makes an effort; indeed, how would others feel if the tables were turned?

I found myself sometimes talking to the interpreter, a huge breach of etiquette as this shuts the client completely out. Communication was a real challenge. Not only did I need to concentrate on talking to the client and not to the interpreter, but also, instead of listening to the client in return, I had to look at the interpreter in order to understand (instead of looking at the client). This makes me wonder how much I miss when I am not focusing on the client. I don't see facial expressions, body language, emphasis, all of which are very important in assessing your client's story or case. Yet, is this disadvantage outweighed by the fact that I am hard-of-hearing? I guess this is an impossible question.

Cristy made a mistake at the end by asking the client if obtaining the same interpreter would be okay. The interpreter (who interpreted this query) pointed out that that was something that we should ask him privately, since, if the client did not feel comfortable with her, that was not something that he would likely tell her directly. Clearly, there are a lot of things to take into consideration in using an interpreter. Overall, the communication with the client seemed to go smoothly. In some ways, of course, dealing with a deaf client is exactly the same as working with a hearing one: you have the same responsibilities to the client, that is, to give him or her the best possible representation that you can; however, you have an additional duty to make a special effort to make sure that they understand you and that you understand them. (And I feel that a part of understanding a deaf person is making an effort to understand their culture as well; for that reason, I'll be very glad when I know enough sign language to use some to at least put a client at ease.)

At the end of the session I had to warn myself that there is another side to this story. I am sure that this large company gave some thought to his firing and the possibility of a lawsuit; so, undoubtedly, they have a story to tell. I, of course, want to believe this client, who is extremely likable and articulate. This is one part of being a lawyer, I suppose; you can't go back in time to witness the events yourself in order to make a judgment as to who has the most truthful account, so you have to operate by means of intuition, experience, and hard work. Still, if this client is relating these occurences truthfully, this is law at its best.

Friday, September 27, 1991

Today I attended training in unemployment law in order to familiarize myself more with the law. Again, the issue of communication arises. Although I could understand the people giving the training, Cristy would have to remind them often to repeat questions that other people would ask (sometimes I could not understand the questions, as I could not see the people making inquiries). It was somewhat frustrating, not from a point of understanding; indeed I understood a lot more than I do in law school classrooms—the room was smaller, although it was packed, and I could see most everyone. What was discouraging was that the speakers had to be reminded countless times to repeat questions. Finally, Cristy wrote a note to one of the speakers and put it in front of the person. Even then the person sometimes forgot.

While I understood most of what transpired at the meeting, I could not help but wonder what the solution was, or if there was one. I have long given up on asking professors to repeat the questions of classmates; in a small setting such as this one, if people do not remember even when constantly reminded, then is there much hope? At one point Cristy asked a question and the speaker asked if she needed to repeat the question; Cristy replied no, as she knew I had understood her. The speaker quickly lapsed back into not repeating the questions.

Wednesday, October 2, 1991

A really draining day, but an exciting one as well. My client came in again so that we could further develop his case. Cristy is stepping back and turning the case over to me (I will be doing the hearing) and to a woman named Christina, who is a paralegal in the income maintenance unit and specializes in unemployment benefits.

I am apprehensive about doing the hearing, as it will be my first. Also, I am not sure how I am going to handle an interpreter myself. GBLS is going to provide some sort of oral interpreter for me, as the interpreter we have been using will be there for the client, not for me. So, there will be two interpreters there, one for a deaf client and one for a hard-of-hearing advocate. It will be a truly challenging situation.

I attended a hearing today involving issues similar to those posed by my client's case. I found that while the hearing room was small and there were relatively few people to keep track of, I realized that I very well could encounter a witness, advocate, or examiner that I found difficult to lip-read. Indeed, in this hearing, I had some difficulty in understanding someone who was seated less than five feet from where I was located. In addition, I observed that there could be moments during which I would need to write notes, converse with the client, or converse with my cocounsel; and thus my attention would be diverted from the speaker, and I would probably lose what that person had said.

I have learned of one method of interpretation, called a CART system, which is taken from courtroom reporting. (I later learned that it stands for Computer Aided Realtime Translation. This technology stems from the use of "realtime reporting," that is, closed-captioning for live television.) The interpreter types in a computer code, which is then translated instantaneously as the deaf/hearing-impaired person reads from the screen. This sounds absolutely perfect for me; however, it costs $60–100 per hour. I was dumbfounded. So, we're going to need to work somehow with an oral interpreter, which I am apprehensive about, having never used any kind of interpreter for myself. As Cristy pointed out, knowing sign would be a great advantage, for then I could utilize the interpreter that the client does. Thus, in some ways, the client, who is deaf, is better off than I, who am hard-of-hearing. Ironic. Does that mean I need to learn to sign in order to accommodate myself to a *hearing* world? Also, why should the state provide interpreters for clients in a courtroom setting or hearing setting, but not provide one for a deaf/hearing-impaired advocate? Perhaps they have never envisioned a deaf person in the courtroom. It seems to me that a strong argument could be made that the court has a duty to accommodate the advocate, as well as the client, as the advocate is a critical part of the client's interaction with the administrative state or the justice system. Under section 504 or some other statute, can courts be forced to accommodate advocates? This is something to definitely explore further.

Meeting with the client was exciting. There is a real thrill to developing a case of your own; however, there is a real responsibility as well. You see the imperativeness of carefully developing your case, combing through it with a fine-toothed comb. And dealing with a deaf client is an extra challenge. Communication takes much longer.

Yet, I learn things that just make me angry and all the more determined to win the case. For instance, the client named several incidents in which the company actually discouraged a friend (hearing, but who signed) from signing to him during meetings (in which they had not provided an interpreter), as they stated it was distracting and creating too much dependence by the client upon the colleague-interpreter. If this isn't discrimination, I'll begin chewing on the rug. It's incredible how insensitive people can be. Just what this stems from, I really can't fathom. There seems to be a compelling need for society to homogenize us all. Yet, we can never all be alike. Indeed, speaking of disability, until medicine reaches a state of perfection, which we are likely never to see, we will always be confronted with infants born disabled or adults who later become disabled, or, perhaps, "physically challenged." Many, if not most, of these people have so much to give. Yet, whether they can is left up to the societal majority, which chooses whether to open the door or shut it. Indeed, not only has this client been shut out of a job that he, in all likelihood, is very qualified to do, but I also may find myself shut out of the hearing, and thus unable to do my job, not because I'm unqualified, but because I have a hearing loss.

So, in many instances, one is left to fight for the chance to compete on a level playing field.

Wednesday, October 9, 1991

In preparing for the hearing, I contacted the Boston Guild for the Hard of Hearing to obtain some statistics on the efficacy of lipreading. I discovered that lipreading is even less accurate than I thought. If someone is completely deaf, lipreading is only about 30–40 percent reliable. I found this startling, and infuriating as well, as there were many instances in which my client was forced to rely upon lipreading and writing of notes. While writing of notes is certainly accurate, it is very time consuming; people thus do not write everything they say— instead, people tend to write main ideas or concepts. So we're going to try to introduce some literature about this as well as an affidavit from the Boston Guild.

Wednesday, October 16, 1991

Today was essentially spent preparing for my client's hearing next week.

In order for the employer to prevail in denying an otherwise eligible claimant unemployment compensation on the grounds of deliberate misconduct, the employer must prove that the employee's misconduct was deliberate, or intentional, and undertaken with the knowledge that such action was contrary to the employer's interest. Furthermore, the employer must also show that this act(s) was the *sole* reason for dismissal of the employee.

In order to refute the evidence we anticipate being presented by the employer, that the client had been given this particular assignment but had not performed it, we will strive to establish that the client had, in good faith, prioritized his work, and that he did not, in any way, intend to subvert his employer's interests. Indeed, in a leading case in which an employee had deliberately refused the orders given to him by his supervisor because the employee deemed other work he was doing to be more important, the Massachusetts Supreme Judicial Court held that such conduct did not constitute "deliberate misconduct in willful disregard of the employing unit's interest" (*Jones v. Director of Div. of Employment Sec.*, 465 N.E.2d 245, 392 Mass. 148 [1984]). Thus, the employee's state of mind is critical in determining whether there has been deliberate misconduct in willful disregard of the employer. In addition, in my client's case, we will attempt to demonstrate, or at least to raise the specter, that there existed other reasons for his discharge, such as his being placed on a performance improvement plan (a probation plan) because of allegedly poor work performance that itself was the result of inadequate accommodation of his disability.

When I spoke with a senior attorney in this area, she stated strongly that while we should definitely bring up the fact that he was discriminated against—as the issue will certainly come up when the examiner, or I, on direct examination, will ask, "Why do you think you were fired?"—we should be careful to stick to the issue at hand, i.e., unemployment benefits and deliberate misconduct.

With that in mind, I spent most of the morning and early afternoon reexamining the voluminous documents our client has given to us, in order to be fully prepared for our meeting in the afternoon.

Christina and I met with the client from about 2:00 until 4:30. I did most of the questioning, which was mostly more fact-finding on my part. I was very pleased with what we accomplished, as I believe some of the information that we dug up was critical in making his case.

The insensitivity of his employer is incredible to me. At one point during the meeting, the client stated that when his supervisor would come across him (the client) and a colleague (who knew some sign language) conversing in sign, the supervisor would demand that they communicate orally. Other communication problems or, perhaps, cultural insensitivity, included an oral warning that the client received, which noted, among other things, the client's tendency to look down or away when not wishing to receive information. According to the client, this was simply a cultural misunderstanding; for example, if he was talking with someone, and that person looked away, then he would look away also, for when deaf people are communicating it is understood that looking at the person is imperative. His supervisor, already hostile, took this as not desiring to receive information. Another incident mentioned in this oral warning was the threatened disruption at a meeting and something to the effect of making colleagues uncomfortable and embarrassed. According to the client, this resulted from a meeting in which no interpreter was obtained, and about which beforehand he had protested vehemently; he had then told his supervisor that he would have to stop people during the meeting or question someone near him in order to find out what was being said. He proceeded to do that at this meeting, and his supervisor was irritated when, at one point, one person was speaking with the client, and then his supervisor spoke to him, and the client told the supervisor to wait, as someone else was trying to tell him something.

Assuredly, some of this may be personality conflicts, as one potential witness observed. (Incidentally, no witnesses would come forward for the client, as all of the people he named to us are still working with this company; I understand that this is not an unusual occurrence.) However, this same witness (again, who refused to testify on his behalf) did state to us that they had definitely discouraged her from communicating to him in sign language in meetings, their reason being that it was distracting and that it created dependence on his part.

In recounting these incidents, I cannot help but think of an observation made by Carol Padden and Tom Humphries in *Deaf in America: Voices from a Culture* (Cambridge: Harvard University Press, 1988): "Deaf people, along with learning about properties of sound and the meanings attached to it, encounter another sobering lesson: the realm of sound very often involves issues of control. It is not surprising that what others use as a central definition of their own lives, sound, should become a powerful tool of control" (100). One senses the pervasive uncomfortableness of "normal" people in being with those that are not like them, especially when that "different" person must call attention to this fact. Indeed, Padden and Humphries also note, deaf people "are very often required to be silent if they cannot master the sound well enough" (101). This refers not only to speech, but also to expressions, movements, and actions, which are discouraged or ridiculed if they are not performed "correctly."

Back to the client, however, the incidents of his differential treatment are legion. For example, in staff meetings once a week, no interpreter was provided. For a seminar no interpreter was provided, thus, everyone attended but the client. In one instance, the client's supervisor, in handing out pay raises, did not speak to him (the client) about his, that is, the supervisor gave no reason for what he felt was a very small increase; yet the client observed the supervisor talking with other people about their raises, for example, about company performance and about their performance. This prompted the client to leave in protest. The client apologized for his walkout the next day; however, this walkout was later mentioned in an oral warning, about a month later.

Again, it sounds as if the client's supervisor was extremely impatient and, in addition, apparently was not particularly well-liked by many in the department. However, in my client's case, the supervisor's impatience and insensitivity were critical to his (the client's) job. And, even more saliently, I feel certain (based on what the client has said) that the supervisor's extreme impatience with him stemmed from the fact that he was deaf.

Another point, which I am sure will come up in the hearing, is the fact that they did accommodate him to some extent. So, I am sure they will attempt to portray themselves as bending over backwards in order to accommodate him, by, for example, purchasing a TTY for his use, and hiring an interpreter on average about 18 times per year. But if one thinks about this, this is not very often. Indeed, this is about once every

three weeks. And, as the client pointed out, these occasions are somewhat misleading; for an all-day training two interpreters would be
provided, one in the morning and one in the afternoon. So, I would
guess the use of an interpreter averaged about once every three and a
half to four weeks, which is deplorable.

Another item that I came across in going through the client's notes
(he documented various incidents during his employment that angered
him; and at a later point, during his probation, his employer required
him to keep a record of any difficulties he encountered) is a hastily and
angrily written note to himself in which he beseeches, "I have learned to
speak and to lip-read. Where are the people to learn sign language in
order to communicate with me?" Indeed. Only one colleague, not a
superior, had the interest to take a sign language class.

Finally, even though I am hard-of-hearing, I do often feel alienated
from the deaf world, although I can empathize with many of their
experiences. For example, today, when the interpreter was speaking
with my cocounsel (after the meeting), I turned to my client and asked
him a question. He understood and responded; I then went on to ask
another question. However, I believe I went too fast or it wasn't easy to
lip-read, because he then immediately and instinctively turned to the
interpreter to interpret. At that moment I did feel oddly guilty, although
I hadn't done anything wrong. Yet, unless one learns the language one
is not truly a part of the community; I can only very marginally speak as
to this experience—I can, of course, speak as to my own. So, I couldn't
help but think, would my client be better off with a representative who
is completely deaf and who would *really* understand? My feeling is that
the answer is a resounding yes.

Wednesday, October 23, 1991

Today I spent in last-minute preparations for the hearing tomorrow. I
composed an opening statement and a closing argument and then ran
these and other last-minute queries by my cocounsel, Christina. In addition, I gathered together all the exhibits I plan to use, then pho-
tocopied and highlighted them for me, the opposing counsel, and the
hearing examiner.

In addition, I spoke by TTY with my client, who called to point out
various places in the documents where he specifically asked how he
could improve his performance as well as other verification for his

contention that he was merely prioritizing his work, rather than refusing to do a specific task. He admitted to feeling nervous about tomorrow. I realized that he needed reassuring, and that was also a very important part of my job; quite frankly, I had been so busy preparing, I hadn't thought about how nervous he would be and how hard this will be for him, to confront his former employer.

I did my best to reassure him that we were prepared, that we would be ready for them tomorrow, and that he should just take a deep breath and relax. I hope I can follow my own advice!! I hope I'm not a nervous wreck tomorrow! In a way I'm excited and looking forward to the hearing, and to doing my best to demolish their case; at the same time, I'm afraid of becoming speechless or losing my train of thought! I guess this is just normal jitters for someone who has never done anything like this before.

Jitters aside, Cristy and I talked today about "reasonable accommodation" of me. We finally were able to obtain a CART reporter for me, although the reporter is very new (this will make two of us!). Cristy then quizzed me as to what I should do if the examiner should happen to give me a hard time about having the reporter; well, under section 504 of the Rehabilitation Act of 1973, any program receiving federal funds cannot discriminate on the basis of handicap. So, the State of Massachusetts, which receives a ton of federal money, cannot discriminate against me by not allowing my use of a reporter. However, whether this leads to the conclusion that the state should pay for the reporter is another question. Cristy and I worked on this today, calling someone at the National Association for the Deaf at Gallaudet; he responded that there was a good case for making them pay. In this instance, we aren't going to push it because we are bringing this assistance with us, rather than notifying the agency ahead of time and requesting accommodation.

Thursday, October 24, 1991

The hearing. Wow. I'm completely exhausted. The bad news is that we didn't finish today; we ran over into the next time slot, so we will have to continue the hearing in three weeks, on November 15. The good news is that today went very well, overall, or so Cristy and Christina seemed to think; we were very well prepared. I really hope it went well. My cross-examination of the employer's witnesses was very effective, but my direct examination of my client was weak in comparison. I thought this was strange; I was more worried about cross! Essentially, I was leading my client too much; I realized this at the time, but I was having difficulty phrasing the questions without leading him. During our meetings the client has tended to go off on a tangent, and we cautioned him before the hearing to be sure to answer the questions and listen carefully. Well, in some ways we were overprepared—I couldn't get him to elaborate enough! According to Christina and Cristy this wasn't a disaster, and overall the direct went well.

Still, I was pleasantly surprised about how enthused Christina and Cristy seemed about how today went. For me it was somewhat of a fog; it was hard to assess how we were doing. And, I'm so nervous about the outcome in this case; we have the truth on our side—I just hope that we can win with this. I know we should win, but, as we all know, the truth doesn't always prevail. I just want to win so badly for him.

Some parts of the hearing were definite highlights. One (low) note-worthy point was an objection the other representative made to Christina's writing notes to me during the hearing, offering me sugges-tions on my cross-exam. He argued that since she had presented herself only as my supervisor and not as cocounsel, that she should not be advising me, unless she planned to conduct the examination and cross-examination. Well, I wasn't prepared for that one, and neither was Christina. Since she had already presented herself as my supervisor, she did not push herself as cocounsel. And I deferred to her on that. Actu-ally, it turned out okay, as I was fine on cross-exam; however, I felt that the other counsel was clearly being extremely adversarial in making this objection.

The other dispute with opposing counsel we clearly won. He ob-jected to my introduction into evidence as an exhibit two letters that the client had written requesting interpreters, plus a letter from their hu-man resources director refusing further assistance. I was very ready to show how they were relevant to the issues at hand; essentially, I argued that this evidence demonstrated that other reasons likely existed for his dismissal. After I gave an explanation, their legal representative com-pletely backed down; it was great!

As far as the interpretation went, it was wonderful. The computer screen was set up to my left; the reporter did not sit beside me, but instead sat on the other side of the room. I generally understood almost all of what everyone said when I was looking at them, but when, for example, my client or Christina would write me a note or when I would look down to write notes to myself, I would have to take my eyes off the speaker and then I would lose track of what was being said. So the CART technology worked beautifully. That is, when I would look down, I would then return to look at the screen to see what I had missed in the interim.

Also, the client benefited from the CART, something that we had not anticipated! He would frequently read the screen to double-check the interpreter, especially before responding to a question; in addition, he would read the screen to ensure that the interpreter had understood his previous response before he would go on to answer the next question.

I'm not sure, though, how the hearing examiner felt about the case. He was hard to read. Some questions he posed I felt were very fair, even favorable for us; others I felt were rather accusatory. That's another thing that I need to focus on—it doesn't matter what anyone else in that room thinks, only what the examiner thinks.

One thing that made the hearing rather intimidating was that they had four witnesses on their side; however, only two testified today. They declined to examine the others because of the lack of time (and, I think, lack of relevance). So, they were prepared.

Imagine, though, 12 people in one room (me, the client, Christina, Cristy, the other legal representative, their four witnesses, the examiner, the interpreter, and the reporter) and trying to consider all of them. Well, actually, I just tried to focus on one at a time, and some I didn't consider.

One terrific feeling was that of not being at a disadvantage because of my hearing impairment because of this technology. Still, as I know, and as Cristy and I tentatively explored yesterday, how available this will be to me when I get out to practice, whether in a state or federal government capacity, private practice, legal services, or even in my judicial clerkship, is a completely open question.

Wednesday, October 31, 1991

Today I spent in going over notes from the hearing and preparing for a meeting with my client tomorrow; we now have a firm date and time for the second part of the hearing—November 21 at 1:00 P.M.

The experience of preparing for the hearing has been a terrific one; and doing it (so far) has been a tremendous experience as well. It has made me see how even bright and intelligent deaf persons can be subtly and not-so-subtly, but devastatingly, discriminated against, and how many of us are conditioned to accept it, as we don't want to make waves by calling attention to ourselves, by illuminating our differences. For example, my client didn't make an initial request for interpreters when he began his job; he just assumed that, because his employer knew he was deaf and because the employer had provided an interpreter for the initial job interview, that everything would work out fine. Later when trouble ensued with a very impatient (and I'd say prejudiced) supervisor, only then did he begin requesting interpreters and accommodation. However, he felt he couldn't push to the point of jeopardizing his job. For example, at a point when the company was in difficult financial times, the client withdrew his request for an interpreter and resubmitted it when times were somewhat better. This, however, places the person in a precarious catch-22 situation; he's damned if he doesn't request an interpreter and he's damned if he does.

Friday, November 1, 1991

Today I met with my client and Christina for about two hours in further preparation for the second part of the hearing. Christina and I clarified some items that came up at the first hearing. I also asked the client to prepare a list of times that he had sought assistance and had been denied—so as to show that he was truly trying to keep his job.

A few interesting items came up while we were on break (an interpreter needs a break after around thirty to forty-five minutes in order to remain accurate): the interpreter and the client were discussing oralism (a method of learning in which deaf kids are to use lipreading and vocal skills only) versus teaching using ASL (American Sign Language). The client had gone to a private, oral school. The interpreter responded that she thought that oral schools were "a form of child abuse." The client, however, vigorously disagreed. Unfortunately, because of time, I was not able to inquire further as to why the client agreed with oral methods (after all, he relies almost entirely on sign language during our meetings). I did also learn, however, that none of the client's family learned sign language. To me, that is practically child abuse—I would want to communicate with my child fully, and if that meant learning sign language, then I would learn it.

One other item of note is that the client received cassette tapes of the hearing from the hearing examiner. According to Christina and Cristy, the other side (the employer) likely asked for these tapes and DET made a mistake and sent them to the wrong party, for tapes are only sent at a party's request (and a considerable expense must be paid). So, it looks as if they are really getting prepared for the next stage.

Later, in speaking with Cristy about the case, she noted that my client is not necessarily unlike those that GBLS serves—he has no source of income at this point in his life, like many of GBLS's clients, who may manage sufficiently during much of their lives, but an economic downturn or other circumstances may cause them to become impoverished.

Wednesday, November 13, 1991

I spoke with my client briefly by TTY. I had asked him to prepare a list of efforts he had made to retain his job, i.e., asking for interpreters, asking for suggestions to improve his job performance, asking to move to another department, working overtime, and so on. He is to come in tomorrow and we are to discuss it. One interesting bit of information is that the client found an article in the *Boston Globe* about a week ago stating that his company had been sued by the federal government for fraud and overcharging the government for defense contracts. Whether we can use this information is doubtful; I feel sure we can't, but it does illustrate to some extent, I suppose, the moral scruples of some in the company.

Cristy and I then went for a late lunch where we intended to talk about the hearing but ended up on politics and life in general. One interesting item that did come up, however, was that of my upcoming graduation. I just mentioned that I was debating whether or not to attend, as I didn't enjoy very much my college graduation because, among other reasons, I couldn't understand (or hear) a word of what was said at the ceremony. Cristy insisted that I demand some sort of accommodation by the law school so that I would understand what was going on, rather than attend and not understand, or simply not attend. Maybe this is the time to revisit the school's disabilities coordinator and see if she has any ideas. I am not especially hopeful, as in the past I have found the office not particularly helpful. Well, maybe I need to give it another try. Still, do I just attend, take my chances, and adopt a who-cares attitude if I cannot understand? Or do I demand to be placed in the front (which would be fine with me, if there were a chance that I could hear; however, given the size of the event, I doubt that this will be much help) or even more radically, demand some sort of CART technology so that I may fully participate in the ceremony? How do I feel about being stared at by classmates, who have probably never seen such technology? Sometimes it's hard to choose which battles are worth fighting and which are better just to leave alone, for your own personal peace of mind; for me, if I became upset by everything I don't understand, I am sure I would have been committed long ago. Some things that used to bother me don't bother me as much now as I become older. Other things bother me more. So, again, another situation presents itself and a decision (or a nondecision, a decision in itself) must be made. I think I'll sit on this one for a while.

Thursday, November 14, 1991

I am apprehensive about the second hearing; I am sure their representative will be much better prepared and will be on the attack. The only thing to do is be ready for him and go on the counterattack. Fortunately, this client is extremely interested in his case and is very willing to meet as often as is needed.

After the client left, I spent time musing further on what my strategy should be for the second part. I spoke with Cristy about this, and she offered some suggestions for preparing for the redirect. The rest of the afternoon I spent at a computer, generating my redirect, keeping in mind everything my client has said in our meetings, the facts, the law, and what has already been stated at the previous hearing by both sides.

Wednesday, November 20, 1991

Today I spent in last-minute preparations for the second hearing. I went over with Cristy my closing argument and my redirect of my client, and she offered some suggestions. Also, I met with my client for about two hours. This proved to be extremely helpful. First, I should state that we did not have an interpreter, since we were meeting on very short notice. However, our communication went relatively smoothly. Since there were only the two of us, he could concentrate on lipreading me, and I could concentrate on lipreading and listening to him. Sometimes we resorted to note writing, and I often would have to catch myself from saying something to him when he was looking away or reading. In some ways it is strange. I have met with him before, and now this meeting, without an interpreter; and yet, in this hearing I am strongly emphasizing his lack of interpreters and communication difficulties. Is this somewhat hypocritical?

Well, I have rationalized that it is not that hypocritical. If our communications constituted more than one-on-one, I feel that both the client and I would insist on an interpreter. Yet, one could ask, weren't many of his interactions on the job one on one? Well, yes, many of them were. Yet, there can still be difficulties in one-on-one communications. For example, I had to be extremely patient, to make sure I understood him (my difficulty in understanding did not just result from my hearing loss, but also from his, as his speech is not easily understood) and also that he understood me. Sometimes both of us would write down what we were saying to make sure that there were no misunderstandings. So, his employer needs to be patient and understanding as well in order for this client to realize his maximum potential. According to the client, this is where he ran into considerable difficulties; his immediate supervisor was very impatient with him, which caused him great stress on the job. Earlier supervisors apparently had been more understanding. Still, all the understanding in the world isn't going to help him in a group situation, such as a meeting or a training, or even among several colleagues engaging in a work-related discussion. People only have limited patience to repeat and explain to someone who doesn't understand. So, interpreters were essential to his work.

Well, back to the substance of our meeting. We uncovered some information in his time sheets showing that he *had* logged time (which he had forgotten about) on this particular project, over which he was fired. This will be extremely beneficial to us in showing his state of mind—that is, even though he complained about this particular job, he still began work on it, and thus had the intention of completing it. That was exciting, almost as thrilling as finding the smoking gun of your adversary! So, we will definitely introduce this information. In addition, I went over with him the questions that I plan to ask him tomorrow, and the form that his answers should take.

So, I think I'm ready for tomorrow!

Thursday, November 21, 1991

Well, the hearing! In a way, I can't believe it's over—I've spent so much time in preparing for this. (We, of course, don't know the decision yet; we should find out in seven to ten days.)

First of all, the opposing representative, who was to finish his cross-examination of my client, chose not to resume cross-exam. I couldn't believe this; perhaps the client had been so strong earlier that he felt that it would be useless to continue with examination. Still, it did not make for a very effective opening. For us, on the other hand, it was great; I then was able to immediately resume my direct exam (redirect), which went extremely well overall. A few times, though, I became a little nervous; for example, when I asked the client a question about a particular incident, he answered in the negative when he was supposed to answer in the affirmative! It took me a second to regain my composure; I then realized that he had forgotten this incident and didn't know what I was talking about, even though we had just talked about it yesterday! So, I was then left to decide whether to pursue the point, a relatively minor one (and possibly be forced to ask some sort of leading question), or whether to just abandon this. I decided to keep on questioning to get the client to see what I was asking for. On the second try, he finally saw where I was going, and responded correctly.

After redirect, the other representative proceeded to redirect his own witnesses. Again, another surprise. Their witnesses began to lie (specifically, concerning two points). One witness stated that the client's assignments weren't necessarily listed in the order of priority on his probation plan; of course, when she said this, my client began to go crazy and furiously write me notes. The second witness, a supervisor, stated that the client had not communicated with him in any way about this project, that is, had not told him (the witness) that this project was going to take him additional time to complete (despite the fact that the client had logged into the automated system that he had spoken with his supervisor about the extra time needed for this project). Again, the client became angry. Well, from this I learned that it can be difficult to confront a lie from a witness in cross-exam, unless you have conclusive proof that they are lying. And, also, don't be surprised when witnesses lie. I suppose the real surprise here was that they did not begin lying before now. But this wasn't terribly damaging to us as they had already admitted that the client had never refused in the past to do any particular task (this occurred at the last hearing). So, of course, I brought that up again today in cross, as it would be very difficult for them to retract past statements. Also, the redirect of their witnesses allowed me to focus on a third direct of my client. Since there arose completely conflicting testimony, it was essential for us to rebut this in a third direct.

After a third direct, we gave our closing arguments. Fortunately for us, the opposing representative's closing was not particularly strong (he was not especially forceful, and his points were not, I thought, made in a very clear fashion). This gave us an excellent opportunity to again appeal to the examiner as to why this client was entitled to benefits.

All in all, the hearing was a lot of fun and exciting to do. Both my cocounsel and my client seemed very happy with how the hearing had transpired. The client was extremely appreciative (but still apprehensive) and I felt we had done the best possible job that we could do.

Wednesday, November 27, 1991

Well, we won the hearing!!!!!!

We received a notice and an opinion today. In reading the opinion, I was extremely pleased to see that the examiner noted the insufficient provision of interpreters (this should help the client if he should decide to bring a claim for employment discrimination), and that the claimant was doing his job to the best of his ability. Also, he found that the claimant had not refused to do this particular task, and that he had acted in good faith in prioritizing his work—all things that we had consistently emphasized in the hearing. I was happy to see that he had believed my client's version of events!

There were a few items in the opinion which that may give pause to the client and, as Cristy noted, that may cause him to be a little less than completely satisfied with the opinion. For example, in the findings of fact, the hearing examiner states, "The claimant is deaf and mute and communication, except in the presence of a trained interpreter, is difficult."

We never stated that the client was mute. In fact, he speaks frequently; this is how he managed to communicate on the job (in conjunction with writing). Also, the examiner certainly saw the client communicate with me and others by speaking, before and after the hearings, or at various breaks during the hearings. But, I suppose, for some, if you are deaf, you are mute, an incredibly negative and false stereotype. Indeed, my client was extremely articulate and very bright—quite the opposite of mute. With the use of this word, one almost harkens back to *deaf and dumb,* which leads one to wonder exactly what the examiner saw in this client. I suppose, for us, in some ways, it could have been beneficial if the examiner saw him (the client) as somewhat helpless. Yet, this is very untrue. Yes, he was treated unfairly and has a right to be very angered by the treatment he received; but he is far from meek, accepting, helpless, and mute.

Actually, the client can communicate very well in a nonhearing world, and marginally in a hearing one; his communication in a hearing world varies with the patience and understanding of the other conversant and with the situation. However, he certainly doesn't have to have a trained interpreter at his side at all times.

So, while we got across the great need for better communications, it seems that the examiner received a picture (or perhaps these were his own preformed perceptions) of an extremely dependent, helpless man, which is far from the truth.

However, I suppose the bottom line is that we won; the client will receive benefits; he will have a much better chance of obtaining employment (as the examiner did not deem him insubordinate); and he has a better opportunity to file an employment discrimination suit.

Wednesday, December 4, 1991

Well, today was my last day at GBLS. It's definitely been a short semester! I met with my client today, the first I had spoken with him since the hearing, and since the decision. He was extremely pleased about the examiner's decision and thanked me repeatedly, which was certainly gratifying for me, and helped to make it all worthwhile!

We also went over the examiner's decision carefully, as he had many questions. One thing I had not thought about was his receiving an answer in the form of the examiner's opinion. He said when he received the opinion in the mail, he was not sure initially whether we had won the case or not. He then frantically contacted some friends to have them read the opinion, and finally a sister-in-law, who was an attorney; after hearing the opinion, the sister-in-law told him he had won the case. The more I thought about this, the more I realized that receiving an opinion could be confusing for a claimant, as the opinion is not necessarily explicit, and could be confusing for someone not used to legalese, or, especially, if one's reading skills are not particularly strong.

I'm not exactly sure what will happen with his case at this point. Cristy is talking with other people at GBLS to determine whether GBLS will keep the case or will refer it out for the next stage (likely an employment discrimination suit against his employer). From what I understand, there are advantages and disadvantages on both sides. Since we already have the case and know the issues and the client, it is certainly convenient and perhaps efficient to keep the case; however, someone outside of GBLS (such as at the Disability Law Center) may know more about employment discrimination law, especially in terms of disability law. Also, there is the question of this now turning into a fee-generating case, which it looks like it very well may. There are some restrictions regarding Legal Services accepting fee-generating cases, so GBLS may have to refer it out.

Whatever GBLS decides to do, I feel sure that Cristy and others, but particularly Cristy, will make sure that he has a strong advocate for the next stage in his case. So, I feel that he is in good hands, and I feel good about the part I played—he now is in a significantly better situation to file an employment discrimination suit, emotionally, financially, and legally, than he was in several months ago.

And I learned that using the CART technology was a tremendously liberating experience for me. If I looked away to read or write notes or turned to my client or cocounsel, I only had to return to the computer screen to ascertain what I had missed in the interim.

I would like to note here that my exposure to this technology caused me to realize that I could have benefited greatly from such accommodation at law school. Indeed, the popular Socratic teaching method makes it impossible for me to follow everything that is going on in a law school classroom. While I usually do not have too much difficulty in following the professor, understanding students' queries or responses, especially in (usually) large classrooms, poses a real and often insurmountable challenge. Unlike my experience at GBLS, the law school never affirmatively sought to discuss with me, or to investigate on its own, various accommodations that might have allowed me to participate more fully in the law school experience.

I recognize I have some responsibility to make clear my needs; I also recognize that I have not pushed the law school as hard as I might have. The reasons for this are very complex and are something that I am thinking very hard about.

On the Vision and Practice of Participation in Project Head Start

Lucie E. White

Introduction

Head Start is one of the few federally funded welfare programs that commands widespread bipartisan support. Though it is best known as a federal preschool program for poor children, Head Start's authorizing law targets parents as well as children. That law requires every Head Start grantee to invite the participation of parents in several ways. All Head Start programs must invite parents into the classroom, as observers or volunteers. Parents must be given priority when staff are hired. Programs must help parents develop educational and enrichment activities that respond to their interests and needs. But perhaps the most innovative, and anachronistic, element of Head Start's law of parent involvement is the requirement that each grantee convene a parent policy council to help make basic management decisions for the program. This requirement has its roots in the legislative mandate of "maximum feasible participation" of clients in all programs, like Head Start, that were funded through the 1964 Economic Opportunity Act.

Over the last quarter century, most War on Poverty programs have disappeared. Head Start, in contrast, has flourished. In many communities Head Start has become an informal gathering place for poor women. And women all over the country have testified that being involved in Head Start has changed the course of their lives. In contrast to other government-sponsored social welfare programs, which clients often describe as sites of state-sanctioned scrutiny, discipline, and humiliation, Head Start has offered women a modicum of safety. For some, it has provided something of a "homeplace," to borrow Afrofeminist critic bell hooks's term.[1] On the margins of the program's officially sanctioned parent involvement routines, some Head Start women have found—or made—psychic shelter for themselves in a harsh world. They have made it a place to affirm, rather than shrink from, the stigmatized social identities that are imposed upon them as poor women of color, with children, on the public dole; a place to nurture bonds of "family" that are not sanctioned by either biological kinship or the law; a place to challenge the false promises of liberal-paternalist social policy and the subordinating logic of the bureaucratic state, instead of having to feign deference toward it; a place to learn, and subvert, the rituals through which citizenship is acted out.

Head Start's founding architects did not design the program to nurture either autonomy or community among poor women. Nor does its authorizing law identify this project as the program's goal. Yet somehow, as Head Start has been enacted by poor women, the program has been made to work toward that goal. Through the efforts at self-respect, solidarity, critique, and citizenship that converge at Head Start—moments that taken singly seem episodic, uncertain, contradictory, and of little consequence—poor women, in an altogether down-to-earth way, have made the law of a particular social program into a practice of social justice.

This essay seeks to make that practice momentarily visible by profiling the work of Corva Marshall,[2] a client at a Head Start site in rural North Carolina. The essay draws upon four taped conversations with Ms. Marshall, which took place from December 1991 through June 1992 in the course of research that I am doing on the impact of Head Start's parent involvement component on the lives of poor women.[3]

Neither the North Carolina Head Start site nor Corva Marshall's own story are typical in any rigorous sense. Rather, her words give us one of many pictures of how women interact with the legally constituted space of the Head Start program, both finding opportunity and making community in the shadow that the law casts. Through Corva Marshall's story, we can see how the intricate forces of personal history,

---

1. See bell hooks [Gloria Watkins], *Yearning: Race, Gender, and Cultural Politics* (Boston: South End Press, 1990), 41–49.

2. Corva Marshall is a pseudonym.

3. I am conducting this research at Head Start sites in rural North Carolina and south central Los Angeles with funding from National Science Foundation grant SES 9022787.

temperament, and aspiration, always overlaid by the strictures on imagination that the language imposes, are what come together to give an unruly, multiple, lived meaning to the letter of the law.

The essay begins with a brief sketch of the Head Start law and its contradictory mandate for parent involvement. It then surveys the social landscape of the North Carolina Head Start site. It then moves on to Corva Marshall's story. I rely largely on Corva Marshall's own words to describe Head Start in one community and to interpret the program's meaning in one woman's life. Ms. Marshall's "own words" are inevitably shaped by the rhetoric about the program that she had absorbed from official program pronouncements, and from the popular culture. This rhetoric has its roots in the efforts of Head Start's early advocates to design a poverty program that could secure universal political support. To do so, they appealed to widely shared, but also deeply contested, cultural norms—norms that exhorted poor women to transform themselves . . . into wage-earning, home-focused, quiescent, and politically empowered . . . middle-class moms. Thus, when we listen to Corva Marshall's "own words," we hear a woman repeating the contradictory features of this image, straining to make them fit. In her effort, however, she infuses this constricting rhetoric with her own good sense, reshaping the law's received meanings to further the project of her own life.

The Law's Mandate

Project Head Start grants federal funds to community action programs, social service agencies, nonprofits, churches, and school systems to provide preschool education and social services to families whose incomes fall below federal poverty guidelines.[4] The program was launched by President Lyndon Johnson in the spring of 1965, as part of his War on Poverty. The program's authorizing legislation, the Economic Opportunity Act of 1964,[5] required that all of its programs "be developed, conducted, and administered with the maximum feasible participation of . . . members of the groups served."[6]

---

4. For the current program year, these guidelines provide that a family of four is eligible for Head Start services if its gross annual income is below $13,400. See ACYF-IM-91-08 (Memorandum issued by U.S. Dept. of Health and Human Services, Administration of Children, Youth and Families, Apr. 9, 1991).

5. Public Law 88-452.

6. P.L. 88-452, Section 202(a)(3).

Head Start was designed by an "expert" committee appointed by President Johnson. For the most part, this committee conceptualized the program within a "deficit" model of poverty; they envisioned Head Start as a way to compensate poor children for the cultural and educational deprivation that they were assumed to suffer, and to enculturate them in the middle-class values of the public school. But a dissenting group in the founding committee saw poverty more as a product of race and class subordination than cultural pathology. They hoped that Head Start might implement the "maximum feasible participation" requirement in a way that would give poor women the skills and incentives to seek broad institutional change. Through their influence, parent involvement—not just in the classroom, but also in program management—became one of four official components of the program, along with education, health-nutrition, and social services.[7]

In 1970, in response to grassroots protests,[8] Head Start's parent governance feature was spelled out in an official agency transmittal[9] that was subsequently appended to the program's regulations and remains in effect today.[10] These regulations require that each local Head Start grantee convene a "policy council," at least 50 percent of whose members must be parents of Head Start children, elected by their peers. The policy council has the legal responsibility to approve the agency's annual budget and personnel decisions. The council must also approve the program's personnel policies and its criteria for selecting children. In addition, the council has broad authority to consult with the staff on the curriculum and other program features. Federal monitors periodically review local programs to make sure that the policy council meets regularly and discharges its responsibilities. Grantees can be defunded if they do not secure policy council approval for personnel decisions and grant applications.[11]

---

7. See Robert Cooke, *Improving the Opportunities and Achievements of the Children of the Poor* (memorandum prepared by Planning Committee, Project Head Start, for the Office of Economic Opportunity, 1965).

8. Interview with Mamie Moore, March 1989, Atlanta, GA.

9. See Office of Child Development-Head Start, Transmittal Notice 70.2 for Instruction I-30, Sec. B-2, 8/10/70.

10. See 45 CFR Section 1304.5–5, Parent Involvement Plan content: Parents, area residents, and the program; 45 CFR Section 1304 et seq., Appendix B—Head Start Policy Manual: The Parents.

11. For example, in 1989, the Tenth Circuit Court of Appeals upheld a decision by HHS to defund a local Head Start grantee that had failed to obtain policy council approval for a personnel decision.

In addition to the requirement that parents, through the policy councils, participate in the "process of making decisions about the nature and operation of the program,"[12] Instruction I-30 also mandates three other forms of parent involvement in Head Start. Each local program must enable parents to participate in the classroom "as paid employees, volunteers or observers." It must provide educational and social activities for parents "which they have helped to develop." Finally, it must assist parents in "working with their children."[13]

In its introduction, Instruction I-30 envisions parent involvement as a catalyst for far-reaching structural change:

[s]uccessful parental involvement enters into every part of Head Start, influences other antipoverty programs, helps bring about changes in institutions in the community, and works toward altering the social conditions that have formed the systems that surround the economically disadvantaged child and his family.[14]

Over the last two decades, however, agency literature has stated more modest objectives for parent involvement, drawn largely from empirical research on the client governance experiments that proliferated in social programs in the early 1970s.[15] In this more modest formulation, parent involvement can accomplish three goals. It can help commit parents to the program and foster habits of involvement in their children's education; it can help parents develop leadership and management skills; and it can help tailor local programming to clients' needs.[16]

The Site

In the hilly, red-clay central region of Carolina, an imaginary line separates the stubby farm-plots of the northern Piedmont from the cotton plantations that extend to the south. This land was seized and settled by

---

12. Transmittal 70.2, at 2.

13. Id.

14. Transmittal 70.2, at 1.

15. See, e.g., Robert Yin et al., *Client Organizations: Increasing Client Control Over Services* (Rand Corporation Monograph, 1973).

16. For one example of the extensive series of agency publications addressing the parent governance requirement, see, e.g., Associate Control, Research and Analysis, Inc. *A Handbook for Involving Parents in Head Start* (prepared for Head Start Bureau under contract no. HEW 105–78–1021, 1980).

fiercely independent Scotch-Irish and German Protestants over two
centuries ago. Some came south from the congestion of Pennsylvania,
to carve modest farm-plots out of the hills. And others pushed north
from the cloying hierarchy of the coastal plain, to extend the cotton
economy deep into the oak and maple woods. These folks' descendants
still pride themselves on their small-farm self-reliance. They are the
kind of people who go to church every Sunday and put up enough
homegrown vegetables in July to feed their families for the entire year.
Yet many of the region's European settlers, particularly those who came
up from the south, did not clear their land or plant their cotton with
their own hands. Rather, this work was done for them by vast extended
families of African slaves.

A major east-west highway dissects both the county and its only
real town, connecting the large city that lies fifty miles to the west with
the popular Atlantic beaches that lie a hundred and fifty miles due east.
That town is both the county's seat of government and the only place in
the area where you can get a real selection of fast food. If you turn south
off the highway at Hardee's and follow the road up the hill, you will
reach the center of town. An imposing postbellum courthouse and jail, a
standard feature in these small southern county seats, dominates the
landscape. A plaque in the courthouse lobby, donated by a local
citizens' group in the 1960s, commemorates the slaves in the county
who remained loyal to their masters during the Civil War. About a
block from the courthouse, a sleek brick and plate glass public library
occupies a corner lot. A fire station stands nearby. Beside it, a bright
blue sign, reassuringly emblazoned with a white "H," points down a
small road away from town. Several professionals' offices—doctors,
dentists, lawyers—are clustered along this path.

On the streets, you can feel that this is one of those places where
white people are outnumbered, and where jobs are scarce. Indeed,
about 60 percent of the county's population is classified by the census as
Black, and of this group, well over half live below the federal poverty
line. Groups of African Americans, mostly middle-aged men, are gathered, "loitering," at just about every corner. No whites are visible, except inside their cars or behind the counters of the few white people's
stores at the top of the hill—a farm supply depot, a drugstore with a
forlorn soda fountain, an insurance agency, and a white-ladies' dress
shop displaying bold-colored women's fashions from a bygone era.
Smaller black folks' stores encircle these shops as the streets spread out

in every direction from the courthouse, down the hill. Some of these stores display rap tapes and skin lighteners in their cluttered windows. Others sell tobacco, boiled peanuts, fried pork rinds, potato chips, soft drinks, and beer. You have to go to the next county to buy hard liquor without breaking the law.

Halfway down the hill, what looks like it used to be the local A&P is now the county Department of Social Services, where poor people go for their food stamps and AFDC. Nearby, another large storefront, once a discount furniture store, has been transformed by flags and banners into the county's Republican headquarters for the fall election. People get their groceries down the hill, at two shopping centers on the main highway east of town. There, they can shop at Winn Dixie, Food Lion, Kmart, Eckerd's, and Pick and Pay. At these buzzing, brightly lit establishments, which border expanses of asphalt, blacks and whites seem to mix easily, naturally, as they wait to hand cash, plastic, or food stamps to young white girls poised at state-of-the-art, optically sensitive, computerized cash registers.

At the west side of town, set just off the main highway, stands a pair of run-down buildings that look like they might have once been a public school. The larger building is an elegant red-brick structure, built with the subtle artistry of Depression-era schoolhouses. It is a single storey, with a dozen classrooms jutting from a hallway that runs to the left and right of the building's entrance and an auditorium extending to the rear. The building is in disrepair: there are several broken windows, and white paint is peeling from its main door. Inside, the classrooms have poster-board signs on their doors: Tax Advice, Weatherization, Homeless Outreach. These signs are the only clue that the building, once the county's all-black high school, is still in use. It now houses the remains of the county's War on Poverty.

The smaller of the two buildings is set off to one side of the first, closer to the highway. This structure has a fenced yard where a few harsh gray playground structures—swings, a slide, a jungle gym—sit beneath a few scattered pine trees in the grass. The building itself, of cheap shoe box 1960s construction, is a block of four classrooms with no interior hall. Each classroom has its own exit to the play yard and is linked to the opposite classroom by a stale-smelling bathroom with two tiny walled-off toilets and a common sink.

In contrast to the forlorn appearance of the older main building, this smaller structure is obviously in use. Three of the classrooms appear to be laid out for very small children. In each, a frayed red rug is spread on the floor in front of the blackboard. Off to one side are three small tables, each surrounded by eight little chairs. Waist-high shelves line the walls and extend into the room, dividing it up into alcoves just large enough to allow four or five children to play. These shelves are crammed with blocks, tattered puppets, board games, a few books, and an odd assortment of beat-up plastic toys. An old gray record player, with a stack of records beside it, sits on top of one of the shelves. Large signs, cut out from colored construction paper and taped to the walls, announce that one corner of the room is for "housekeeping," another for "science," a third for "manipulative skills," and a fourth for "reading." Along one wall is a wooden board with eighteen toothbrushes hanging from little metal hooks. Above each hook is a piece of masking tape with a name carefully printed on it in block letters— "Antoineisha," "Kayleisha," "Luscious," "Lafayette," "Mautavius." Childish paintings, in broad angry strokes of yellow and red and blue, are tacked up to bulletin boards. Each of these paintings is labeled in broad-tipped black marker with one of these same names.

The fourth classroom is set up as an office and parent activity room. A small refrigerator and microwave are set on a counter in one corner. Two schoolteacher's desks are angled toward each other a few feet away. About twenty folding chairs are arranged in rows in the center of the room, facing two long tables set up end to end across the front of the room. Framing the blackboard are two bulletin boards. Tacked to one are notices to "employees," printed in small gray type. The second bulletin board, captioned "parents," displays a few photographs of awkward, proud women, and yet more notices, about "Child Abuse" and "HIB vaccinations" and "Bus Pick-up Schedules."

To one side of the gravel walkway that connects this classroom's exit to the parking lot and the highway beyond, stuck into the grass, is a wooden sign with profiles of two obviously African American children crudely outlined in black paint. Below these figures, the words "County Head Start Program—from the parents, 1987" are somewhat uncertainly blocked out in red paint.

Corva Marshall

Corva Marshall is a tall, wiry, Christian woman of African descent. She is about thirty, the oldest of six children, and the single mother of a

Head Start son. Her mother supported the family by working in a sewing mill. Her father had occasional jobs in lumber mills and was often away from home. She "started very young, having to take care of people. . . . Basically I had to grow up fast."[17]

As a child, Corva remembers herself as very shy—"just unsure about myself"—and she didn't like her name.

She attended one of the early Head Start programs in her county, at her elementary school. Her memories of this experience are sporadic but uniformly positive—drawing, coloring, "laying on the floor and . . . we drew each other's body figure."[18] For some reason that she doesn't really understand, Head Start was "the start of me being a little more secure.   It helped me to start establishing responsibility."[19]

Corva entered first grade after the schools in the county had already integrated. She has forgotten how race affected her school experience in the early grades. But by the time she got to high school,

> you knew how to read people a little bit more. . . . You could see the lines between black and white and you could . . . really actually see them doing more for the white students and putting the blacks, you know, they just did whatever, and kind of left aside. . . . Sometimes depending on where your mind is at far as being stable, some kids cannot deal with that. And some, you know, that makes them fight that much harder to prove themself.[20]

For complicated reasons, perhaps having something to do with her "mom's characteristics," her being the oldest, or her own inner drive,[21] Ms. Marshall was one of the lucky ones who can take humiliation and turn it into determination. But many of the kids around her were not quite so resilient; she could see them getting "a raw deal." And for some reason, that bothered her: "I feel like I sense anybody's pain when they were going through changes. . . . I could sense it myself."[22]

---

17. Interview number 1, page 6, lines 30–31, 40. This and all subsequent quotations from Corva Marshall are taken from the transcripts of interviews with her conducted on Dec. 12, 1991, and Feb. 5, March 3, and June 25, 1992, in North Carolina. The citations are to typed transcripts of these interviews.

18. 1, 5, 1.

19. 1, 6, 40–42.

20. 1, 9, 4–16.

21. 1, 10, 39–47.

22. 1, 11, 44–49.

When she was in high school, Ms. Marshall didn't think to build a career around this unusual talent she had for sensing other people's pain. Instead, after washing dishes at the local fish camp as a young teenager, she took cosmetology courses in high school. She graduated with pretty good grades, got her state cosmetologist's license, and rented some space in a local beauty parlor. After a while she left her fledgling business to take a job making biscuits at Hardee's on the early shift. But she found that "I can't get up no more at 3:00 in the morning."[23] So she went back to making her living in the beauty business, washing and dyeing and straightening her neighbors' hair.

When her son turned four, even though she had a babysitter, she put him in a group day-care center. She made this decision for several reasons:

> I wanted him to start developing his educational habits, . . . to start interacting with other children . . . with both races or all races, . . . and to deal with people . . . to learn how to share, . . . to play with other kids and just, basically to get him involved with community type things.[24]

Her son was a very determined child; he loved his mamma; and he was great at sports. But he also had something wrong with his speech:

> He just can't form the words exactly right, . . . he know what he tries to say and he says it in a sentence, but sometimes it just get tangled up and I have to listen real hard.[25]

After a few months, she followed the path of her own mother and enrolled her son in Head Start. She made the switch because she was afraid that at the private day-care center her son wasn't getting enough to eat.[26] She also made it because she wanted him to have "more school atmosphere than just playing atmosphere."[27] She had decided that it was time for her son's education to start.[28]

---

23. 1, 14, 43.
24. 1, 18, 44–51.
25. 1, 16, 31–35.
26. 1, 19, 19–26.
27. 1, 20, 10–11.
28. 1, 18, 46–47.

Corva Marshall is happy about the changes that she feels Head Start has made in her son:

> It has helped him tremendously in sharing, and the speech. . . . [H]e loves his teachers. . . . He sits quieter. He raises his hand, and he has a thousand questions. He always has a lot of questions, but they're more sensible now. [H]e's always talking about the other children. . . . [H]e has a lot of friends now, where he wasn't able at one time to play well.[29]

After her own childhood memories of Head Start, she expected it to do good things for her son. She was surprised, however, to discover the program's effects on herself.

For Corva Marshall, getting involved in Head Start worked like a mirror, enabling her to look squarely at the course of her life. What she saw through that mirror was a complex reflection, the reflection of a woman with a desire, and a talent, for listening to other people and for feeling with them when they had been made to feel worthless:

> I listen to all the horror stories about people just going off losing their minds, and I couldn't help but feel like these people have some problems and there's nobody for them to go to express their problems and it's just building up and all of a sudden they explode. . . . I just not gonna be satisfied to think that all these people are just mean. I just think they have problems and with the pressures with the way society is today . . . there's got to be some way to reach some of these people. . . . And I feel like the best way to start is with the children, . . . by the time they get to teenhood they won't be totally gone, . . . maybe we can catch it by then. . . . I remember when we were in middle school, we used to go to the guidance counselor . . . and we discussed things. . . . [I]t takes a certain type person to talk to someone. . . . they need to be able to talk to all kinds of people. . . . I know for a fact that . . . [the white guidance counselors are] intimidated by darker skinned people, especially black boys, because they've been put into a stereotype . . . if you have a certain look about ya, you know, long hair, and you just look hard and ruggy, cut off jeans jacket. . . . Regardless of how, if I have to go and take karate classes and everything else that

29. 1, 21, 2–33, passim.

it takes I'm gonna let them kids know that they're not gonna get over on me, cause I'm there to help them.[30] . . . I know I can't reach everybody, but if I just reach one or two persons . . . who are on the bitter end, on the end of their rope, whether it be to kill someone or to commit suicide, I just feel like if that person has somebody that they can talk to, it might make a difference.[31]

She speculates that her need to listen is what drew her away from washing dishes and into styling hair. For in her beauty parlor, Corva Marshall could talk with her clients about their fears and their futures, especially the teenage girls.[32]

It was not until she got involved in Head Start, however, that Corva Marshall finally decided to pursue her childhood goal in a more straightforward way. She had always wanted to be a high-school guidance counselor, and "[Head Start] helped me to be more inspired about going back to school."[33]

Corva Marshall isn't sure quite how Head Start had this effect. In part, it was the regular parent meetings. These informal gatherings gave her day-to-day support in coping as a single parent. More importantly, however, the meetings gave her an opportunity to practice her skill, and thereby to affirm her commitment, of mutually supporting other women. The experience dissolved for her any clear line between what she "took away" from these meetings and what she "gave." For the talk at these meetings—the listening, remembering, confessing, cajoling, critiquing—broke down familiar distinctions between provider and consumer, helper and victim, us and them:

> [W]e basically get together and talk. . . . A lot of the parents are single parents, so we support each other. . . . Some are going to school, some are working, some are just home with the kids, but you know, we kind of help each other. It's good to know that no way is the wrong way. . . . [W]e kind of motivate each other. Plus, being a single parent is depressing. It really can be very depressing. So therefore, we concentrate on the parent. There's a lot of people who want [to go back to school . . . to get a good job, . . . to get

30. 3, 24–27, passim.
31. 3, 32, 14–20.
32. 3, 28, 9–10.
33. 3, 24, 6–8.

involved with your child at their school or whatever] but they don't have anybody to talk to about it. And that's where the parent involvement comes along. . . . They want to know other people who did it. . . . You can relate to somebody else's situation. . . . You know, it's sad to say, I think a lot of situations are made for the people who are already down for 'em to stay down a lot of times. Because, that's just the way the system is. A lot of people can be helped, . . . but they don't know which way to go, so they just taking it as is.[34]

Though her participation in parent meetings was surely important, her work on the program's policy council played an even larger role in inspiring Corva Marshall to go back to school. Although Ms. Marshall considers herself shy, she has also always been curious. At the first parent meeting that she attended, she knew that she wanted to get more involved in Head Start. The policy council seemed an intriguing opportunity.

[F]rom day one when we had the very first parent meeting at the recreational center and the policy council was brought up, I knew I wanted to be on the policy council. . . . I remember going to [the parent involvement coordinator] and saying something about it. And then I said something to my son's teacher whenever I saw her. . . . I didn't know what it involved, but all I knew is that it was something that I had a chance to voice my opinion about some things, and that's what I wanted to do.[35]

Without much competition from the handful of other women who showed up at parent meetings, Ms. Marshall got her wish.

Participating on the council was very important for Ms. Marshall, but it was not an experience that empowered her in any simple way. Indeed, especially at the beginning of the year, she felt quite uncomfortable at council meetings. She was one of the younger council members, and therefore she felt herself to be even more intimidated than some of the older women.[36] The meetings seemed like a litany of "yes ma'am's" to the director's agenda. The parents sat there in silence, too intimi-

---

34. 3, 23–25, passim.
35. 3, 34, 40–44; 3, 35.
36. 3, 11, 3–14.

dated to raise questions about the proposals that the director put before them:

> [A] lot of times when things are presented to us, it's just a yea and nay situation.[37] . . . [W]e don't really know what we're making decisions on.[38] . . . [A] lot of times I feel like the council vote, I included, and really not knowing the facts about the situation, but just going on assumption that [the director] has done her job.[39] . . . [W]e could vote all day long, but for our vote to mean something . . .[40] I don't think we've had a lot of impact.[41]

But she was eager to make the most of the opportunity that the council offered, so she simply determined that she would feel more at ease:

> All I can do is the best that I can and that's all that they can expect of me, and once I start looking at it in that, in that aspect I feel more comfortable.[42]

The other women noted this determination and Corva Marshall's leadership potential. At midyear, the policy council's chairperson unexpectedly resigned, and several women asked Corva if she would agree to run for interim policy council chair:

> I said, "Well." The problem I had was with the parliamentary procedure. I said, "I just don't know the procedure properly." . . . [Then the parent involvement coordinator] said "Well, Corva, I think you will make an excellent chairperson." And you know, when a person tells you to do something long enough, you feel a little more confident. It's just like somebody telling you [you] can't do something, and then after a while you start thinking "I can't do it, because I've been told I can't do it."[43]

---

37. 2, 33, 13–15.
38. 2, 35, 21–30.
39. 3, 12, 48–51.
40. 2, 36, 19–22.
41. 2, 8, 15.
42. 3, 11, 12–14.
43. 3, 21, 29–36.

In spite of the fact that the director supported another candidate, Corva Marshall won the election.

As chair, she no longer felt that she could sit back and let the director do the talking:

> [As chairperson] you want to be more or less a leader.[44] . . . I want to know what I'm doing. I want to go through the procedure correctly.[45] . . . I'll just practice the best that I can with the parliamentary procedure and just hope . . . I know a little bit about it so I have a little something to go on. And the fact that I want to learn is a plus. . . . I could just come in to have somebody read off word for word what I'm supposed to say, but I don't want it to be like that . . . because it's part of my responsibility as chairperson to know or at least strive to try to learn as much as I can and then let it go with the flow a little bit. In other words, it's more or less a challenge to me.[46]

So Corva took up the challenge of learning more about the program and the council's role. She learned about the teachers' responsibilities and, consequently, began to respect them more.

> They have a lot of paperwork, a lot of meetings they have to go to, seminars, a lot of literature they have to read.[47] . . . In the beginning we fill out all those papers, and I don't know what we think they do with the papers. We think they trash them or they just put them back in lost and found, but, you know, they have to really go back and look at those files and compare it to the beginning, to the middle, to the end of the year, and look at the progress. It just helps me not to take their job so for granted now that I understand what all they had to go through.[48]

She learned something about Head Start's budget:

> The budget is thousands of dollars, thousands of dollars for this, for that. And people fail to realize how much it cost to run a

---

44. 3, 10, 48–49.
45. 3, 11, 4–7.
46. 3, 11, 3–48.
47. 2, 5, 33–37.
48. 3, 3, 44–52.

program like this. I was looking at the dental [budget]. The dental
bill I think was like $17,000. . . . [A] couple of children needed
anywhere close to almost $2,000 of work done on an individual
child, because of the decay—the way the teeth were in such bad
shape.[49]

But she was determined to learn more:

I can look at the budget now. I can sit and look, but I would really
like to sit one-on-one with [the director] and figure out why some
money is spent more on one category, why it is so much for this
particular category.[50]

Corva Marshall's self-education made her a loyal supporter of the
Head Start program:

[I]t's a blessing really for a lot of these parents, because I couldn't
begin to realize or imagine how some of the children's teeth, or
other things, go unnoticed or undetected, because most parents,
sad to say, feel like a child doesn't need to go to the dentist until
they have a tooth ache. I like Head Start because it just doesn't look
at the education aspect. It thinks of the health, it thinks of the
overall atmosphere of the child, it's living in the child, you know,
and it hits everything.[51]

But her self-education about the program also made her see that
the parents, through the policy council, had substantial, but entirely
unrealized, formal powers:

The policy council has responsibilities that I would have never
thought that the parents of the children of Head Start would have
any decision over.[52] I don't think that any of the members but a few
may be aware of [these responsibilities]. . . . It has a lot of power,
and I think we all took it for granted, because I took it for granted
until I got into it more. I had no idea, you know. We can question a

---

49. 3, 8–9, 51–52; 11–22.
50. 3, 8, 33–38.
51. 3, 8–9, passim.
52. 2, 4, 29–32.

lot of things that . . . we might not feel comfortable about, and we don't have to brush it under the rug.[53]

She came to understand these powers most fully through a training session on the policy council that she attended at a parent conference. She came away from this session determined to figure out how her own program's council could begin to exercise some of its powers:

> My problem is I would like to know how we can go about applying the power that we have . . . that's what I want to learn more about. . . . [I]f there was any doubt in our mind, we could postpone the hiring [of a candidate] to get more detail about this person. . . . [I]t's in our power to do that, but as far as when to do that and how to do it, [that] is the weak problem, the weak point of it.[54]

She had a feeling that if the council could realize its potential powers, its powers to hire staff and to allocate funding, the program, and the larger community, would improve. For one thing, teachers who were carefully screened by the council would be much more likely to work effectively with poor families:

> [S]ome of the teachers, I'm sure that they study their credentials and everything[55] . . . [but] you need to be a people person dealing with this because you're touching a lot. First of all, the children most of the time come from a very sensitive background. And the parent is probably in a delicate situation. . . . [I]t's usually a single parent home, and they're usually on, you know, working with the social service program, and you need to be an understanding person of this situation.[56]

In her vision, the screening process should be exhaustive:

> [The candidates should] come to the policy council meeting . . . be introduced to us, in person . . . for us to ask questions so we can just get a feel for that person . . . because every parent wants their child to be in an atmosphere where they are going to feel comfort-

---

53. 4, 11, 21–26.
54. 4, 10–13, passim.
55. 4, 16.
56. 4, 17, 1–8.

able. . . . Maybe [we could] spend the day with [the candidate], in the classroom, and watch how they do. I would like to be able to just sit back and watch, observe how this applicant is going to go throughout the day. Can she handle it?[57]

In addition to improving the quality of Head Start's staff, Corva Marshall had the sense that a policy council that was more in command of its own collective powers could also have an impact on the wider community. For, in her view:

If enough parents get involved and protest a certain situation, that's the only way you are going to get any change most of the time.[58]

In Corva Marshall's judgment, the policy council started to work better over the course of the year. The women began to feel more comfortable together, more familiar with the routines of council meetings. After a particularly "good" meeting, she noted that

There was a little bit more discussion about certain topics. . . . It's not like [the director] has the last word on everything. . . . [The parents were] making sure they knew what they were voting for. . . . [T]here wasn't as much tension. . . . [I]t moved rather smoothly, and we carried out the business. . . . I learned more, and I expressed myself more, and I think a lot of people expressed themselves. . . . [W]hat we have now seems more like a policy council. . . . It's sort of coming together. . . . I enjoyed it.[59]

But still, during her short tenure as chair of the council, she didn't manage to awaken her colleagues to their full powers. There were just too many changes in the group that year, "faces come, faces go."[60] And Corva, like the other council members, was just too busy hassling with her own life.

Yet her learning that year about the council—about the gap between its legal promise and its real, enacted power—was very important for Corva Marshall. This learning turned out to be more important

57. 4, 18, passim.
58. 3, 10, 17–20.
59. 3, 12–14, passim.
60. 3, 13, 43–44.

to her than the more tangible benefits of her policy council tenure, like her new engagement with her son's education, her new confidence about speaking in public, or her new savvy about Robert's Rules. It was even more important than her new friends. For that learning—her mental grappling with the council's unrealized promise—cast light on a similar gap that she was starting to acknowledge in her own life:

> A lot of times deep down inside I know I have the potential to do things . . . but sometimes I need a little push from somebody else to get it out of me.[61]

Somehow, by feeling the power gap within the policy council—and by assiduously studying her experience—Corva Marshall became able to see, and stand up to, a similar disjuncture in her own life.

Through her reflections about her experience in Head Start, and especially on the policy council, Corva Marshall discovered, or more accurately devised, three strategic lessons. The first of these lessons was about the power that comes from asking questions, even when those questions feel very hard to ask. She describes what she learned from council meetings:

> It's just helping to open up our eyes to questions, to just being able to . . . voice your opinion just to know behind closed doors what things are.[62] I'm realizing that if there is any bit of doubt, just question it so it is clear in your mind. . . . A lot of times it's questions that we might think . . . sound stupid, but a question is a question to me. I don't think there's no limits on how smart or how dumb a question is.[63]

The second lesson was about the power that comes from looking closely, with patience, at the details of the everyday routines that one is lulled into taking for granted. She describes what she learned from participating in the annual review of program performance that federal guidelines require each policy council to conduct:

> [W]e look at the teachers, we look at the students. See if the teachers are doing their job, in coherence with the [performance

61. 3, 21, 46–48.
62. 2, 30, 35–41.
63. 3, 12, 48–52; 3, 13, 1–5.

standards]. . . . And then we look at the children and see if they are
coming along the way they should be. . . . Going into details and
really behind-closed-doors type seeing of what goes on. . . . I'm
beginning to understand different things that were new to me in
the beginning.[64]

The third lesson was about the power that comes from mutual
support. We have seen how the power of mutual support was brought
home to Ms. Marshall through her experience in classroom-level parent
meetings.[65] But she also experienced the power of solidarity as she
battled against the shyness and discomfort that sought to keep her
quiet:

> Whenever one person starts asking questions or expressing their
> opinion, . . . other people start doing that. I noticed that with this
> meeting. I could sense [it] in the last meeting, but this meeting was
> . . . I felt like [it] was a good meeting.[66]

It was through these three strategies—asking questions, looking
closely, and seeking practices of mutual support—that Ms. Marshall
was able to trust the promise that the policy council presented, but at
the same time name its failure. And it was through these same three
strategies that she came to accept, critique, and finally change the
course of her life.

The discrepancy between the policy council's formal promise of
power sharing and its ritualized, staff-dominated reality has led pro-
gressive scholars to dismiss these councils as a fairly crude instrument
of co-optation, of class and race domination.[67] Yet ironically, it was
precisely this discrepancy—the gap between the council's democratic
promise and its obviously compromised practice—that gave Corva
Marshall the insight and will that she needed to change her life. Or
rather, it was Corva Marshall's own *reading* of her Head Start

---

64. 3, 2, 7–40.

65. See text and notes, supra.

66. 3, 14, 9–12.

67. See, for example, Mary Klenz, "Parent Involvement in Head Start and the
Reproduction of Class" (unpublished master's thesis, University of North Carolina at
Charlotte, 1993), concluding on the basis of field observations that meaningful involvement in Head Start policy councils is precluded by the structures of class and race
hierarchy that shape interactions between parents and staff at council meetings.

experience—what she made of the gap between the promise and the practice that she encountered in the policy council—that enabled her to make changes in her life.

For instead of reacting to this gap with outrage, or withdrawal, like some of her peers, Corva Marshall found it to be a compelling moral puzzle. This puzzle compelled her to ponder her own shyness, her own complicity in the pervasive silence at council meetings. This puzzle enticed her to seek innovations in the council's structure and the parents' practice, changes that might strengthen, and focus, their voice.

This puzzle also challenged Corva Marshall to spell out her vague intuition that the program would indeed be improved if the parents used their power. She groped for the words to make this intuition clear. Gradually, she came to understand that parents on the hiring committees would make a huge difference, because they could tell which applicants would be likely to respect and empathize with the poor. She came to understand that with veteran parents in charge of new parent orientation and educational programming, the vitality of parent involvement could finally begin to improve. And she came to understand that if parents worked with the staff in budget planning, funding allocations would better reflect the community's needs.

In March of her year in Head Start, Corva Marshall enrolled in a degree program in counseling at a community college about forty miles from her home. It wasn't easy for Ms. Marshall to go back to school. Although she had finished high school, that was almost ten years ago, and she had taken a vocational track to learn her trade of doing hair:

> I took my placement test and I was kind of disappointed with myself. . . . I don't use a lot of paragraphs doing hair.[68]

Once she started school, her schedule had a dizzying pace:

> [I'll] drive to [college] early in the morning [after I] see my son get on the bus at a quarter to seven. . . . [H]opefully I could be finished [with classes] by 12:00, 12:30 at the latest, because I want to start my appointments here at least by 2:00. . . . And I still got to spend time for my son. . . . [On the week-ends] I am busy with church. I guess it's a blessing that I don't have a boyfriend at this time.[69]

68. 3, 31, 34–41.
69. 3, 30–31, passim.

Yet her first term at school went very well:

I came out with an A and a B. . . . it was a great learning experience. . . . I made a lot of new friends and it was wonderful.[70]

She is planning to transfer to a four-year college when she com-
pletes her A.A. degree in counseling. And she thinks that eventually she
would like to use her counseling credential, and all of her hands-on
experience, in a parent involvement staff position with Project Head
Start.[71]

To Corva Marshall, then, participating in the Head Start program
has meant both analyzing the program's failure and responding to its
promise. It has meant gaining in personal autonomy—acknowledging
her fears, affirming her talents, acting upon her private goals—but
doing this work through practices of mutual support. Corva Marshall's
experience has blurred the rigid conceptual boundaries between community and self-interest, and between co-opted and fully franchised
political power. The policy council's failed promise drew forth intense
moral energy from Corva Marshall. This was energy that she in turn
could draw upon to take on the Head Start program, actively, on her
own terms, remaking it into a kind of homeplace in the shelter of which
she could nurture her own life.

70. 4, 29, 14; 4, 30, 33, 37.
71. 4, 31, 6–9.

Afterword: Constancies and Commonalities in This Volume's Law Stories

Gary Bellow and Martha Minow

Starting with the story of Gladys and Rita, the stories in this volume concern people who are relatively powerless in both the legal system and the society at large. None of the clients described here paid for the legal help they received. All of their lawyers and legal workers provided help to them under auspices that emphasized access and vindication as primary values. Stories so situated may not offer any guide to understanding the vast realms of legal work driven largely by economic motives, but they surely provide a unique window on what has come to be called public interest practice. It may surprise and trouble some to note how many conflicts and tensions remain in this practice, even with economic pressures held somewhat in check.

Even within this small subset of the bar, the practices described in these stories reflect a very wide range of contexts, including such diverse settings as a Head Start program, the bankruptcy court, a juvenile detention center, and an unemployment benefits bureaucracy. In most of these settings the legal rules have far less to do with results than might be supposed from attending a law school class or consulting the writings and treatises that contain the "rules of law" that "govern" the proceedings. Rather, routines established by bureaucracies, political and personal interests, and plain luck set the overarching frameworks for results. Whatever choices do appear for the legal workers and their clients, choices about how to argue and how to behave, and even choices about what choices to make or seize, they are embedded in these realities.

This seems to us the most obvious common ground among the stories included here. Although they touch on many themes, each of them explores, in some way, the impact of context on choice, and the salience of identity in shaping motives and options. We offer here elaborations on these themes, remaining mindful, indeed hopeful, that others will make very different sense of the stories we have included.

Context

The authors draw on an array of legal frameworks in charting the fate of the contested claims that they describe. Lenora Lapidus tells of a probate court asked to act in the "best interests of the child" and return the child to her mother. Staughton and Alice Lynd write about a legislator pressed to introduce a bill that would enhance the protection afforded retired workers whose former employer is seeking bankruptcy. Lucie White portrays a Head Start program administrator facing diverse responses by parents to the federal program's requirement of parental participation. In these and other essays, the specifics of each situation—its participants, setting, and culture—are critical to the outcome.

At the same time, all the essays can be read against a backdrop of familiar, media-shaped images of what legal controversies entail in contemporary America: first, there are wrongs, defined in terms of enacted rules or established norms; then, there are individuals who seek to right the wrongs, or obtain compensation for them, by directly challenging the wrongdoer. Finally, the claims are presented, through oral and written argument, to functional, relatively neutral institutions designed to handle such disputes. The results reflect the quality and character of the claims presented in this process.

What we believe the stories included here offer is an understanding of how such images change when examined against descriptions of law-in-operation. In Lenora Lapidus's troubling account of her efforts to help her client regain custody of her child, her adversary is not a contentious partisan, but caution and routine operating in an institutionalized culture of public agencies that assume risks without examining them, defer to experts whose judgments are never independently evaluated, and treat delay as an inevitable, costless feature of their operation. Changing such a culture without producing a reckless deference to parents' wishes over children's needs requires efforts much more complex than what is implied by the image of a heroic lawyer righting a wrong.

Similarly, in Lynn Weaver's thoughtful description of her advocacy of unemployment benefits for her deaf client, the underlying problem, as she frames it, is not the agency's misinterpretation of the governing rules concerning her client's entitlement to benefits. Instead, the deeper problem is a widely shared complex of beliefs and attitudes among agency personnel that cannot, or will not, sufficiently individualize judgments to consider how a hearing-impaired employee could function effectively in the workplace. A legal institution constituted in this way presents very different problems for advocates than an institution that is, for whatever reason, clearly violating some established rule or norm (although the Americans With Disabilities Act, adopted after these events, creates a new norm of individualized accommodation).

Indeed, particular institutional cultures and dynamics define whether and in what sense established rules can even be raised in a dispute. Two of the stories, for example, again and again emphasize how initiatives on behalf of clients can be effectively stymied by the absence of any forum to hear the clients' claims. Nell Minow sets out the barriers to shareholder efforts to hold corporate officers accountable. Alice and Staughton Lynd, in their depiction of the struggle of retirees against a bankrupt company's decision to foreclose their benefits, emphasize how the difficulties in finding a forum to present their clients' claims interfered with their clients' efforts to be heard.

Gritty detail similarly complicates the image of criminal cases as an adversarial combat between good and evil, power and powerlessness. Abbe Smith struggles with how it felt to be a criminal defense lawyer suddenly thrust into the role of a victim's advocate. Charles Ogletree recounts how the experience of working as a public defender on behalf of a young man seemed to require far more of himself than simple courtroom defense. For both of these storytellers, it is the narrowness of the criminal justice system's conception of the attorney role, and the limited room it offers for influence within the lawyer-client and victim-prosecutor relationship, that define their experiences and their clients' vulnerabilities.

To be sure, the contexts described by the authors may not fully or adequately capture the problems experienced by the clients or advocates in their narratives. The stories give little attention, for example, to beginnings outside of an explicit legal frame; that is, to the times when the problems were not seen by participants as legal problems at all. They also say very little about the competing demands—personal and professional—that an advocate inevitably experiences as he or she guides a case to conclusion. Each case is, thus, pictured as more free-standing and independent of the advocate's own continuing personal life and ongoing involvement in the legal field in which he or she practices than seems plausible.

Nevertheless, the conceptions of legal conflict and the dispute-presenting settings depicted here provide a valuable antidote to shallow or sentimentalized depictions of legal work. They also make clear that public interest lawyering, whether conducted in Legal Services or public defender offices or in other venues, is carried on in the face of powerful pressures supporting the status quo. There may be times when effort and craft will open up large possibilities for changing a given institution or practice. Reforms of the institutional arrangements described here can be made; many are underway. But the rigidity and resistance of the processes and arrangements evoked by this book call for something more subtle and more ambitious than reforms of particular rules, or even particular institutions, if they are to be changed. Rather, they require an acute awareness of the openings, gaps, and ambivalences that exist on the ground in each setting. Whatever the room to maneuver in any legal context, maneuvering is rarely as easily accomplished as scripted versions of legal action may suggest. In each of these stories, questions of appropriate and possible conduct become problems of strategic intervention, problems of action in the face of resistance and constraint. Each of the authors finds he or she must take these constraints as the starting point for the strategies, and often the goals, that are pursued.

Agency

How, then, do the lawyers and clients depicted in these chapters respond to the institutional realities they encounter? What strategic opportunities do they exploit or shape? Within or despite the constraints they describe, many of the authors recount successes. Abbe Smith does succeed in exercising influence in her less familiar role, persuading the prosecutor to seek exclusion of testimony about her client despite his earlier failure to object to its introduction in court. Lynn Weaver alters the outcome of the unemployment administration's judgment. Alice and Staughton Lynd, who powerfully recount their clients' vulnerabilities, do obtain a restoration of a good portion of their benefits in the very forums that seem so unavailing. Others proved far less successful in achieving their own and their clients' goals. When they fail, what are the reasons? When they succeed, how much can their own choices be credited?

One answer to these questions—clearly suggested by many of the chapters—is sheer perseverance. In law work, will itself, along with words (and sometimes wisdom), is strategy. People can exit from conflict and take the consequences. Indeed, professionals can and often do exit, and guide, legitimate, or force the exit of those they represent. But exit is not the route taken by the legal workers in these stories. Lapidus tells how she returned to court again and again, more than forty times in an eighteen-month period. Ogletree continues his connection with his client before, during, and after the judicial hearing and pursues ends that adjudication did not and perhaps could not offer. Minow pursues avenue after avenue, as do the Lynds, to work against the exclusion of their clients from centers of power or influence. Given the frustrations, disappointments, and constraints that these stories present, the repeated choices to persevere in these accounts are striking.

Equally important responses to questions concerning the sources of action in effective law work are skill, imagination, and judgment. In chapter after chapter, arguments are framed and presented; adversaries are influenced, maneuvered, and positioned. Clients' and lawyers' voices are intermingled, or separated, the clients acting on their own or pushed to pursue strategies that lawyers could not successfully carry out themselves. This is the central theme of Alice and Staughton Lynd's description of the efforts of the members of Solidarity USA to regain their lost retirement and health benefits. It is a significant dimension of what can be learned from Lucie White's powerful account of how one woman gained and exercised power in the course of participating in Head Start's parental participation component. And it is the source of the warning, posed by Anthony Alfieri, that strategic skill and commitment can, themselves, blind attorneys to the ways clients' interests and voices can be silenced by those that represent them. There is a craft dimension of legal work that needs to be far better understood.

But these possibilities should not lead us to evoke images of action in law work more grandiose and dramatic than seem to be supported by the authors' accounts. Members of the legal profession, despite lawyers' protestations to the contrary, have self-interested reasons to prefer spacious accounts of lawyers' work and its significance. Popular culture often reinforces images of lawyers as heroes and villains. Even the academic literature on lawyering, although less complimentary and more cognizant of the pervasive bureaucratization of much of the legal order, regularly depicts lawyers as powerful enough to be "double agents" or shapers of significant events.

As the stories in this volume make clear, the problem with those descriptions is that law work is almost exclusively word work, done in a variety of settings among people of varying status and influence. Lawyers' tools are words. Within the institutions of public and private bureaucracies, in courtrooms, in legislatures, on telephones, and in one-on-one meetings with clients and adversaries, legal workers use words to help clients get what they want or to avoid what they do not want. Lawyers use words to press at the cracks of closed doors and to persuade the doorkeepers to open them. The drama, if there is one, is created through precise, carefully constructed statement; there is not much action of a heroic nature.

Moreover, law work is performed over time, usually with far more lag and waiting time than television and movie renditions of trials convey, and with accomplishments, when success is achieved at all, far more limited and incremental than are typically depicted in recent fiction about law or autobiographical accounts of highly publicized legal conflicts. Perhaps there are too many words reported in these stories and not enough descriptions of silence, body language, waiting, and down time. Whether done by lay persons, law students, or lawyers, law work most commonly involves pushing and pulling within some more or less rule-guided institution. One could elevate the seriousness and detail of his prosaic definition, but Holmes probably had it right when he described law practice as a "shopkeepers' art," concerned with agreements, sales pitches, or plans designed to avoid some predicted disaster. It is difficult, and seriously misleading, to make these events and interactions more dramatic and significant than they are.

Indeed, even within the small subset of public interest practitioners referenced here, Holmes's description is surprisingly accurate. What these essays offer to the probing reader is not uplift, but useful insights into the ways these prosaic arts are performed, the choices they entail, and the ends they serve.

Identity

In the course of their involvement, the legal workers in these stories gave definition to their commitments, to their clients' claims, to their clients as individuals, and to themselves. The basic tool of law practice—words—became a vehicle, not only of persuasion, but of invention and reinvention of the identities of those affected by the legal process. One reading of the stories assembled here would examine how "law talk" works to define both speaker and audience, altering and creating identities and self-understandings of those it touches.

In some instances, the outcome of a legal dispute turns almost entirely on how an individual is characterized and understood. This is obvious in family law, where the issue may be as concrete as who a child's father is, or as profound as who is a good parent. When lawyers and clients in such cases develop alternate ways to characterize their clients, the effort may profoundly affect both the client's and the lawyer's sense of self. In representing a woman who had lost custody of her child, Lenora Lapidus confronted the system's labeling of her client as "a bad mother." No particular legal rule or procedure mattered as much as that characterization. Once having been assigned, that label became a very difficult one to replace or reformulate. Could Lapidus re-present her client as a good mother? As a person who once had been a bad mother but no longer was? The usual difficulties of this task were compounded by Lapidus's own identity as a student and a young person. Could she secure the authority to author the identity of her client as a good mother? Could she find a comfortable way to shape her client's identity before the court without seeming to control or dominate that client? In the essay, Lapidus found herself searching for ways to convey her client's voice, perhaps because the legal proceedings offered so little space for the client to speak for herself.

In representing a man who was deaf and who lost his job, Lynn Weaver needed to alter the characterization given by his employer of his conduct at work, while simultaneously challenging stereotypes of disabled persons on which the characterization was grounded. Although her client was deemed unresponsive to his supervisor at work, he could be presented as able and competent, if only the employer had provided minimal accommodation. In developing this line of argument, Weaver confronted her own experiences as someone with a hearing impairment. She viewed the effects of disability from a different angle when she realized how she may have miscommunicated with the client in the same ways that others at times had miscommunicated with her. Advocating for someone else seemed to grant Weaver more room to think about her own needs and entitlements—especially her own claims for accommodation in the legal system itself.

Issues of identity also arise as lawyers accept or construct their own roles as advocates. Inhabiting a lawyering role may lead to identification with one kind of client or a particular side of a case. Performing that role in particular ways may set sharp limits on the very process of self-definition that legal conflicts foster.

As we already noted, the two essays set in the criminal context explicitly deal with tensions between role and identity. Abbe Smith reexamines how her role as a criminal defense attorney predisposed her against the prosecutorial perspective and complicated her ability to assist the victim of a horrible crime. A woman was murdered and another attacked; they happened to be lovers. Everyone involved in the case conceded that the defendant acted in response to the sight of two lesbians enjoying a quiet romantic moment. How would Smith accommodate her identities as defense attorney and as someone personally appalled by this defendant's motivation? Could she draw upon her knowledge of strategies and gambits available to the defense to secure a conviction, or a particular disposition? Working on behalf of the one woman who survived the crime, could Smith protect her from abuse or misuse by either the prosecution or the defense in a system explicitly tilted to favor the defendant? Reflecting on her role in the case also afforded Smith a chance to think more deeply about herself.

Charles Ogletree is faced with the apparent limitations of his role as defense attorney when he represents a juvenile who might avoid punishment but who would, then, probably commit more offenses until again apprehended. In "doing his job," Ogletree remains acutely aware of his own identity as an African American raised in an inner city. He represents someone who could have been his friend or even himself as a youth. Did these parallels between their lives give Ogletree a special obligation, or opportunity, to stretch the usual lawyer's role and become a role model or father figure for his young, poor, Black male client? Or would responding to such a bond strain the proper stance of the zealous criminal defense attorney and the boundaries of work needed to preserve a lawyer's energy and ability to serve other clients?

Such questions inevitably evoke the dangers of paternalism, an issue that occupies all the legal workers in these essays. The very definitions of *lawyer* and *client* create hierarchy because the lawyer has knowledge, professional expertise, and status that the client often lacks. Alfieri, for example, describes the lawyer who took his cues from the legal rules and the routine aspects of legal services delivery, only to realize how this process produced a picture of the client as dependent and helpless rather than dignified, strong, and choosing. Alfieri's essay raises questions about the sources of the imposed identity. Did the legal framework itself call for a particular picture of the client in order to make the food stamps application process move smoothly or successfully? Or did the lawyer need to construct the client's identity as a dependent person in order to ease his handling of so many cases each day? Or to support his own constructed identity as a legal services do-gooder? What conceptions of his identity would lead a lawyer to look for other versions of the client's identity? How does recasting the client in terms of her strengths affect the lawyer's own sense of himself and his role?

Finally there is the question of the effects of legal experience itself on identity. Many of the stories suggest that identities forged in law-oriented conflicts and maneuvers can challenge imposed patterns of passive victimization. Lucie White's examination of parents participating in Head Start found people who might be viewed by some as dependent and powerless. Yet they drew upon their identities as mothers to enlarge their self-confidence and capacities for action. One woman in particular developed a career and took steps to realize it. White explores how the woman's identities as both a mother and an alumna of the Head Start program contributed to these developments. Each participant in White's essay is affected differently by the ways the parental participation dimensions of Head Start disempower or empower the individuals who take part in the program.

Similarly, in their essays, Alice and Staughton Lynd and Nell Minow present specific struggles designed to surmount the passive victimization of retirees disowned by their union and their former employer, and stockholders ignored by corporate managers. The Lynds show how the retirees sought to position themselves as rightful claimants rather than victims; the Lynds also themselves tried to foster a political movement approach to the problem rather than minister to individual clients in need. In the course of efforts to work through the maze of bureaucracies, bankruptcy procedures, and legislative politics, at least some of the retired people they represented did become politically engaged and active. The Lynds capture a conversation in which some of the retirees tried on the identity of "radical" and claimed an alliance with early radicals, also known as the nation's founders and drafters of the Constitution. Although they record great frustrations with the legal systems they encountered, the Lynds also report some successes, of which the most notable seems to be the retirees' new identities as activists.

When Nell Minow examines what avenues were and were not available to shareholders organized through institutional investors such as pension funds, the image of shareholders as wealthy fat cats disappears. These shareholders are merely small pensioners remote from the channels of communication and power. When a major company decided to spend money in ways of no use to these shareholders, this powerlessness became absolutely apparent. Minow heard of the situation and essentially invented a client—the shareholders behind the institutional investors. She also invented a role for herself as an alternative kind of advocate in a world dominated by the insular and self-interested shareholder derivative suit bar. Sorting through the layers of public and private governance rules to find ways to demand accountability to the shareholders, Minow raises questions about who is the client. Even more profoundly, she asks who really is the corporation. What lies behind the legal fiction that the corporation is a person? One of Minow's most intriguing discussions concerns the low-level bank clerk who took seriously her identity as guardian of the interests of the investors when she questioned the proxy statement announcing the decision to finance Armand Hammer's autobiography and art museum. The bank clerk lacked any legal authority to object. Without her effort to flag the issue, however, there would be no story to tell.

There is much that is compelling and satisfying in what was accomplished in these stories. Yet it is also fair to note how often these authors, with all their dogged and resolute concern for the causes and clients they embrace, felt they had to shape their claims, and often their identities, to fit expectations of what is appropriate and acceptable within specific contexts. Whether this tack ignored opportunities for deeper challenges to the status quo they faced remains an open question. The storytellers' own tones and descriptions of strongly felt limitations may be the best guide to the nature of the systems in which they work, and the abilities of those they serve to alter or avoid these systems.

Questions

Each of the stories raises questions for reformers. Should reformers focus on changing rules or changing bureaucratic routines? Is it better to seek discretionary rules to grant lawyers more room to maneuver within institutions or better to seek clear rules that could limit failures and abuses by bureaucrats? Should questions of identity be fair game for strategic lawyering or are they too important, too fragile, or too personal to justify that approach?

The stories also invite questions for those, in law school and in practice, who are becoming lawyers. Is it more important to master the routines of law practice or to search for ways to break the routine? What is the proper place of the personal and intimate in working on behalf of clients? How can one maintain a proper tension between commitment and distance, and between going for whatever the client could get compared with evaluating what would be right or just?

The questions for clients are similarly numerous. Should lawyers be trusted? Should other professionals be enlisted before or during legal proceedings? Should nonprofessional, community-based approaches be pursued alongside or instead of legal strategies to meet the needs of poor or disadvantaged people?

Finally, the essays suggest questions for those who study human experience. Law stories have stories within them—stories told by their authors and subjects to persuade, console, or understand others. How do law stories illuminate the place of stories in human lives? How do legal workers make meaning of their experiences? Do emotional rather than analytic patterns govern more powerfully in crafting narratives from painful or confrontational encounters with the law? What kinds of stories can communicate the intensity and richness of experiences that will permit readers to make their own interpretations while offering portrayals that are recognizable to participants?

The story form selects and moves forward; inventive storytellers let us see the very process of selection they employ and the resistance of memory and experience to their embodiment in narrative. Our hope is to find more of such storytellers, to prompt and produce more stories, more questions, and more ways to organize and reorganize our understandings of law and life.

Contributors

Anthony V. Alfieri is an associate professor of law at the University of Miami School of Law where he teaches civil procedure, lawyering, and ethics. He has long served as a legal advocate for poor people working with both legal aid and grassroots community organizations. He has published widely on poverty law, ethics, and the legal profession.

Gary Bellow is the Louis D. Brandeis Professor of Law at Harvard Law School and Faculty Director of the School's Clinical Programs. He is the author, with Bea Moulton, of the *Lawyering Process* (New York: Foundation Press, 1979), and numerous articles on clinical teaching, law practice and the delivery of legal services in low income communities.

Lenora M. Lapidus is the 1994–1996 John J. Gibbons Fellow in Public Interest and Constitutional Law at Crummy, Del Deo, Dolan, Griffinger, and Vecchione in Newark, New Jersey. As a Gibbons fellow, Ms. Lapidus litigates a broad range of constitutional and public interest cases on behalf of poor and underrepresented individuals in New Jersey. Her current caseload includes issues concerning termination of parental rights, battered woman's syndrome self-defense, mandatory HIV testing, affordable housing, prisoners' rights, and New Jersey's death penalty. Ms. Lapidus also serves as an adjunct clinical law professor in the Constitutional Litigation Clinic at Rutgers Law School. Previously, she litigated abortion rights cases at the Center for Reproductive Law and Policy in New York and served as a law clerk to the Honorable Richard Owen in the United States District Court for the Southern District of New York. Ms. Lapidus graduated cum laude from Harvard Law School in 1990. While a law student, she represented low-income clients in domestic, housing, and public benefits cases through the Harvard Legal Aid Bureau. The story told in her essay, "Maintaining the Status Quo: Institutional Obstacles in a Child Custody Dispute," involves the case of a woman Ms. Lapidus represented in a divorce and custody proceeding while a student attorney at the Harvard Legal Aid Bureau.

Alice and **Staughton Lynd** work as attorneys at Northeast Ohio Legal Services in Youngstown, Ohio. They have jointly edited *Rank and File: Personal Histories by Working-Class Organizers* (3d ed., New York: Monthly Review Press, 1988); *Homeland: Oral Histories of Palestine and Palestinians* (New York: Olive Branch Press, 1994); and *Nonviolence in America: A Documentary History* (2d ed., Maryknoll, N.Y.: Orbis Books, 1995).

Martha Minow is a Professor of Law at Harvard Law School. She is the author of *Making All the Difference: Inclusion, Exclusion, and American Law* (Ithaca, N.Y.: Cornell University Press, 1990); the editor of *Family Matters: Readings on Family Lives and Law* (New York: The New Press, 1993); and co-editor with Austin Sarat and Michael Ryan of *Narrative, Violence, and the Law: The Essays of Robert Cover* (Ann Arbor: University of Michigan Press, 1992).

Nell Minow is a principal of Lens, Inc., which enhances the value of focus companies through use of shareholder ownership rights. She formerly was president of Institutional Shareholder Services, Inc., which advises institutional investors on issues of corporate governance, including analysis of more than 6,400 companies' proxies each year. Ms. Minow is a graduate of Sarah Lawrence College and the University of Chicago Law School. With Robert A. G. Monks, she is coauthor of *Power and Accountability*, published in 1991 by HarperBusiness, and *Corporate Governance*, a textbook published by Blackwell in 1995.

Charles Ogletree is a professor of law and the director of the Criminal Justice Institute at Harvard Law School. He has written extensively on legal issues, particularly those focusing on the criminal justice system. He is coauthor of a book, *Beyond the Rodney King Story*, which examines police conduct in minority communities. Professor Ogletree served as a public defender for eight years in the District of Columbia, representing adults and juveniles in criminal cases.

Abbe Smith is the deputy director of the Criminal Justice Institute at Harvard Law School, a clinical instructor in the school's criminal defense clinic, and a lecturer on law in Harvard's Trial Advocacy Workshop. A graduate of Yale College and the New York University School of Law, Ms. Smith was an assistant defender at the Defender Association of Philadelphia from 1982 to 1990. Ms. Smith has written on feminism and criminal law, juvenile justice, indigent criminal defense, police misconduct, and clinical legal education. Abbe Smith is also a cartoonist, with a published collection of cartoons entitled *Carried Away: The Chronicles of a Feminist Cartoonist* (Bridgeport, Conn.: Sanguinaria Press, 1984).

Margaret Lynne Weaver was born in Eden, North Carolina. She graduated from Duke University in 1989, summa cum laude, with a B.A. in political science, and received her J.D. from Harvard Law School in 1992. Following law school, she clerked for Chief Judge B. Avant Edenfield, United States District Court, in the Southern District of Georgia. Ms. Weaver is presently with the law firm of Hunton and Williams in Raleigh, North Carolina, where she concentrates on antitrust, intellectual property, and trade regulation matters.

Lucie White is a professor of law at Harvard Law School. Her work focuses on law, lawyering, and social change. She teaches courses in civil procedure, social welfare policy, and community-based advocacy around poverty issues. She is currently writing an ethnography of women in two local Head Start programs, as an example of law's potential to support grassroots community-building work among poor women. She has also written about lawyer-client roles, social power, and institutional arrangements in contexts of extreme poverty, as well as change-oriented lawyering practices in apartheid South Africa.